Library of Congress Cataloging-in-Publication Data

Curtis, Michael Kent, 1942–
    No state shall abridge.

    Includes index.
    1. United States—Constitutional law—Amendments—
14th—History.   2. Afro-Americans—Civil rights—
History.   3. Slavery—Law and legislation—United
States—History.   I. Title.
KF4757.C87   1986   342.73'085   86-6309
ISBN 0-8223-0599-2

To

Deborah F. Maury

and

Matthew Fontaine Curtis-Maury

Contents

Foreword

The best introduction to this important book by Michael Curtis was effectively provided by the Attorney General of the United States, Mr. Edwin Meese, on July 9, 1985. It appeared in the form of his major address to the American Bar Association, in Washington, D.C. The subject of the Attorney General's nationally reported speech was the extent to which the Bill of Rights does or does not apply to the states. It is the same subject to which Mr. Curtis devotes himself in *No State Shall Abridge*. This foreword is in turn but a bridge, an invitation as it were, to cross over from the Attorney General's address to Mr. Curtis's response.

In his remarks to the ABA, Mr. Meese shared with the assembled lawyers his satisfaction with certain recent Supreme Court decisions he described as tending to undo "the damage" previously done by what he referred to as the "piecemeal incorporation" of the Fourth Amendment to the Constitution through the Fourteenth Amendment. The "damage" to which the Attorney General referred was damage he associated with a set of significant Supreme Court cases decided principally during the tenure of the Warren Court—cases in which search-and-seizure practices by state law enforcement officials had been examined by the Supreme Court under Fourth Amendment standards. To the extent that recent Supreme Court decisions reviewing state search-and-seizure procedures reflected a somewhat more relaxed view on the Court, namely, that the states may *not* be bound to observe the same standards constitutionally required of federal law enforcement agents, Mr. Meese regarded the new cases as both welcome and encouraging. They tended, as he said, to undo "the damage" previously resulting from the Warren Court's use of the "incorporation" doctrine.

These recent developments, the Attorney General felt encouraged to suggest, might not represent an isolated trend. Rather, they might be taken to reflect a new willingness on the part of the Supreme Court to reconsider the entire incorporation doctrine, which it was the object of his address to have his audience reflect upon. "[N]owhere else," the Attorney General said, "has the principle of federalism been dealt so politically violent and constitutionally suspect a blow as by the theory of incorporation." And "nothing can be done," he counseled his audience, "to shore up the intellectually shaky foundation upon which the [incorporation] doctrine rests."

The doctrine to which the Attorney General referred is a familiar doctrine in American constitutional law. It is the doctrine that the enactment of the Fourteenth Amendment put an end to the dispute respecting the exemption of the states from the Bill of Rights. It is that exemption the Attorney General suggests may in fact never have been given up and, indeed, may even now be reclaimed.

Turning to the church-state clauses of the First Amendment, the Attorney General implied that these provisions, too, may not apply to the states or at least not apply in anywhere near the same manner as they apply to the national government. (Indeed, it was in the context of addressing these clauses, rather than the Fourth Amendment, that he spoke of the "constitutionally suspect . . . theory of incorporation.") And if that is so, then may not the states each be free to support religion in a variety of ways foreclosed to Congress? Mr. Meese left no doubt of his own view that they may.

The relationship of the Bill of Rights to the states was thus the very subject of the Attorney General's address, prompted by what he regarded as encouraging developments in the Supreme Court itself. Indeed, in November, spiritedly responding to published criticism of his ABA address (Anthony Lewis of the *New York Times* accused the Attorney General of seeking to "repeal legal history"), Mr. Meese took up the challenge altogether cheerfully. "Now, as we approach the bicentennial of the framing of the Constitution," he declared to members of the Federalist Society in Washington, "we are witnessing another debate concerning our fundamental law. It is not simply a ceremonial debate, but one that promises to have a profound impact on the future of our Republic."

There may be, of course, a bit of hyperbole in the Attorney General's view. It may bespeak undue confidence in anticipating certain appointments to the Supreme Court, or it may exaggerate the impact that such expected "debate" might have. Even so, assuming the foundations of the incorporation doctrine are truly as shaky as the Attorney General believes, his expectation is scarcely unreasonable. If the grounds for associating the Bill of Rights with the Fourteenth Amendment are not there, it is difficult to say why that observation should not now count—why it no longer matters. And, indeed, so far as the importance of the subject itself is concerned, it is difficult to imagine a more consequential subject than this one, short of pulling back the Bill of Rights even from the federal government itself.

Whether, for instance, the free speech and press clause of the First Amendment applies only partly to the states, equally to the states, or not at all to the states is obviously an issue of great consequence. Whether the Seventh Amendment right to trial by jury (even in a civil case involving but twenty-one dollars) is binding on the states matters as well, although doubtless not nearly so much. But whether as a general proposition the whole regime of the Bill of Rights is carried across the boundary of federalism (literally "tittle for tittle and jot for jot"), whether only parts of it are thus transposed, or whether indeed virtually none of it applies is—as the Attorney General says—no mere "ceremonial" question. It is, rather, a question so consequential as to make it appear astonishing that the answer could possibly be thought doubtful at this late date, virtually two centuries after the ratification of the Bill of Rights itself and more than a century after the ratification of the Fourteenth Amendment.

And yet, for many very serious people, the question is still doubtful, even as the Attorney General suggested. The question raised publicly by the Attorney General in his ABA address has been raised repeatedly by others, many of whom preceded him by decades and indeed by generations. The fact is that Mr. Meese's point of view does not stand alone; it is no late Reaganite novelty, and it has troubled some of the most serious scholars (and judges) of our constitutional history.

Moreover, contrary to what most people might have supposed, the Supreme Court itself has never quite settled on a single rationale in associating the Bill of Rights with the Fourteenth Amendment. Within the existing case law, for instance, one will find no less than four "doctrines" differently relating the Bill of Rights to the states via the Fourteenth Amendment. There are, in brief, at least two positions a number of justices have taken additional to the mutually exclusive primary positions—of full association or of no association.

The strongest of these positions is of course that of full association (or "incorporation" as it is called). And in sharp contrast to the Attorney General's thinking, Mr. Curtis does not think that that foundation is shaky at all. To the contrary, he believes it is sound—indeed that it is overwhelming. In this book he undertakes to show why.

Necessarily, Mr. Curtis's book is not a quick or an easy read; nothing that undertakes a conscientious review of sources appropriate to a subject such as this one can be reduced in that way. Much better than any quick or easy read, however, *No State Shall Abridge* provides the most powerful response to doubts respecting the incorporation doc-

trine yet published. One will not know the full strength of the incorporation case without reading this book. But I need to say no more, since
this invitation is now complete. The Attorney General wrote the real
foreword, last July.

William W. Van Alstyne
March 1986

Acknowledgments

Many people have given me encouragement and help in connection with my work on the Fourteenth Amendment and the Bill of Rights. Although they have provided help and encouragement, they cannot be held responsible for ideas contained or mistakes made. One of the gifts of the best teachers is to encourage students to pursue their own ideas. The teacher deserves much of the credit, but he or she deserves none of the blame. Similarly, those reviewing a long and complex project may help the writer avoid some mistakes. To help a writer avoid all would require an undertaking equivalent to that which produced the manuscript.

For encouragement in pursuing my work on the Fourteenth Amendment I want to thank particularly Professors Leonard Levy (whose encouragement has been constant and crucial), William Van Alstyne, Louis Lusky, and Henry J. Abraham. The Frances Lewis Law Center at Washington and Lee University has a lawyer-in-residence program where I spent a month working on the book. For the help and support of people at Washington and Lee I am particularly grateful.

Professors Roger Groot, L. H. LaRue, and Brian Murchison at Washington and Lee all read large portions of the manuscript and helped me to improve it. An anonymous person read and reread the manuscript for Duke University Press with meticulous care and made many suggestions, large and small, which substantially improved the quality of what I had written. My law partners Michael Okun and Davison Douglas and Martha Johnson and my wife Deborah Maury also read much of the manuscript and made helpful suggestions. My brother Tom Curtis, a gifted writer and editor, did much to improve the book's style. Professor Robert Kaczorowski read chapter 6 and made helpful suggestions, and Professor William Van Alstyne also made helpful suggestions.

I am grateful to Norita Speaks with the Greensboro Public Library for her assistance in ordering roll after roll of newspapers on microfilm; to the Wake Forest, Connecticut, Ohio State, North Carolina, and West Virginia Law Reviews, which have published earlier versions of some of the ideas set out here and which, to the extent of their copyright interest, have given permission to reprint. Margaret Williams at Washington and Lee Law School provided invaluable assistance in preparation of the manuscript, as did Beverly Erskine and Diane Becker. The Frances Lewis Law Center provided me with two research assistants, Carl Hankla and Jonathan Rak, who worked hard and did a superb job.

My law partners have generously tolerated and encouraged this project.

To all of these people and to the many others who have assisted me in this project, I give my sincere thanks. Finally, I acknowledge my debt to those academic pioneers who have looked at the relation between the crusade against slavery of the Fourteenth Amendment and the Bill of Rights.

This book is far better than it would otherwise have been because of all the help and encouragement I have had. Had I the insight and judgment to understand and follow all the critical suggestions of those who read the manuscript, the end product might have been significantly better. The views expressed are my own, and not the responsibility of those whose help or encouragement I have acknowledged.

Introduction

Current Controversy

The idea that the federal Bill of Rights protects liberty of speech and press, freedom of religion, and other basic rights from violations by the states has become commonplace, even for lawyers. Indeed, many Americans probably accepted this commonplace when careful lawyers knew it was not so. From 1833 to 1868 the Supreme Court held that none of the rights in the Bill of Rights limited the states.[1] From 1868 to 1925 it found very few of these liberties protected from state action.[2] Those the states were free to flout (so far as federal limitations were concerned) seemed to include free speech, press, religion,[3] the right to jury trial,[4] freedom from self-incrimination,[5] from infliction of cruel and unusual punishments,[6] and more. State constitutions, with their own bills of rights, were available to protect the individual, but too often they proved to be paper barriers.[7]

Most, but not all, scholars believe that the Supreme Court was right, at least as a matter of history, up to 1868. They believe, that is, that the founding fathers did not intend for the Bill of Rights to limit the states.[8]

In 1868 the Fourteenth Amendment was ratified. Section 1 provided:

All persons born or naturalized in the United States, and subject to the jurisdiction thereof, are citizens of the United States and of the State wherein they reside. No State shall make or enforce any law which shall abridge the privileges or immunities of citizens of the United States; nor shall any State deprive any person of life, liberty, or property, without due process of law; nor deny to any person within its jurisdiction the equal protection of the laws.

A reasonable reader might conclude that the Fourteenth Amendment was intended to change things so that states could no longer violate rights in the federal Bill of Rights. The reader might think this was what was intended by the language, "No state shall make or enforce any law which shall abridge the privileges or immunities of citizens of the United States." I believe that the reader would be right.

The thesis is intensely controversial. It has never, for instance, been accepted by the United States Supreme Court, although the Court has haltingly reached much the same result by gradual incorporation of most of the rights in the Bill of Rights as limits on the states under the due process clause, a development that reached fruition in the 1960s.[9] Historical justification for this selective incorporation of rights under the clause of the Fourteenth Amendment that says "No state shall deprive any person of life, liberty, or property without due process of law" has also been controversial.[10] Here again, at least as to all procedural guaranties—the right to jury trial, the right against self-incrimination, the right to counsel, and the like—the reading is also historically correct.

The idea that the framers of the Fourteenth Amendment intended guaranties of the Bill of Rights to limit state action has been rejected by many legal scholars. These scholars have treated their rejection as "amply documented and widely accepted."[11] The historical argument for applying the Bill of Rights to the states has been treated as "conclusively disproved,"[12] and the evidence for it marshaled by Justice Hugo L. Black[13] has been denounced as "flimsy."[14] One scholar tells us that "it is all but certain that the Fourteenth Amendment was not intended to incorporate the Bill of Rights."[15] Another assures us that the idea that the Fourteenth Amendment was designed to apply the Bill of Rights to the states has been "discredited . . . in a study with which even activists concur."[16] A noted professor of law says that the application of the religious guaranties of the Bill of Rights to the states occurred "solely at the whim of the Court."[17] Still another tells us that it is now "generally accepted" that the framers of the Fourteenth Amendment intended no restrictions on government regulation of speech.[18]

It may well be that most professors of constitutional law who have ventured an opinion on the question—and it sometimes seems most have—have reached the conclusion that application of the Bill of Rights to the states under the Fourteenth Amendment was, as a matter of history, a mistake. Still, such opinions have usually been expressed in passing, as a minor feature of the author's work, and not after exhaustive investigation of the historical sources. Among scholars who have studied the historical sources in detail, opinion is more divided. Most of this group seem to agree that the Fourteenth Amendment *was* intended to apply the Bill of Rights—or at least most of them—to the states.[19]

Skepticism in the scholarly and judicial community as to the intent of the framers of the Fourteenth Amendment has begun to have extreme political and judicial manifestations, often not intended by the skeptics.[20] In a recent book, *Government by Judiciary*, published by the Harvard University Press, Mr. Raoul Berger has called for a "rollback" of decisions applying the Bill of Rights to the states.[21] There are indications that some are willing to respond to the trumpet call.

One federal judge has found the Supreme Court's decision applying the First Amendment guaranty of free exercise of religion to the states "a result oriented decision which cannot be supported by historical data."[22] Still, the judge recognized that he was bound by the decision. Another federal court has not been so timid. It ruled that none of the guaranties of the Bill of Rights applies to the states.[23] Although the decision was promptly reversed,[24] it indicates a changing judicial climate, one in which federal protection for many liberties in the Bill of Rights may be frozen out of existence.

Mr. George Will, whose columns are widely circulated, has announced that "the Court took a radically wrong turn when it 'incorporated' the First Amendment into the fourteenth amendment."[25] Senator John P. East, Republican of North Carolina, has asserted that the framers of the Fourteenth Amendment did not intend to apply the Bill of Rights to the states, and he has introduced legislation designed to free the states and localities from federal protection for liberties in the Bill of Rights. Attorney General Edwin Meese has flirted with similar ideas.[26]

The idea that protection of human liberty under the Bill of Rights against state action is the result of judicial whim or judicial usurpation eats like acid at the legitimacy of federal protection of civil liberty. The current Supreme Court seems unwilling to embrace the proposed rollback.[27] Still, pervasive skepticism about the legitimacy of application of the Bill of Rights to the states may be a factor in encouraging the recent trend in Supreme Court decisions toward restricting individual liberty and expanding government power. Indeed, one scholar who has questioned the historical legitimacy of federal protection of Bill of Rights liberties has suggested that the Court begin a rollback of civil liberty by more restrictive readings of particular guaranties.[28] For whatever reason, the Court has given an increasingly strict construction to the rights of the individual and an increasingly broad construction to the power of government.[29]

In particular cases and for particular Justices, whether the states are bound by the literal provisions of the Bill of Rights or by subjective notions of what the Justice finds essential to liberty has had profound significance. The clearest examples are the cases in which Justice Lewis

F. Powell, Jr., agreeing with four of his colleagues, found that the Sixth Amendment *did* require unanimous juries, but nonetheless in which he found that the Fourteenth Amendment did *not* require full or literal application of the Sixth Amendment to the states. The upshot was that states could convict persons in criminal cases by nonunanimous juries.[30]

Justices Powell, Warren E. Burger, and William H. Rehnquist insist that the guaranties of the Bill of Rights are not literally incorporated by the Fourteenth Amendment—so that certain procedures constitutionally required by the Fifth Amendment are not necessarily required by the Fourteenth.[31] Justice Rehnquist believes that "not all of the strictures which the First Amendment imposes upon Congress are carried over against the states by the Fourteenth Amendment."[32]

Lawrence Tribe, of Harvard Law School, suggests that additional Court appointments by President Ronald Reagan could produce reconsideration of the rule holding that guaranties of the Bill of Rights limit the states.[33] The legitimacy of applying the Bill of Rights to the states has practical consequences now and, unfortunately, may have more in the future.

How can it be that so many able writers of widely different political views have concluded that the Fourteenth Amendment was not designed to make Bill of Rights liberties a limit on the states? Part of the explanation, but only part of it, is that most who have expressed opinions on the subject failed to do the tedious job of wading through the historical sources. Another reason may be simple lack of interest. Henry Monaghan suggests that professors of constitutional law are "problem solvers by training" and "unsympathetic to being bound by chains of the past."[34] The assumption that study of relevant legal history admits the controlling power of the "chains of the past" has led many to treat history as irrelevant.

Another part of the explanation for the current conventional wisdom is that the historical sources are initially confusing to minds steeped in modern approaches to constitutional law. Because the job of looking at the congressional debates is so massive, and because the sources themselves are initially somewhat opaque to the modern reader, law professors and others have naturally looked to secondary studies. One study, that done by Charles Fairman,[35] has been particularly influential.

Prior Fourteenth Amendment Scholarship

Fairman wrote in 1949 in response to a dissenting opinion by Justice Hugo Black in the 1947 case of *Adamson v. California.*[36] At the time

Black wrote his dissenting opinion in *Adamson* the Supreme Court applied to the states only those rights the Justices considered implicit in the concept of ordered liberty. Many of the rights in the Bill of Rights were then thought not to fit into this category—including rights such as jury trial in criminal cases and protection against double jeopardy and self-incrimination.[37] The process of selective incorporation—by which so many of the guaranties have since been applied to the states—was then not far advanced.

In *Adamson* Justice Black argued that the Fourteenth Amendment was intended to overrule earlier Supreme Court decisions and to make the first eight amendments to the Constitution a limitation on the states.[38] Justice Black showed that the privileges or immunities clause was the primary device used to accomplish this end and that reference to privileges or immunities was a reasonable way to apply the Bill of Rights to the states.[39] Justice Black also relied on the due process clause of the Fourteenth Amendment.[40] By his reference to the due process clause, in addition to the privileges or immunities clause, Justice Black made his argument more congruent with prior Supreme Court decisions that had held some guaranties of the Bill of Rights binding on the states through the due process clause. His partial reliance on the due process clause, however, also made it easier for critics to ignore the main thrust of his argument. Three Justices joined in Black's dissent, so it looked as if it might soon become the law.

Justice Black's thesis was promptly attacked by Charles Fairman, then a professor at Stanford.[41] Fairman was horrified at the thought that the Fourteenth Amendment might require the states to obey all of the Bill of Rights, including even the right to civil jury trials.[42] Fairman examined the debates surrounding the adoption of the amendment, later construction of the amendment by Congress in the years immediately following its passage, contemporary newspaper accounts, and other sources. He concluded that the amendment in general and the privileges or immunities clause in particular were not intended to make the Bill of Rights applicable to the states.[43] Fairman read most of the evidence to show the framers of the Fourteenth Amendment understood it simply to incorporate the Civil Rights bill, passed in 1866. Since Fairman seemed to read the Civil Rights bill only to protect rights under state law, his analysis appeared to show that none of the rights in the Bill of Rights were to be applied under the Fourteenth Amendment except for the due process clause, which was written specifically into the amendment. That clause, Fairman believed, did not include any other Bill of Rights liberties—e.g., the right to civil and criminal juries or the right to free speech.[44]

What, then, according to Fairman did the framers expect the privileges or immunities clause to mean? "Pretty clearly there never was any such clear [inclusive and exclusive] conception."[45] After "brooding over the matter," Professor Fairman "slowly" concluded, however, that "implicit in the concept of ordered liberty" was about as close as one could come to the "vague aspirations" that the framers had for the clause.[46] Such an interpretation had the advantage, at least, of explaining why guaranties of the Bill of Rights such as freedom of speech were mentioned in connection with the clause.[47]

The framers of the Fourteenth Amendment emerge from Professor Fairman's article as men with, at best, only a vague idea of what they were doing. Although scholars often accept most of Fairman's negative conclusions, many refuse to accept his argument that a selective incorporation was intended.[48] This reluctance is understandable. Fairman's conclusion on this point seems at war with the burden of his argument. As the scholarly opinions cited above show, Fairman's article has been accepted as gospel by many legal scholars.[49] It did much to sharpen the debate on the intended meaning of the Fourteenth Amendment.

Still, Fairman's article suffered from defects. First, it ignored much of the larger historical context out of which the Fourteenth Amendment grew, including the crusade against slavery and for civil liberty during the years from 1830 to 1866. Because Fairman read only the debates on the Fourteenth Amendment and the Civil Rights bill and read these from the standpoint of legal orthodoxy, he was unable to make much sense out of many things that leading Republicans said. Fairman failed to look at debates on the Thirteenth Amendment and Reconstruction, overlooked much evidence that tended to contradict his thesis,[50] denigrated the evidence of intent to apply the Bill of Rights to the states that he did find,[51] and made much over the failure to find evidence explicitly indicating an intent to apply the Bill of Rights to the states.[52] For example, he shows that there is little evidence from Republicans in state legislative debates on ratification showing an intent to apply the Bill of Rights to the states. The negative evidence loses much of its force, however, when one understands that Republicans often agreed not to say anything on the subject, content simply to wait and vote.[53]

An Antislavery Analysis
of the Fourteenth Amendment

This book examines the Fourteenth Amendment in light of the antislavery crusade that produced it. The amendment declared an antislavery constitutional interpretation. It reflected Republican legal theories, theories that were often at variance with conventional constitutional doctrine. Indeed, when read in light of Republican constitutional theory, much that seems confusing in the congressional debates leading up to the Fourteenth Amendment becomes clear. No one will ever be able to reduce the debates to perfect harmony. But the hypothesis advanced here makes sense, rather than nonsense, of what leading Republicans had to say.

Republicans accepted the following tenets of antislavery constitutional thought. First, after the passage of the Thirteenth Amendment abolishing slavery, blacks were citizens of the United States.[54] Republicans held this view even though the *Dred Scott* decision[55] was to the contrary. Second, the guaranties of the Bill of Rights applied to the states even prior to the passage of the Fourteenth Amendment. Most Republicans held this view even though the Supreme Court had ruled to the contrary in the case of *Barron v. Baltimore*,[56] decided in 1833. Third, the privileges and immunities clause of the original Constitution[57] protected the fundamental rights of American citizens against state action.[58] Fourth, the due process clause of the Fifth Amendment protected all persons from enslavement in the District of Columbia and in the federal territories.[59]

To understand Republican ideas, I have looked in detail at the debates on the Thirteenth Amendment and on Reconstruction. In those debates shortly before the 1866 passage of the Fourteenth Amendment, Republicans tend to spell out their views that rights in the Bill of Rights limit the states. By eliminating slavery, Republicans thought they were ridding the country of the institution that had diverted the course of the law and kept the courts from nationalizing civil liberties. With the removal of slavery, the Constitution was expected by many to spring back to its original purposes—those set out in the Declaration of Independence and in the preamble. It would become a document protecting liberty.[60]

I have examined debate on the Civil Rights bill for two reasons. First (as in the case of the Thirteenth Amendment debates and debates on Reconstruction), the debate on the Civil Rights bill illustrates Republican constitutional doctrine. Second, the Civil Rights bill has been treated as evidence that the Fourteenth Amendment could not have been designed to apply the Bill of Rights to the states. The act, so the argument goes, was designed to protect blacks only from discrimination in certain rights under state law—the right to contract, testify, inherit, and to protections of state civil and criminal law. Since some supporters of the amendment said it was equivalent to the Civil Rights bill, the amendment, some scholars insist, could not have protected Bill of Rights liberties.[61] In fact, the argument is based on a mistaken

reading of the act. Statements made about the equivalence of the bill
and the amendment are consistent with application of the Bill of
Rights to the states.[62]

The primary method used here is detailed analysis of historical
texts. A prime text, of course, is the amendment itself. Others include
Republican and antislavery party platforms, antislavery constitutional
tracts, newspaper accounts of speeches, and, most of all, the text of
debates in Congress. These provide a rich source of material on
Republican ideology and constitutional analysis. On careful analysis,
these texts provide support for the proposition that the Fourteenth
Amendment was designed to apply the Bill of Rights to the states.

My analysis of the purposes of the Fourteenth Amendment has
been enriched and guided by earlier scholars who have looked at the
connection of antislavery legal thought, civil liberties, and the Fourteenth Amendment and by those who have looked at Reconstruction
in general.[63] Most influential on my thought is the major scholarly
attack on Fairman's article written by W. W. Crosskey, then a professor
at the University of Chicago. Crosskey was one pioneer in reading the
congressional debates in light of antislavery legal thought.

Crosskey insisted that the amendment should be understood in
light of "old Republican" constitutional ideas. These included a reading of the privileges and immunities clause of article IV, section 2 to
mean that the citizens of each state would be entitled to all rights of
citizens of the United States in every state; a reading of the Fifth
Amendment guaranty of due process to require the government to
supply equal protection in the rights to life, liberty, and property; and,
finally, a belief that the guaranties of the Bill of Rights were limits on
the states even prior to the framing of the Fourteenth Amendment.[64]
Although my interpretation now diverges from Crosskey's in some
significant ways, I still believe that his work brilliantly illuminates the
forgotten relation of the Fourteenth Amendment to the Bill of Rights.

Other works have also helped me to understand the context in
which Republicans spoke. These include Jacobus tenBroek's classic
Equal under Law,[65] which looks at the antislavery origins of the Fourteenth Amendment (including unorthodox ideas about the scope of
the Bill of Rights) and draws conclusions on the Bill of Rights question
somewhat different from those reached here; William Wiecek's *Sources
of Antislavery Constitutionalism in America*; works that examine southern suppression of free speech in the years before the Civil War; and
studies of Reconstruction.[66]

The privileges or immunities clause of the Fourteenth Amendment
and even the often maligned work of Professor Crosskey on this
subject are enjoying an academic renaissance. Since I first wrote on

the Bill of Rights issue in 1979 a number of scholars have looked again at the history surrounding the amendment.[67] Additional scholarly support for the thesis that the Fourteenth Amendment was designed to apply the Bill of Rights to the states can now be found in the work of Harold Hyman and Wiecek and of others. If recent scholarship is any indication, there is reason to hope that the privileges or immunities clause may once again enjoy the central role in protection of civil liberties envisioned for it by its framers.

The Search for Meaning

The provisions of the Constitution, as Hans Linde has noted, "reflect a series of decisions concerning the organization of government, its powers, and limitations that were made by particular men at particular moments in history."[68] A look at what the people who framed the Fourteenth Amendment intended as far as the protection of civil liberty was concerned is a worthwhile endeavor. Analysis of problems that confronted Republicans and led them to think the amendment necessary sheds light on what their purposes were. Understanding the threats to civil liberty that shaped the amendment shows the vitality of its purposes for our own time.

Proof that the amendment was designed to nationalize the protection of civil liberties provides legitimacy for the general endeavor of protecting rights in the Bill of Rights.[69] In one way this fact seems obvious. Justices and politicians regularly appeal to the intent of the framers in an effort to legitimize their decisions. Opponents of application of the Bill of Rights to the states appeal to history to justify their opposition. As C. Vann Woodward has noted, political movements in America have always sought to gain control of history. Woodward cites the commissar in George Orwell's novel *1984*: "Who controls the past controls the future, who controls the present controls the past."[70]

It is easy, as Woodward does so well, to criticize the search for historical legitimacy. We may seek from history more than history can provide. The fact that the likely intent of the framers of a constitutional provision (narrowly read) may provide one form of legitimacy does not mean that it provides the only form. Still, appeal to historically existing common values is one characteristic of a community. Where valid, the appeal should not be discarded simply because the method may not answer all possible questions correctly from the critic's point of view.

Modern critics have been quick to reject historical sources of legitimacy as inadequate and to look for others.[71] More careful examination of the history shows that conceding the historical record to those favoring a "strict construction" of individual rights is often premature.[72]

There is a sense in which scholars, like generals, are always fighting the last war. An emerging problem of American constitutional law may be to find sources of legitimacy to oppose the contraction of basic rights. If the historical purposes of a constitutional provision are viewed as providing such a source, or perhaps as the irreducible minimum standard for constitutional rights, history provides one tradition against which at least some calls to restrict individual liberty may be tested.

The problem of legitimacy of Supreme Court decisions is a baffling one for modern scholars. Although most lawyers remain convinced that the process of constitutional adjudication can and should be tested by criteria of legitimacy, there is no agreement as to what the criteria are.[73] Suggestions range from the insistence that original intent must be the sole criteria[74] to insistence on its utter irrelevance and to suggestions for substitutes.[75]

As Charles Miller has noted in his study on the use of history by the Supreme Court,

> The power of the courts to interpret the Constitution, and the expectation that they will supply cogent reasoning in justification of their interpretation, presents a dilemma of modernity peculiar to the American judiciary. No other nation possesses a written constitution (still in use) as old as America's and no other nation worships its constitution with such reverence. Yet we expect the judiciary to be both contemporary and rational when expounding constitutional law.[76]

One factor leading critics to reject the search for original intent is the assumption that following it will unacceptably bind the present to the injustices of the past. The assumption overlooks the possibility that the framers expected certain clauses in the Constitution to be read in light of contemporary conditions.

One of the most rigid announcements of the original intent theory came in the *Dred Scott* decision. In that case Chief Justice Roger B. Taney concluded that free blacks were not citizens of the United States, could not sue in federal courts, and were entitled to none of the protections of the federal constitution.

> No one, we presume, supposes that any change in public opinion or feeling, in relation to this unfortunate race . . . should induce the court to give to the words of the Constitution a more liberal construction in their favor than they were intended to bear when the instrument was framed and adopted. Such an argument would be altogether inadmissible. . . . If any of its provisions are deemed

unjust, there is a mode prescribed in the instrument itself by which it may be amended; but while it remains unaltered, it must be construed now as it was understood at the time of its adoption. [The Constitution] speaks not only in the same words, but with the same meaning and intent with which it spoke when it came from the hands of its framers. . . . Any other rule of construction would abrogate the judicial character of this court, and make it the mere reflex of the popular opinion or passion of the day.[77]

The result in the *Dred Scott* decision is abhorrent. So it is easy to treat the decision as proof that the original intent theory always produces monstrous results. Ironically, Taney's history was as bad as his result. The decision itself was a "reflex of the popular . . . passions" of the day that Taney deplored.[78]

If court decisions are compared to vectors, then history has been one of the forces that are finally reflected in the result. It has never been more, and perhaps never will. Still, the study of history leading to a constitutional provision can improve the quality of judicial decision. It can do so by increasing the number of cases and consequences judges consider and by allowing the judges to consider and follow the purposes and policies that produce the provision.

History is also a potent method for teaching political values. According to Charles Miller, using history in this way, as the Court often does, is consistent with the intent of the framers of the Constitution, for they saw history, particularly the struggle for liberty in seventeenth-century England, as a means of instruction in civic virtue. And they saw the Bill of Rights as a potent teacher of the value of political liberty.[79]

As a practical matter, the values judges bring to the bench have always been an important factor in shaping their decisions. History, the constitutional text, and precedent are all matters that to greater or lesser degree become part of the judges' value system.

Meaning and Intent

The method for determining the meaning of a constitutional text is itself controversial. The Supreme Court has at different times announced rules that differ at least in emphasis. Some Justices may cite James Madison's statements in the first Congress to show that judicial protection of liberties in the Bill of Rights was to be a special concern of the courts.[80] Other Justices show little interest in statements made by the author of section 1 of the Fourteenth Amendment or of the senator who managed it in the Senate.[81]

The meaning of the privileges or immunities clause of section 1 of the Fourteenth Amendment is really a question of the meaning of language. Some argue that extrinsic evidence should not be allowed to contradict the plain meaning of the clause.[82] It is doubtful that words stripped from their historical context ever have plain meaning. At any rate, a look at Republican ideology and Republican legal thought and at what leading proponents said the amendment meant is fruitful because it sheds light on the meaning of the words used. In *United States v. Wong Kim Ark*[83] the Court cited statements made by congressmen in the debates on the Fourteenth Amendment as to what the words in the amendment meant. These, the Court said, were "valuable as contemporaneous opinions of jurists and statesmen upon the legal meaning of the words themselves."[84]

Sometimes the Court says that a constitutional provision should not be construed in light of what its leading sponsors said about it at the time, but rather that courts should "read its language in connection with the known condition of affairs out of which the occasion for its adoption may have arisen" and construe it to further its object.[85] This rule misses the point of investigating the congressional debates, for the debates on the adoption of the Fourteenth Amendment shed light on the condition of affairs leading to its adoption and indeed provide a rich source of evidence on that point. To ignore the words of leading sponsors of a proposal is to reject one source of light on the meaning of the words used. As Professor Monaghan has noted, "Textual language embodies one or more purposes and the text may be usefully understood and applied only if its purposes are understood. No convincing reason appears why a purpose may not be ascertained from any relevant source, including legislative history."[86]

Some argue that the purposes of those who frame and ratify a constitutional provision are difficult to know. That is true in the present case because so many people were involved and so few spoke to the question. It would be useful, for example, if a poll had been taken of all supporters of the Fourteenth Amendment in Congress and in the state legislatures. They could have been asked, "Under section 1 of the fourteenth amendment will states remain free, as they were before the Civil War, to punish political speech, as they punished expression critical of slavery? Will they continue to be free to ignore the other provisions of the federal Bill of Rights?"

No such poll was taken, of course. So the search for the purposes of the amendment requires some criteria. These the reader has a right to know: (1) The language of the amendment is a guide to the purposes of those who proposed it. (2) The meaning of the amendment should be sought in the abuses that produced it and in the political and legal philosophy of those who proposed it. (3) The congressional debates are a further guide to meaning. In evaluating the debates one should look primarily to statements of those who supported the amendment and not primarily to statements of opponents. (4) The remarks of leading proponents are entitled to great weight. And the greatest weight of all should be given to the statements of members of the committee that reported the amendment to Congress.

These criteria give disproportionate weight to the views expressed by some congressmen as opposed to the views of others. The views of those who speak are given weight over the views of those who do not. The views of the supporters of the proposal are given weight over the views of those who oppose it. The views of the leaders of the Senate and House Judiciary Committee receive greater weight than those of an ordinary representative. Greater weight is given to statements in Congress by members of the committee reporting the amendment—in this case, the members of the Joint Committee on Reconstruction. The views of the author of section 1 of the amendment and of the committee members assigned to explain its purposes to the Congress should receive the greatest weight of all. These are the people to whom other representatives would most likely have looked for guidance.

In our republican government the Constitution is treated as emanating from the people. The purposes of the people in 1866 are not knowable directly, if at all. Looking at statements of leading proponents of the Fourteenth Amendment makes the task of determining purposes more nearly attainable. It is consistent with a realistic recognition of the disproportionate influence of elites in the political process. By narrowing the scope of the inquiry to the purposes of leading Republicans with reference to the Fourteenth Amendment and the Bill of Rights, the question of purpose is more easily answered. But the answer may be less compelling as a rule of constitutional law for the future. Furthermore, the attempt to use congressional purposes as a guide to constitutional law is confronted by a paradox, for at least some Republicans accepted the legitimacy of an evolving constitution and of law as a progressive science.[87] And some may have rejected the use of history as a guide to meaning.[88]

There is still another paradox in the attempt to learn the meaning of section 1 of the Fourteenth Amendment. To the framers of the Fourteenth Amendment the meaning of the privileges or immunities clause, of the due process clause, and of the equal protection clause were of secondary importance. The questions of primary importance had to do with political power, particularly the power of the rebellious southern states and of the leaders of the rebellion.

After the defeat of the southern states, the ratification of the Thirteenth Amendment abolishing slavery, and the assassination of President Lincoln, his successor, Andrew Johnson of Tennessee, insisted that the rebellious southern states were entitled to immediate representation in Congress. The Constitution in article I, section 2 provided that representation in the House should be based on the number of free persons in the state and three-fifths of all other persons—that is, of slaves. With the end of slavery the former slaves would be counted as free persons for the purposes of representation. The result was that the representation of southern states would be much increased.

For years before the Civil War, southerners and their allies had dominated the federal government. After four years of civil war and untold suffering, it now seemed that the leaders of the rebellion might return to political power on the backs of their disfranchised black population. To Republicans this would be an intolerable result.

All agreed that the southern states would eventually return to the Union as states. The burning issue of 1866 was, when and on what conditions? This was the question that occupied congressmen and other politicians. The crux of that question was the issue of political power.

In the Thirty-ninth Congress and in the campaign of 1866 overwhelming attention was devoted to the question of political power. Shall rebels rule? There were endless variations on the theme—efforts to show that Congress was consistent and reasonable in requiring conditions for readmission and that the president was unreasonable and inconsistent in not requiring further conditions beyond the abolition of slavery and the repudiation of the rebel debt. Most of the political rhetoric of the day was devoted to the subject of political power.

Closely connected to the question of political power was the question of the Union debt. If the Republican party became the minority party, would the war debt be repudiated? Would the Democratic coalition require taxpayers to pay the rebel debt or perhaps compensate slaveholders for the loss of their slaves?

There are five sections and 428 words in the Fourteenth Amendment. Three-fourths of the substantive sections deal with subjects other than the rights of citizens.

Section 2 of the amendment dealt directly with the question of political power. If states disfranchised a portion of their male population over the age of twenty-one (except for participation in rebellion or other crime), their representation in the House would be proportionately reduced.

Section 3 also dealt with the question of political power. It disqualified from office those who had taken an oath to support the Constitution and then engaged in rebellion. By a two-thirds vote of each house Congress could remove the disability.

Section 4 protected the debt of the United States, including pensions for soldiers. It also prohibited the states or the federal government from paying the rebel debt or from compensating slave owners for the loss of their slaves.

Of the 428 words in the Fourteenth Amendment, 67 were relevant to the Bill of Rights question—the citizenship, privileges or immunities, and due process clauses. If one adds the enforcement clause, the total rises to 81. In discussions of the amendment in Congress and in the campaign of 1866, the ratio of words related to due process, privileges or immunities, and equal protection to words related to the other questions discussed by the amendment is even smaller.

Distressingly, the issue that seems primary to us today, the meaning of section 1 of the amendment, received relatively little discussion. Questions of political power that are far removed from current concerns received overwhelming attention. The questions we ask today about what section 1 of the amendment meant were not the questions Republicans were typically most determined to talk about.

In a sense, of course, they were right. For if the political question had been answered as President Johnson had wished, there never would have been a Fourteenth Amendment at all, much less a Fifteenth Amendment granting blacks the right to vote.

The fact that the legal meaning of section 1 was not the focus of discussion in 1866 underscores the difficulty of answering the question of what section 1 meant to Republicans. There are very direct statements from two leading congressional Republicans indicating that section 1 of the amendment will require the states to obey the Bill of Rights. No one explicitly denied that it would have that effect. Beyond that, however, much of the evidence is partially hidden in generalizations—and is to be found in history, and ideology, and legal thought long forgotten and in what legal theories meant to Republicans in 1866 instead of what they mean to us today.

Republicans often suggested that the Fourteenth Amendment would protect all rights of citizens or all constitutional rights. They often said that it would secure an equality of basic rights to citizens. Although Republicans were emphatic on these points, the content of the rights secured received less attention. So to understand the content of "all rights of citizens" in the minds of Republicans requires a detailed historical inquiry.

In following the long and winding trail in search of one purpose of section 1 of the Fourteenth Amendment, I hope to have the reader's patience and understanding. I am looking for probable Republican understanding of a question to which they devoted comparatively little direct attention. Several reasons for the lack of attention are clear. Republicans were playing for the higher stakes of political power. And they took for granted much that we would like them to have discussed instead of to have assumed. Part of the effort of this book will be to uncover those assumptions.

At most, history can point to the likely purposes of section 1 of the amendment. Historical background, Republican ideology, the text of the amendment, congressional debates, and evidence from the ratification process all combined can point to probable purposes. Because of the number of people involved and the lack of direct evidence as to what many of them thought about the meaning of section 1, absolute certainty is impossible.

Statements by Republican congressmen were made in a particular context. Their views were shaped by their experience of the assault on civil liberties that occurred during the crusade against slavery and by a political ideology that emphasized the Declaration of Independence and the rights of the individual. Abraham Lincoln evoked this context when he spoke of the Declaration of Independence.

I think the authors of that notable instrument intended to include *all* men, but they did not intend to declare all men equal *in all respects*. They did not mean to say all were equal in color, size, intellect, moral developments, or social capacity. They defined with tolerable distinctness, in what respects they did consider all men created equal—equal in "certain inalienable rights, among which are life, liberty, and the pursuit of happiness." This they said, and this meant. They did not mean to assert the obvious untruth, that all were then actually enjoying that equality, nor yet, that they were about to confer it immediately upon them. In fact they had no power to confer such a boon. They meant simply to declare the *right*, so that the *enforcement* of it might follow as fast as circumstances should permit. They meant to set up a standard maxim for free society, which should be familiar to all, and revered by all; constantly looked to, constantly labored for, and even though never perfectly attained, constantly approximated, and thereby constantly spreading and deepening its influence, and augmenting the happiness and value of life to all people of all colors everywhere. The assertion that "all men are created equal" was of no practical use in effecting our separation from Great Britain; and it was placed in the Declaration, not for that, but for future use. Its authors meant it to be, thank God, it is now proving itself, a stumbling block to those who in after times might seek to turn a free people back into the hateful paths of despotism. They knew the proneness of prosperity to breed tyrants, and they meant when such should re-appear in this fair land and commence their vocation they should find left for them at least one hard nut to crack.[89]

Since Republicans spoke and acted in a particular legal and historical context, it is that context that I now examine.

Chapter 1

From the Revolution to the Bill of Rights

and Beyond

From the Revolution to the Bill of Rights

When the American colonies rebelled against Great Britain, the rebels gave their reasons in the Declaration of Independence: "We hold these truths to be self-evident: that all men are created equal; that they are endowed, by their Creator, with certain unalienable rights; that among these are life, liberty, and the pursuit of happiness. That to secure these rights, governments are instituted among men, deriving their just powers from the consent of the governed." The rhetoric, of course, was more advanced than the reality. Blacks were held as slaves in the colonies, not even all white males would get the vote for another sixty years or so, and all women were disfranchised and deprived of important liberties. Still, rhetoric has a way of shaping reality. By the twentieth century America was closer to the ideals of the Declaration than it was in 1776. The words of the Declaration itself were a factor in bringing about the change.

According to the Declaration, people have unalienable rights to liberty. The ideology of the revolutionary generation shaped the later American Bill of Rights. This revolutionary ideology combined and wove together both the natural rights of man and the historic rights of Englishmen.[1] The colonists emphasized natural rights and historic liberties as a result of their view of government. Government was naturally hostile to human liberty and happiness.[2] Political power was essentially aggressive.[3] The Continental Congress in its Address to the Inhabitants of Quebec quoted Marquis Beccaria:

"In every human society . . . there is an effort, continually tending to confer on one part the heighth of power and happiness, and to reduce the other to the extreme of weakness and misery. The intent of good laws is to oppose this effort, and to diffuse their influence universally and equally."

Rulers, stimulated by this pernicious "effort," and subjects animated by the just "intent of opposing good laws against it," have occasioned that vast variety of events, that fill the histories of so many nations.[4]

The rebellious colonists dealt with the problem of aggressive political power by several devices: separation of powers, an independent judiciary, the right of people to have a share in their own government by representatives chosen by themselves, and an insistence on the natural and historical rights and liberties of citizens reflected in revolutionary bills of rights of the several states.[5]

By 1787 delegates from the states had drafted a constitution to replace the Articles of Confederation. Juxtaposed to the ideology of the Revolution was the reality of slavery. Although the framers declined to use the word, their constitution contained clauses designed to protect the institution. As Luther Martin, member of the Constitutional Convention from Maryland, put it, the framers had avoided "expressions which might be odious in the ears of Americans, although they were willing to admit into their system the things which the expressions signified."[6]

One of the most significant constitutional advantages extended to slavery was that each slave was counted as three-fifths of a person for purposes of representation in the House of Representatives. In addition, the importation of slaves could not be banned by the federal government until 1808, and this provision could not be amended. Provision was also made for the return of fugitive slaves: "No person held to service or labor in one State under the laws thereof, escaping into another, shall, in consequence of any law or regulation therein, be discharged from such service or labor, but shall be delivered up on the claim of the party to whom such service or labor may be due."[7] In addition to provisions explicitly protecting slavery was the absence of explicit power to remove it. In the Virginia ratifying convention James Madison assured his fellows that the Constitution did not allow interference with slavery in the states.[8]

These concessions to slavery produced some protests. George Mason, delegate from Virginia and a leading advocate of a federal bill of rights, complained that delegates from South Carolina and Georgia were more interested in protecting the right to import slaves than in promoting "the Liberty and Happiness of the people."[9] Luther Martin's criticisms were more fundamental and prophetic. Slavery, Martin insisted, "is inconsistent with the genius of republicanism, and has the

tendency to destroy those principles on which it is supported." It habit-
uated people to tryanny and oppression.[10]

Some framers rationalized the compromise with slavery on the
assumption that the institution would soon die out. In truth, however,
a compromise was made in the interest of the Union. While the framers compromised with slavery, they took steps to prevent its spread to
new states. Particularly after the adoption of the Bill of Rights the
Constitution reflected the Jekyll-and-Hyde character of the nation.
The nation sought simultaneously to protect liberty and slavery.

When the Constitution replaced the Articles of Confederation, proposals to preface the Constitution with a Bill of Rights had been
rejected. As a result, George Mason, a delegate to the Constitutional
Convention from Virginia, objected to the proposed Constitution:
"There is no declaration of rights: and the laws of the general government being paramount to the laws and constitutions of the several
states, the declaration of rights, in the separate states, are no security."[11]

Mason's concerns were shared by others, including Thomas Jefferson,
then ambassador to France. In December 1787 Jefferson wrote James
Madison about his thoughts on the proposed Constitution. After indicating what he liked, Jefferson went on to what he did not like. First
among these was "the omission of a bill of rights providing clearly and
without aid of sophisms for freedom of religion, freedom of the press,
protection against standing armies, restriction against monopolies,
the eternal and unremitting force of the habeas corpus laws, and trials
by juries in all matters of fact triable by the laws of the land and not by
the law of Nations."[12] Jefferson rejected the idea that trial by jury
should not be guarantied because some states "have been so incau-
tious as to abandon this mode of trial."

> It would have been much more just and wise to have concluded the
> other way that as most of the states had judiciously preserved this
> palladium, those who had wandered should be brought back to it,
> and to have established general right instead of general wrong. Let
> me add that a bill of rights is what the people are entitled to against
> every government on earth, general or particular, and what no just
> government should refuse, or rest on inference.[13]

Madison responded to Jefferson that he also favored a bill of rights
but had never thought the omission a material defect. First, he thought
the rights were reserved by the manner in which federal powers were
granted. Second, he thought there was reason to fear that "a positive
declaration of some of the most essential rights could not be obtained
in the requisite latitude." Third, the jealousy of state governments
against the federal government would afford a security. And finally,

"because experience proves the inefficacy of a bill of rights on those occasions when its control is most needed. Repeated violations of these parchment barriers have been committed by overbearing majorities in every state."[14]

Writing back to Madison from Paris, Jefferson said Madison had missed an argument in favor of a declaration of rights that had great weight with him, "the legal check which it puts into the hands of the judiciary."[15] Jefferson admitted that experience had often proved the inefficacy of a bill of rights.

> But tho it is not absolutely efficacious under all circumstances, it is of great potency always, and rarely inefficacious. A brace the more will often keep up the building which would have fallen with that brace the less. There is a remarkable difference between the characters of the Inconveniencies which attend a Declaration of rights, and those which attend the want of it. The inconveniences of the Declaration are that it may cramp government in its useful exertions. But the evil of this is shortlived, moderate, and reparable. The inconveniencies of the want of a Declaration are permanent, afflicting and irreparable: they are in constant progression from bad to worse.[16]

After the ratification of the Constitution, Madison led the congressional fight for a bill of rights. The amendments Madison first suggested included proposals designed to secure all of the rights that were finally set out in the federal Bill of Rights. In addition, Madison proposed to provide that "no state shall violate the equal rights of conscience, or the freedom of the press, or the trial by jury in criminal cases."[17] Although most of Madison's proposals were adopted, many in the very language in which he proposed them, his proposal for these explicit limitations on the power of the states was not.

In Congress Madison made his famous, and ultimately effective, argument in favor of the adoption of a Bill of Rights.

> It may be thought that all paper barriers against the power of the community are too weak to be worthy of attention. I am sensible they are not so strong as to satisfy gentlemen of every description who have seen and examined thoroughly the texture of such a defense; yet, as they have a tendency to impress some degree of respect for them, to establish the public opinion in their favor, and rouse the attention of the whole community, it may be one means to control the majority from those acts to which they might be otherwise inclined.[18]

Madison considered and finally rejected the argument that the limited powers of the federal government were a sufficient security for liberty. The general government had a right to pass all laws necessary to collect its revenue, so "may not general warrants be considered necessary for this purpose"?[19] Finally, Madison picked up and elaborated the argument that had been made earlier by Jefferson.

> It has been said, that it is unnecessary to load the constitution with this provision, because it was not found effectual in the constitutions of the particular States. It is true, that there are a few particular States in which some of the most valuable articles have not, at one time or another, been violated; but it does not follow but they may have, to a certain degree, a salutary effect against the abuse of power. If they are incorporated into the constitution, independent tribunals of justice will consider themselves in peculiar manner the guardian of those rights; they will be an impenetrable bulwark against every assumption of power in the legislative or executive; they will be naturally led to resist every encroachment upon the rights expressly stipulated for in the constitution by the declaration of rights.[20]

So, in the end, the Bill of Rights was proposed by the Congress and ratified by the states.

The Bill of Rights Goes to Court

Not until 1833, apparently, in the case of *Barron v. Baltimore*,[21] did the United States Supreme Court consider whether or not rights in the federal Bill of Rights limited the states. Barron contended that the City of Baltimore had diverted certain streams so that sand was deposited around his wharf, making it of little value. As a result, Barron said, his property had been taken for public use without just compensation.

In *Barron* the Supreme Court might have held: (1) that the rights recognized in the Bill of Rights were basic liberties of the citizen that no government, state or national, had power to deny; (2) the Constitution was the supreme law of the land; and (3) consequently, acts of the states infringing rights in the Bill of Rights were void. As W. W. Crosskey has shown, some commentators and some state courts had read the generally phrased rights in the Bill of Rights in this way before *Barron* was decided.[22]

The Supreme Court rejected this approach. Chief Justice John Marshall noted that the original Constitution expressly limited the power of the states in certain respects: "In every inhibition intended to act on State power, words are employed which directly express that intent." The application of such clauses to the states, Marshall said, is not "left to construction. It is averred in positive words." If states had been concerned about additional safeguards to liberty needed to prevent encroachments of their own governments, Marshall insisted, they would have amended their own constitutions. "Had Congress engaged in the extraordinary occupation of improving the constitutions of the several States by affording the people additional protection from the exercise of power by their own governments in matters which concern themselves alone, they would have declared this purpose in plainly intelligible language." But, Marshall argued, no such result was intended. The Bill of Rights was adopted because of the fear of abuses of power by the federal government. It simply had no application to the states.[23] Most scholars have concluded that Marshall's reading of the intent of the framers of the Bill of Rights was correct.[24] James Madison had proposed to make only a few Bill of Rights guaranties a limit on the states. That Congress rejected even this proposal seems to indicate that *Barron* was correctly decided.

Although Chief Justice Marshall had strong nationalist tendencies, the decision in *Barron* was a vindication of states' rights. Although Marshall had relied on natural law particularly in the protection of property, the decision left the states free to nullify basic rights, including the right to property.[25]

The decision in *Barron* never mentioned slavery, but it seems unlikely that the issue can have been far from the minds of the Justices. The abolitionist William Lloyd Garrison had launched the *Liberator* in 1831[26] just two years before the decision in *Barron*. Nat Turner's rebellion (a massacre of plantation families by blacks) had left southern whites with a conviction that abolitionist propaganda was incendiary—the seditious spark likely to provoke a slave rebellion.[27]

Barron avoided troubling questions. It promoted the stability of the Union at the expense of liberty. It left southern states free to suppress speech and press on the question of slavery and left them free to deny procedural and substantive rights to blacks. That the decision may be the most reasonable reading of the constitutional text is, of course, only part of the explanation for it.

The next time the Supreme Court considered the matter, also in 1833, the contention that the federal Bill of Rights prohibited state infringements of trial by jury was given short shrift: "As to the amendments to the Constitution of the United States, they must be put out of the case: since it is now settled that those amendments do not extend to the states."[28]

The Court looked at the application of the Bill of Rights to the states again in 1845, in the case of *Permoli v. New Orleans*.[29] New Orleans had passed an ordinance making it unlawful to expose any corpse in any Catholic church. The penalty for violation was a fine of fifty dollars. Permoli, a Roman Catholic priest, had violated the ordinance. In the action against him he contended that the ordinance violated the First Amendment of the United States Constitution, since the corpse was exposed as a part of a Catholic funeral. The Supreme Court rejected the First Amendment argument summarily. "The Constitution," the Court noted, "makes no provision for protecting citizens in their respective States in their religious liberties; this is left to State constitutions and laws; nor is there any inhibition imposed by the Constitution of the United States in this respect on the States."[30] Permoli's case was dismissed.

Although the Supreme Court considered the application of the Bill of Rights to the states settled, others did not. In *Nunn v. Georgia,*[31] decided in 1846, the Georgia Supreme Court considered an act that prohibited carrying weapons. The Georgia constitution seems to have lacked any protection for the right of bearing arms. At any rate, the Georgia court relied on the Second Amendment to the United States Constitution. First, the Georgia court cited a number of decisions under the constitutions of other states protecting the right to bear arms.

> It is true, that these adjudications are all made on clauses in the State Constitution; but these instruments confer no *new rights* on the people which did not belong to them before. When, I would ask, did any legislative body in the Union have the right to deny to its citizens the privilege of keeping and bearing arms in defense of themselves and their country? . . .
>
> If this right, "inestimable to freemen," has been guarantied to British subjects since the abdication and flight of the last of the Stuarts and the ascension of the Prince of Orange, did it not belong to our colonial ancestors in this western hemisphere? . . . Has it been . . . forfeited here by the substitution and adoption of our own Constitution? . . . On the contrary, this is one of the fundamental principles upon which rests the great fabric of civil liberty, reared by the fathers of the revolution and of the country.[32]

While the Georgia court relied on the Second Amendment to the federal Bill of Rights, still it was "aware that it has been decided, that this, like other amendments adopted at the same time, is a restriction upon the government of the United States, and does not extend to the individual States."[33] But, in spite of decisions to the contrary, the Supreme Court of Georgia held that the Second Amendment limited the state legislature.

The language in the *second* amendment is broad enough to embrace both Federal and State governments—nor is there anything in its terms which restricts its meaning. The preamble which was prefixed to these amendments shows, that they originated in the fear that the powers of the general government were not sufficiently limited. Several of the States, in their act of ratification, recommended that further restrictive clauses should be added. . . . But admitting all this, does it follow that because the people refused to delegate to the general government the power to take from them the right to keep and bear arms that they designed to rest it in the State governments? Is it a right reserved to the *States* or to *themselves?* Is it not an unalienable right, which lies at the bottom of every free government? We do not believe that, because the people withheld this arbitrary power of disfranchisement from Congress, they ever intended to confer it on the local legislatures. This is a right too dear to be confided to a republican legislature.[34]

In another case the Supreme Court of Illinois assumed that the due process clause of the Fifth Amendment limited the states,[35] though in this case the court seems simply not to have been aware of the decision in *Barron v. Baltimore*. In fact, state courts or judges in Alabama, Connecticut, Georgia, Iowa, Illinois, Kansas, Massachusetts, Missouri, North Carolina, Rhode Island, Tennessee, Texas, and Vermont suggested that the specific rights in the federal Bill of Rights limited the states after the decision in *Barron*.[36] Other state courts explicitly held, to the contrary, that the Bill of Rights did not apply to the states.

Some Democratic politicians (notably Stephen A. Douglas) and some southern Democrats also believed that the guaranties of the Bill of Rights limited the states.[37] Indeed, some southerners seem to have been moving toward an interpretation of the due process clause by which it would have protected the right to hold slave property even in free states.[38]

The idea that the guaranties in the Bill of Rights limited the states, as well as the federal government, was also advocated by opponents of slavery. Indeed, the experience and ideas of people opposed to slavery shaped the Fourteenth Amendment. The Fourteenth Amendment, of course, is the vehicle by which the Supreme Court (much later) held that the states are required to obey at least most of the guaranties of the Bill of Rights.

Chapter 2

The Historical Background

of the Fourteenth Amendment

Slavery and Civil Liberties, 1787–1864

The history out of which the Fourteenth Amendment grew was that of slavery, sectional conflict, secession by the South, victory by the North, abolition of slavery, and the problem of the status of the newly freed blacks and the rebellious southern states.[1]

After 1830 slavery became a divisive political issue. Should slavery be allowed to expand into the territories? What rights did southerners have to northern assistance in recapturing fugitive slaves? The more explosive of these issues was the expansion of slavery into new territories. Most northerners, and at first even most abolitionists, accepted the constitutional theory that slavery in the states was beyond the reach of Congress. But, expansion of the institution to the territories was a far different matter.

In the Northwest Ordinance of 1787, Congress prohibited slavery in every part of the West under congressional jurisdiction.[2] After 1787, however, southern slaveholders demanded and received increasing concessions in favor of the expansion of slavery.

In 1820 controversy erupted in Congress over the admission of Missouri as a slave state. Missouri was finally admitted with slavery, but slavery was prohibited in the remainder of the Louisiana Purchase lying north of latitude 36 degrees, 30 minutes. After the Mexican War and further territorial expansion, the slavery question was raised again. Efforts to extend the Missouri Compromise line were defeated. Instead, the Utah and New Mexico territories were opened to slavery. In Oregon and certain other territories slavery was forbidden.[3]

The Kansas and Nebraska territories had been included in the Missouri Compromise as areas in which slavery was forbidden, but escalating southern demands led Congress to abrogate the compromise. Under the Kansas-Nebraska Act of 1854 the territories would be admitted as states "with or without slavery as their constitutions may provide."[4] Instead of having Congress prohibit slavery, the question was to be left to the people of the territory, or so it seemed. Congress provided for appeal on the slavery question from the territorial court to the United States Supreme Court.

The Kansas-Nebraska Act immediately ignited a political firestorm. Only seven of the forty-four northern Democrats in the House who voted for the Kansas-Nebraska bill won reelection. At the same time the Republican party was being born—founded in large part on hostility to the "slave power." The party's rise was meteoric. By 1856 with the candidacy of John Charles Frémont, it had made a strong run for the presidency.[5]

Southerners were not satisfied, as it turned out, to leave the question of slavery to the voters of the territories. They ultimately insisted that slaveholders had a constitutional right, protected by the due process clause, to take and hold slaves in any territory. Chief Justice Taney gave their argument his stamp of judicial approval in his opinion in the *Dred Scott* case.

But the arguments for the extension of slavery did not stop there. Congressman John A. Gilmer of North Carolina cited the *Dred Scott* decision to support his argument that new states could not confiscate slaves imported during the territorial period.[6] On November 17, 1857, the newspaper, the *Washington Union*, an organ of the Democratic party and particularly of President James Buchanan, argued that emancipation in the northern states had been an outrageous attack on property rights and that state laws prohibiting slavery were unconstitutional.[7]

As a sectional party created by the controversy over slavery, the Republicans had a vested political interest in promoting the controversy.[8] The common ground occupied by Republicans was opposition to the expansion of slavery. At first, most Republicans agreed that slavery was illegal in the territories but that Congress could not interfere with the institution within the states. Although they initially recognized limitations on government power to attack slavery directly, Republicans remained steadfastly against slavery. Slavery, as Lincoln said, was to be put in the "course of ultimate extinction."[9] Most Republicans hoped to destroy slavery within the southern states by developing local opposition. They expected federal patronage and free flow of antislavery literature through the mails to nurture opposition that would grow and eventually destroy the institution.[10] Once freedom of speech and of the press were restored in the South, Republicans believed they would have more votes there than Democrats did in the North.[11]

The territorial question, as Don Fehrenbacher has noted, was only a skirmish line in a more extensive struggle.[12] Lincoln emphasized that although the immediate question was the expansion of slavery into the territories, Republicans should "never forget that we have before us the whole right or wrong of slavery in this Union." For Lincoln, the fact that slavery was morally wrong everywhere was the linchpin of the argument against its expansion.[13]

Even if Republicans stuck to their position that Congress could not prohibit it in the southern states, southerners recognized the threat Republicans posed to slavery. There was the clear and present danger that, as southern leaders warned, "cohorts of federal office holders, abolitionists may be sent into our midst" and postmasters would "load" the mails "with incendiary documents." One southern newspaper warned that Republicans hoped to use nonslaveholders in the South as a "great lever" to "extirpate slavery."[14] In addition to agreeing on a policy of containment of slavery, Republicans also shared a libertarian view of government—a libertarianism that was shaped by their experience with the crusade against slavery in the thirty years before the Civil War.

As public criticism of slavery increased in the 1830s, so did attempts by slaveholders and their allies to stifle antislavery speeches, publications, and actions. To protect slavery, slaveholders and their allies tried, with considerable success, to restrict the rights of whites and free blacks. Many opponents of slavery responded by emphasizing legal rights belonging to persons and citizens under the Constitution and Bill of Rights. To defend free blacks, they insisted that free blacks were citizens. Since many threats to the liberties of free citizens came from the states, they developed a legal theory by which the states as well as the federal government could not deny the fundamental rights of American citizens.

Reacting to the restrictions on liberty that resulted from slavery, Republicans made concern for protection of the rights in the Bill of Rights a central part of the ideology of the Republican party. By 1866 leading Republicans accepted the doctrine that the states could not restrict the fundamental liberties of American citizens. The doctrine had been central to the effort to protect opponents of slavery and had been, and remained, pivotal in the effort to protect free blacks threatened by racism.

Prior to the Civil War prejudice against blacks was extensive. Even free blacks in the North often were prohibited from testifying in cases where a white was a party[15] and, in some northern states, they were barred from entering or remaining in the state.[16] Before the war many

Republicans considered free blacks citizens and opposed denial of these basic civil rights to blacks.[17] Other Republicans were less sympathetic with the rights of free blacks. Although they opposed slavery and opposed its extension into the territories, they did not necessarily support civil rights for blacks.[18] Some even hoped to colonize them in Africa.[19]

By the time congressional debate on the Fourteenth Amendment got under way, the political stock of blacks had reached an all-time high. Black troops had fought for the Union, slavery had been abolished, and most Republicans considered blacks citizens entitled to basic civil, but not necessarily political, rights. Before the Civil War protection of blacks and slaves had threatened the Union. But during the Civil War abolition of slavery was associated with the cause of the Union. Emancipation was justified initially as a war measure designed to deprive the South of the assistance of slaves. In 1864 Lincoln concluded that the 140,000 or so black soldiers, seamen, and laborers supporting the Union cause were crucial to its success. "Take from us and give to the enemy [this black support]," Lincoln wrote, "and we can no longer maintain the contest."[20]

Republicans had always been politically strongest in their attack on the slave power and politically weakest in their assertion of rights for blacks. Racism was a potent weapon for Democrats.[21] During the Civil War a new synthesis began to emerge. Protection for blacks was associated with defeat of the slave power. Abraham Lincoln led a united Republican party in national abolition of slavery—a goal advocated only by a handful of radical political abolitionists just a few years before.

The primary goal of the abolitionists was being realized. Blacks were not to be deported but were to be incorporated into American society. Under the Civil Rights Act passed just prior to the Fourteenth Amendment, blacks would be recognized as citizens and would receive at least the basic rights to own property, to sue and be sued in court, and to enjoy the same legal protection as white citizens.[22]

The years of discrimination against blacks are an important part of the history leading to the Fourteenth Amendment. But a crucial part of the history leading to the Fourteenth Amendment is the relation between the concern for the protection of civil liberties and the crusade to abolish slavery. The confrontation between slavery and liberty went back years before 1854, when the Republican party was founded. Both politically active abolitionists and others repeatedly invoked the Bill of Rights in their agitation against slavery. Sometimes they appealed to the Bill of Rights as a shield against federal action; sometimes, in spite of the 1833 decision of *Barron v. Baltimore*,[23] they cited it as a limitation on both the states and the federal government.

836, for example, Congress considered federal suppression of very publications. Abolitionists had conceived a plan to print numbers of antislavery publications and to mail them throughout the country. Southerners insisted that such tactics threatened slave revolts. Sacks of abolitionist literature were seized and burned in Charleston, South Carolina.[24]

Amos Kendall, postmaster general under President Andrew Jackson, concluded that the states could legally ban abolitionist publications. One clause of the Constitution that might provide protection for abolitionist literature was article IV, section 2, which provided that the citizens of each state are entitled to all privileges and immunities of citizens in the several states. Kendall, however, relied on a narrow reading of the clause. He insisted that it did not provide the citizen of Massachusetts any greater rights to mail antislavery publications to South Carolina than the citizen of South Carolina would have under state law.[25]

Following Kendall's suggestion, President Andrew Jackson recommended that Congress prohibit circulation through the mails of "incendiary publications intended to instigate slaves to insurrection." The proposal did not go far enough to suit Senator John C. Calhoun of South Carolina. He proposed a bill to prohibit postmasters from mailing any publication "touching on the subject of slavery" when the addressee's state prohibited its circulation. Daniel Webster opposed the bill because it violated the First and Fourth Amendments.[26] William Plummer, a former senator from New Hampshire, published a pamphlet attacking Calhoun's bill. The pamphlet asserted that First Amendment rights of speech and press were protected against both federal and state interference.[27]

As antislavery agitation increased in the 1830s, a number of southern state legislatures passed resolutions demanding that northern states pass laws to suppress antislavery expression.[28] Most northern legislatures and leaders were equivocal or worse in response. (New York, for example, noted that mob action made legislation unnecessary.) The Vermont legislature, however, responded with a resolution passed in 1836 that "neither Congress nor the State Governments have any constitutional right to abridge free expression of opinions, or the transmission of them through the public mail."[29]

Starting about 1830 southern states adopted laws restricting freedom of speech and of the press in an effort to suppress antislavery ideas.[30] In 1836 Virginia made it a serious crime for a member of an "abolition" society to enter the state and "advocate or advise the abolition of slavery."[31] In addition, laws were passed making it a felony to circulate books that denied the master's right to property in his slaves.[32]

A Louisiana statute imposed harsh penalties on anyone who spoke or published language that had a tendency to produce discontent among free blacks or excite insubordination among slaves.[33] Similar laws existed in other southern states.[34]

Proslavery public opinion, mobs, and vigilance committees made extensive resort to antiabolitionist laws unnecessary.[35] Still, there were some prosecutions. In 1858 over fifty Republican congressmen endorsed Hinton R. Helper's book attacking slavery, *The Impending Crisis*. One hundred thousand copies of an abridgment were prepared, to be circulated as a Republican campaign document.[36] Meanwhile, southerners who circulated the book faced criminal prosecution. An indictment for circulating the book was brought in Virginia, but the defendant was not brought to trial.[37] In North Carolina, Daniel Worth was indicted for circulating the book. He was convicted and sentenced to twelve months in prison. On appeal, he claimed that his conduct was protected since the book was circulated only among whites. The North Carolina Supreme Court rejected this defense. For books that had the "evident tendency . . . to cause slaves to be discontented and free negroes dissatisfied," circulation with the intent to propagate the books' ideas was criminal, whether it be among whites or blacks.[38]

Southern states passed laws requiring postmasters to rifle the mail and to notify justices of the peace if they found publications "denying the right of masters to property in their slaves and inculcating the duty of resistance to such right."[39] Under such a law the *New York Tribune* was banned by a Virginia postmaster in 1859.[40]

In addition to being legally restricted from spreading antislavery doctrine, abolitionists were the victims of mob violence.[41] In these cases local authorities often failed to make any effort to protect the victims.[42] Nor were attacks limited to abolitionists. A meeting for Frémont, the Republican presidential candidate, was broken up in Baltimore in 1856.[43] In fact, in the Lincoln-Douglas debates Stephen Douglas attacked the Republicans as a sectional party and, as proof, offered the fact that the Republicans were not able to proclaim their doctrines in certain sections of the country. Lincoln responded by pointing out that Douglas could not proclaim democracy and denounce monarchy in Russia.[44] Threats of violent retaliation against those with antislavery sentiments were even made on the floor of the United States Senate. Senator Henry S. Foote of Mississippi threatened an antislavery senator, John P. Hale of New Hampshire, with lynching if he came to Mississippi.[45]

To a remarkable degree, civil libertarian concerns appeared in the political platforms of the major antislavery parties. Though none advocated interference with slavery in the states where it already existed, the platforms illustrate concern for liberties set out in the Bill of Rights. The very slogan of the Republican party in 1856 was "Free Speech, Free Press, Free Men, Free Labor, Free Territory, and Frémont."[46]

In the mid-1850s Republicans gave detailed attention to events in the Kansas Territory. By the Kansas-Nebraska Act, Kansas had been opened to settlement under the doctrine of popular sovereignty—the people of the territory themselves would decide the slavery question. Kansas promptly and literally became a battleground between pro- and antislavery factions. Illegal proslavery voters from Missouri invaded the state and elected a proslavery legislature. The legislature passed a stringent slave code providing severe penalties for antislavery expression and a test oath for officeholders.[47] Opponents of slavery in Kansas—including a large number of immigrants from the North who had come in part to save Kansas from slavery—responded by organizing a free state government and constitution. That constitution prohibited both slavery and immigration into the state by blacks, illustrating the fact that not all opponents of slavery favored civil rights for blacks.

So Kansas had two governments. Armed conflict escalated.[48] President Franklin Pierce and the national Democratic administration supported the proslavery government in Kansas.

The issue raised by "bleeding Kansas" was ideally suited to the needs of the burgeoning Republican party. Republicans in their platform of 1856 complained that the national Democratic administration had sanctioned violation of the constitutional rights of the people of the Kansas Territory, including their right to keep and bear arms; the right of an accused to a speedy public trial by an impartial jury; the right of the people to be secure in their persons, houses, papers, and effects from unreasonable searches and seizures; the right not to be deprived of life, liberty, or property without due process of law; and the right to freedom of speech and of the press.[49] The closing paragraph of the 1856 Republican platform asserted that "the spirit of our institutions as well as the Constitution" guaranteed "liberty of conscience and equality of rights among citizens" and opposed "all legislation impairing their security."[50]

In 1856 Congressman John A. Bingham (who later wrote section 1 of the Fourteenth Amendment) spoke to the House of Representatives on the contested Kansas election.[51] Bingham criticized laws passed by the Kansas Territorial Assembly.[52] Kansas was a federal territory. Bingham had no doubt that the guaranties of the Bill of Rights applied to it. Because the legislation criticized by Bingham was identical to that passed by a number of states, however, his comments also indicate how badly he thought the states were abrogating the basic liberties of their citizens.

The Kansas laws made it a felony to aid or harbor an escaped slave.[53] They also made it a felony "to assert that persons have not the right to hold slaves in said Territories," and made it a felony to circulate any writing containing any sentiments calculated to induce slaves to escape from the service of their masters.[54] Bingham attacked the last two provisions as violations of the First Amendment. "Any territorial enactment which makes it a felony for a citizen of the United States, within the territory of the United States 'to know, to argue, and to utter freely according to conscience,' is absolutely void, because it is not consistent with that provision which declares that the Congress of the United States shall not pass any law abridging the freedom of speech or of the press."[55]

Congressman Bingham's deep hostility to the Kansas laws can be gleaned from the following passage from his speech:

Congress is to abide by this statute, which makes it a felony for a citizen to utter or publish in that Territory "any sentiment calculated to induce slaves to escape from the service of their masters." Hence it would be a felony there to utter the strong words of Algernon Sidney, "resistance to tyrants is obedience to God"; . . . a felony to read in the hearing of one of those fettered bondsmen the words of the Declaration, "All men are born free and equal, and endowed by their Creator with the inalienable rights of life and liberty"; . . . a felony to harbor a slave escaping from his thralldom; a felony to aid freedom in its flight. . . . Before you hold this enactment to be law, burn our immortal Declaration and our free-written Constitution, fetter our free press, and finally penetrate the human soul and put out the light of understanding which the breath of the Almighty hath kindled.

. . . .

This pretended legislation of Kansas violates the Constitution in this—that it abridges the freedom of speech and of the press, and deprives persons of liberty without due process of law, or any process but that of brute force.[56]

This history shows that the rights set out in the Bill of Rights were cherished and appealed to by antislavery northerners and were disregarded in the South and elsewhere in the interest of protecting slavery. It shows that many in the North were discontent with the protection the Bill of Rights had received in the states prior to the Civil War.[57] Among these were leading members of the Republican party.

The purposes Republicans had in mind in passing the Fourteenth Amendment should be assessed in light of several factors: the pressing practical and political problems facing the Republicans of the

Thirty-ninth Congress, their view of the history of the previous thirty years, their political philosophy, and their legal ideas.

The Fourteenth Amendment:
Historical Background, 1864–1866

Practical and Political Problems. Republicans in Congress in 1866 shared a number of common characteristics. Many were of New England origin. Often their ideas were shaped by reforming Christianity, which saw the battle over slavery as a battle between good and evil. A number of congressional Republicans had years of experience in the antislavery cause—in the Liberty and Free Soil parties and then in the Republican party.

Though most Republicans had started with the view that slavery in the states was and should be beyond the power of the national government, the Civil War had revolutionized their views. Total abolition of slavery had become part of the creed of the Republican party. The congressmen of 1866 had been elected in 1864. The Republican platform of that year set out the Republican orthodoxy on the question of slavery. "*Resolved*, That as slavery was the cause, and now constitutes the strength of the Rebellion, and as it must be, always and everywhere, hostile to the principles of Republican Government, justice and national safety demand its utter and complete extirpation from the soil of the Republic."[58] As a result of Lincoln's support for emancipation, radical abolitionism had become Republican orthodoxy by 1866.

It is common for historians to emphasize the split between Radical and more conservative Republicans. And such divisions unquestionably existed, particularly on Reconstruction and the political rights of the newly freed slaves. As Michael Benedict has noted in his study of Reconstruction politics, however, there was much agreement among Republicans on fundamentals. Conservative Republicans tended to see Radical proposals not as wrong but as impractical. Radicals saw conservatives as overly influenced by practicality. As Benedict notes, "Their common anti-slavery heritage, their shared desire to guarantee the security of southern loyalists, their determination to realize a Reconstruction that would permanently cement the Union, and their united wish to see justice done to the freed men enabled Republicans to act in fundamental harmony under great pressure despite disagreements."[59]

Another historian of the Civil War era has reached a similar conclusion. According to Herman Belz, the differences between Radical, moderate, and conservative Republicans were differences in

"timing, method and assessment of political reality" instead
ences in ideology or basic objectives.[60]

When the Thirty-ninth Congress assembled in Decembe
faced severe political problems. The South had seceded and
defeated after a bitter war. Southern states were seeking readmission
to Congress and the Union. Slavery had been abolished. Once the
southern states were fully restored to Congress and the Union, they
would, except for the limitations of the new Thirteenth Amendment,
enjoy all the powers and rights they had possessed before the Civil
War.[61]

Republicans had long been troubled by the South's interference
with rights guarantied by the Bill of Rights. After the war, furthermore,
the South apparently believed that its power to regulate its local black
population, short of actual reenslavement, was undiminished. Southern legislatures passed Black Codes denying blacks many important
liberties secured to whites. The codes restricted such basic rights as the
freedom to move, to contract, to own property, to assemble, and to
bear arms.[62] Many northern states had deprived blacks of such basic
rights before the Civil War. But in the changed political climate of
1866 Republicans were unwilling to tolerate such deprivations, as the
passage of the Civil Rights bill would show.

The southern states also passed provisions for the control of black
labor. In Mississippi blacks were compelled to bind themselves to work
for a year and to forfeit the entire year's wages if they left before that
time. The state passed broad vagrancy laws specifically applicable to
blacks. Mississippi penal laws applicable to slaves were reenacted as
applicable to all blacks. Both whites and blacks could be punished by
"corporal punishment, by suspending the party convicted by the
thumbs, not more than two hours in twenty-four, nor more than ten
days."[63]

Last, but not least, the Thirteenth Amendment's abrogation of the
clause by which each slave was counted as three-fifths of a person for
the purposes of representation meant that the rebellious southern
states could expect a substantial increase in their representation in the
House.[64] This last change was the most galling of all. As Don
Fehrenbacher has noted, before the Civil War the power of the South
had been increased by a sort of holding company arrangement. The
South had been the majority section in the Democratic party, and the
party had been the majority party in the nation.[65] In 1866 Republicans faced the prospect that southern states would be counting 100
percent, instead of 60 percent, of disfranchised black former slaves
for purposes of representation.

When the Thirty-ninth Congress assembled in late 1865, southern

representatives were excluded while Congress considered what additional guaranties would be required before their readmission.[66] The
Fourteenth Amendment was the principal additional guaranty ultimately selected by the Congress.

The Republican View of History. Most Republican congressmen agreed
what the history before the framing of the Fourteenth Amendment
meant. Republicans saw events from 1830 to 1866 as a battle between
slavery and freedom, a battle to determine whether the nation would
become all slave or all free. They believed the liberty of all citizens of
the United States hung on the outcome of that battle. They saw slavery
as fundamentally incompatible with a free society. Its survival required
eliminating the basic liberties of all citizens, white as well as black.[67]

Typical of the Republican view was an 1866 speech by Congressman
Tobias Plants of Ohio. Plants was a first-term congressman who studied
law, edited a newspaper, and served in the state legislature before
coming to Congress, and he would later become a state judge.[68]
Speaking early in the Thirty-ninth Congress, Plants first noted that
slaveholders were convinced of their right to hold slaves and to em-
ploy "all the means requisite to their full enjoyment of that guarantee." But "the system would not be secure if men in the slave
States were permitted to discuss the matter in any form; and hence
freedom of speech and the press must be suppressed as the high-
est of crimes; and no man could utter the simplest truths but at
the risk of his life. For more than a quarter of a century the world
knew no despotism so absolute and reckless as that which ruled
the South."[69] Plants then noted that slaveholders demanded the
right to take slaves into any territory of the United States, a right
finally assured in the "immortal infamy of the Dred Scott decision."[70]
But, as slavery moved into the territories, so did the closed society
required to protect it. So, from the dictum in *Dred Scott*, Plants argued,

> naturally unfolded the laws of Kansas, which if in force today, would
> hie you, Mr. Speaker, to the dungeon or the gibbet, if found with a
> copy of the Chronicle or the Globe in your trunk, though used only
> as wrapping paper. And all that was right if slavery was right. But,
> by logical necessity, that same [Dred Scott] decision carried slavery
> with all its consequences into all the States. . . . But if they had a
> right to take and hold their slaves in the free States, they had a right
> to do it in safety, and as they could not hold them safely where
> dissent was permitted, all dissent must be suppressed by the strong
> hand of power. Will any one dare to say this would not have been the
> next step. . . . [O]nly one of two things remained possible—either

the utter destruction of slavery or the total extinguishment of freedom.[71]

Historian Michael Benedict has made a detailed study of attitudes of congressional Republicans toward Reconstruction. By Benedict's calculations about half of the Republicans in the House were Radical. The next-largest group was centrist Republicans.

Benedict rates Plants as a conservative, in both the first and second sessions of the Thirty-ninth Congress.[72] On the issues that divided Republicans — black suffrage and Reconstruction — Plants was unwilling to follow the Radical agenda. Plants' views are significant because they reflect the degree to which conservative Republicans shared basic antislavery assumptions with Radicals.

Plants's conviction that an aggressive slave power had been bent on nationalizing slavery and destroying liberty was a widely shared Republican view. In his 1858 house divided speech Abraham Lincoln had predicted a second *Dred Scott* decision "declaring that the Constitution does not permit a state to exclude slavery from its limits."[73] Nor were such fears totally unfounded. Since Republicans believed slavery was hostile to civil liberty, they had seen its expansionist tendencies as a threat to the freedom of whites in the North.

Speeches by Republicans in the Thirty-eighth Congress, which passed the Thirteenth Amendment abolishing slavery, reflect the Republican view that slavery destroyed constitutional rights. Implicit, and often explicit, in these declarations was their view that the Bill of Rights secured the rights of citizens and protected these rights against interference from any quarter.

Isaac Newton Arnold was a lawyer who had been in Congress since 1860. Arnold had been active in the Free Soil movement of 1848. In 1850 he was a member of the Chicago committee appointed to draw up a protest against the fugitive slave law. He had been elected as a Republican to the state legislature in 1856.[74]

On the radical-conservative continuum, Benedict found Arnold impossible to scale in the first session of the Thirty-eighth Congress and centrist in the second.[75] On questions of slavery and constitutional rights, however, Arnold shared the prevailing Republican view. Looking back in 1864, Arnold complained, "Liberty of speech, freedom of the press, and trial by jury had disappeared in the slave States."[76]

Congressman James Wilson, chairman of the House Judiciary Committee in 1864, was one of the most prestigious Republican congressmen.[77] He insisted that slavery had defied the supremacy clause and nullified the constitutional rights, privileges, and immunities of citizens. "Freedom of religious opinion, freedom of speech and press, and the right of assemblage for the purpose of petition belong to every American citizen, high or low, rich or poor, wherever he may be within the jurisdiction of the United States. With these rights no State may interfere without breach of the bond which holds the Union together."[78]

Still, in the South, "the press has been padlocked, and men's lips have been sealed. Constitutional defense of free discussion by speech or press has been a rope of sand south of the line which marked the limit of dignified free labor in this country."[79] Although Wilson said he "might enumerate many other constitutional rights of the citizen which slavery" had "practically destroyed," he believed he had done enough to prove that slavery "denies to the citizens of each State the privileges and immunities of citizens in the several States."[80]

Representative John A. Kasson was another lawyer who was a veteran of antislavery causes. He had been a delegate to the Free Soil convention in Buffalo in 1848. He subsequently became a Republican and was one of the chief drafters of the Republican platform of 1860. According to the *Dictionary of American Biography*, Kasson was a moderate Republican. Benedict classifies him as an "anti-negro suffrage" Republican in the first session of the Thirty-eighth Congress and as a conservative in the first session of the Thirty-ninth Congress.[81]

During the debate on the abolition of slavery Kasson also referred to the denial of constitutional rights that had resulted from slavery. The privileges and immunities clause, he noted, had been disobeyed in the slave states "for some twenty-five or thirty years past."[82] Kasson apparently considered the First Amendment rights of free speech and press as among those rights secured against state infringement. He noted: "You cannot go into a State of the North in which you do not find refugees from southern states who have been driven from the States in the south where they had a right to live as citizens, because of the tyranny which this institution exercised over public feeling and even over the laws of those States."[83] Slavery "denies the constitutional rights of our citizens in the South, suppresses freedom of speech and of the press, throws types into the rivers when they do not print its will, and violates more clauses of the Constitution than were violated even by the rebels when they commenced this war."[84] According to Kasson, the rebellion against the Constitution had been going on for years.[85]

The proslavery movement had even attempted to suppress freedom of speech and of the press in the North and had impaired the rights of northerners in their states.[86] These attempts had made a strong impression on northerners and had contributed to a rise in antislavery sentiment. Republican Representative John F. Farnsworth of Illinois had been an abolitionist since the 1840s and a supporter of Owen

Lovejoy. He served in Congress from 1862 to 1873[87] with vie\
ing from radical to conservative.[88] In 1864 he noted,

> Then it was, Mr. Speaker, that the slave power got the contr\
> Government, of the executive, legislative, and judicial depar........
> Then it was that they got possession of the high places of society.
> They took possession of the churches. They took possession of the
> lands. Then it became criminal for a man to open his lips in denun-
> ciation of the evil and sin of slaveholding. Then followed those
> scenes of riot and bloodshed in the North, the dragging of Garrison
> through the streets of Boston with a rope around his neck to be
> hanged; the issuing of a message by the Governor of Massachusetts
> Edward Everett, declaring that the men agitating the slavery ques-
> tion were indictable at common law; the indictment in southern
> States of men in the North for anti-slavery publications in the City
> of New York. Then came requisitions upon the Governors of the
> North to surrender the bodies of these men to be taken South to be
> tried; the offering of rewards for the heads of northern men; the
> murder of Lovejoy at Alton; the thrusting of that old patriot, Joshua
> R. Giddings, out of Congress; the attempt to expel John Quincy
> Adams; the throttling of the right of petition; suppressing the free-
> dom of the press; the suppression of the freedom of the mails; all
> these things followed the taking possession of the Government and
> lands by the slave power, until we were the slaves of slaves, being
> chained to the car of this slave Juggernaut.[89]

Some congressmen who spoke of denial of rights to free speech
referred specifically to the right of northerners to speak in the South.
Representative Ebon C. Ingersoll, a Radical elected to fill the vacancy
caused by the death of Owen Lovejoy, referred to the freedom of
speech "which guaranties to the citizen of Illinois . . . the right to
proclaim the eternal principles of liberty, truth, and justice in Mobile,
Savannah, or Charleston with the same freedom and security as though
he were standing at the foot of the Bunker Hill monument."[90] Senator
Daniel Clark complained that slavery had denied constitutional rights
to citizens of other states. He mentioned specifically liberty of speech
and press.[91] Although these congressmen referred to denial of freedom of speech to citizens of other states, they were not simply referring to a narrow or conventional understanding of the privileges and
immunities clause by which northerners would be allowed the same
freedom to attack slavery as people were in the southern states themselves—which is to say none. Instead, they espoused a theory fully protecting freedom of speech against state infringement. Other representatives expressed similar concerns and a similar view of history.[92]

As we have seen in their analysis of the effect of slavery on liberty, these Republican congressmen were essentially correct. Beginning in the 1830s, southern states passed laws abridging freedoms of speech and the press as they applied to slavery. Advocating abolition and denying a master's right to property in slaves were made crimes.[93] Antislavery publications were eliminated from mails in the South, and southern states sought to extradite northerners responsible for anti-slavery publications.[94] What could not be accomplished by law was enforced by mobs.[95] The elimination of free speech in the South affected all Republicans, not just abolitionists.[96]

Guaranties of liberty were also sacrificed to facilitate recapture of fugitive slaves. In several northern states blacks were presumed free, and free blacks were citizens. In the South blacks were presumed slaves.[97] Under the Fugitive Slave Act of 1850[98] blacks living in the North who were claimed as runaway slaves were deprived of the right to testify in their own behalf, to cross-examine witnesses, to benefit of the writ of habeas corpus, and to have a jury trial before they were handed over to the private person claiming them as slaves.[99] So blacks had no right to these procedural protections before they were shipped off to a southern state where their color gave rise to a presumption that they were slaves.[100] Northern personal liberty laws carefully passed to secure basic rights to blacks were invalidated.[101] To make matters worse, the commissioner who decided whether the person brought before him was a fugitive slave received a larger fee if he found the black to be a fugitive slave.[102]

The Civil War put considerable strains on Republican commitments to civil liberties. Once in control of the government and in the midst of civil war, some officials of the Lincoln administration had occasionally suppressed antiadministration newspapers and had arrested Ohio Copperhead Clement Vallandingham for making a speech.[103] These war-time restrictions on free speech produced protests from some Republicans. Horace Greeley protested Vallandingham's arrest.[104] And Senator Lyman Trumbull and Congressman Isaac Arnold addressed a protest meeting about the suppression of the *Chicago News* by General Ambrose Burnside, a suppression based on the paper's repeated expression of disloyal and incendiary statements. In response to a telegram from Trumbull and Arnold, Lincoln rescinded the orders suppressing the paper.[105]

Concern for civil liberties produced some congressional action. The Republican Congress regulated military arrests. An act authorized the president to suspend the writ of habeas corpus during the rebellion. But the secretaries of state and war were required to provide lists of political prisoners to the federal court for indictment or release. Officers in charge of the prisoners were required to obey court orders.[106]

What is surprising is not that Republican devotion to civil liberties wavered when confronted by seditious activity during the Civil War, but that the devotion remained so strong. Its resilience was a tribute to the power of political philosophy.

Republican Political Philosophy. The Republican reaction to the problems of Reconstruction also was molded by political philosophy. Republican congressmen accepted an eighteenth-century view of the relation of man to government. Government existed, as the Declaration of Independence asserted, to protect natural rights of man—inalienable rights to life, liberty, and the pursuit of happiness. Because of the nature of the social compact, all citizens shared their fundamental rights equally.[107]

Although Republicans repeatedly invoked natural rights, for them natural rights did not exclude those protected by the Constitution. Instead, the categories overlapped. Senator James Nye, for example, referred to the "natural and personal" rights protected by the Constitution as a shorthand reference to Bill of Rights liberties.[108] Congressman Columbus Delano noted, "Our democracy protects rights. It was organized for that end not to bestow them." Delano, naturally enough, associated individual liberty with Bill of Rights liberties.[109] Indeed, perhaps the most common Republican refrain in the Thirty-ninth Congress was that life, liberty, and property of American citizens must be protected against denial by the states.

Arguments by Democrats that the protection of fundamental rights would interfere with the legitimate rights of states struck Republicans as absurd. No state retained the legitimate authority to deprive citizens of their fundamental rights because government, at all levels, was designed to protect such rights.[110]

Although Republicans rejected the notion that states could invade the fundamental rights of citizens, they still wanted to preserve the states. They did not want the federal government to supplant them altogether or usurp their basic functions.[111] Several congressmen used an analogy to the solar system. States must be kept within their proper orbit,[112] an orbit that would keep them from colliding with the rights of the individual. But although Republicans wanted to preserve the states, they did not sympathize with the doctrine of states' rights advanced by slaveholders and their Democratic allies in Congress in the years before the Civil War—a doctrine that permitted some citizens to deny the rights of others. States' rights in this sense was seen by Republicans as the cause of the Civil War.[113]

Republican Legal Thought. By 1866 Republicans were strongly nationalistic about protecting the rights of citizens from the hostile acts of states. In fact, a recurring theme in the debates of the Thirty-ninth Congress was the need to protect the rights of citizens and to require states to respect those rights.[114]

In their efforts to protect the basic rights of blacks and the basic civil liberties of all citizens, Republicans faced hostile Supreme Court decisions. In *Barron v. Baltimore*,[115] decided in 1833, the Court held that the guaranties of the Bill of Rights did not apply to the states. In *Dred Scott v. Sandford*[116] the Court held that blacks, even free blacks, belonged to a degraded class at the time the Constitution was written and, short of a constitutional amendment making them citizens, could never be citizens of the United States. As a result, blacks were not entitled to any of the privileges, immunities, or rights secured by the Constitution to citizens, including those in the Bill of Rights.[117] Republicans reacted to these Court decisions by rejecting them.

Antecedents. Republican constitutional theory was influenced by the work of radical abolitionist lawyers and others who wrote before the Civil War. Alvin Stewart was a successful lawyer and leader of the New York State antislavery society. Stewart was also an innovator in the field of antislavery constitutional thought. Born in upstate New York and educated at Burlington College in Vermont, he finally settled in Utica, New York. There he "blended immense learning with mordant humor in ways which juries, and later anti-slavery assemblies found marvelously effective."[118] In September 1837 Stewart announced that instead of safeguarding slavery in the states, the Constitution was in fact an antislavery document that empowered Congress and the courts to free the slaves.[119] Stewart rested this conclusion in part on the due process clause of the Fifth Amendment, which provided that no person shall be deprived of life, liberty, or property without due process.[120]

Stewart's doctrines were soon elaborated by others. Joel Tiffany's *Treatise on the Unconstitutionality of American Slavery*, published in 1849, typifies and summarizes radical antislavery constitutional thought. Tiffany was a lawyer and reporter for the New York Supreme Court. He had been raised in Lorain County, Ohio, a hotbed of abolitionist and then radical Republican thought.[121] As the title of his book suggests, Tiffany concluded that slavery was unconstitutional, even in the states. Slaves were citizens.[122]

This doctrine was not accepted by most Republican congressmen prior to the passage of the Thirteenth Amendment.[123] For one thing, it was difficult to reconcile with American history and several provisions of the Constitution. But with a few significant modifications, such as admitting that slaves were not protected as citizens, Tiffany's theories provided the basis for a plausible civil libertarian reading of the Constitution. Because Tiffany's views are remarkably similar to those expressed by Republicans in the Thirty-ninth Congress, they are worth examining.

Tiffany believed in a paramount national citizenship requiring allegiance by the citizen and protection of the citizen's rights by the national government. All persons born or naturalized in the United States were citizens.[124] The object of the national government was to protect the natural and inalienable rights of each citizen, protection that extended against "the encroachments of foreign nations, and domestic states." After all, "a state might assume the authority to rob a portion of her citizens of their dearest rights."[125]

Tiffany found support for his libertarian reading in the preamble to the Constitution, which announced its objects as establishing justice and securing the blessings of liberty. He wrote that a "careful examination" of the Constitution showed that "ample provision" had been made to protect the rights of citizens "from the despotism of states at home."[126] The rights protected were "all the rights, privileges, and immunities, granted by the constitution of the United States."[127] "Whenever a state shall by its legislation, attempt to deprive a citizen of the United States of those rights and privileges which are guaranteed to him by the Federal Constitution . . . such legislation of the state is void," and the federal judiciary was required to correct the violation.[128]

The "privileges and immunities" of citizens of the United States included "all the guarantys of the Federal Constitution for personal security, personal liberty and private property."[129] Tiffany then asked: "But what further guarantys, for personal security and liberty could a government provide than the constitution of the United States has already provided?" He listed guaranties in the Bill of Rights and "the great writ of Liberty, the Habeas Corpus." Tiffany noted:

[The Constitution] has secured the right of petition, the right to keep and bear arms, the right to be secure from all unwarrantable seizures and searches, the right to demand, and have a presentment, or indictment found by a grand jury before he shall be held to answer to any criminal charge, the right to be informed beforehand of the nature and cause of accusation against him, the right to a public and speedy trial by an impartial jury of his peers, the right to confront those who testify against him, the right to have compulsory process to bring in his witnesses, the right to demand and have counsel for his defense, the right to be exempt from excessive bail, or fines, etc., from cruel and unusual punishments, or from being twice jeopardized for the same offense; and the right to the privileges of the great writ of Liberty, the Habeas Corpus.[130]

Tiffany insisted that the federal government had the power to enforce the guaranties of personal liberty contained in the Constitution. The Bill of Rights was a source of legislative power by which the federal government could directly protect the rights of citizens within the states.[131] To be a citizen of the United States, according to Tiffany,

> is to be invested with a title to life, liberty, and the pursuit of happiness, and to be protected in the enjoyment thereof, by the guaranty of twenty millions of people. It is, or should be, a panoply of defense equal, at least, to the ancient cry, "I am a Roman Citizen." And when understood, and respected in the true spirit of the immortal founders of our government it will prove a perfect bulwark against all oppression.[132]

Tiffany read "privileges and immunities" to include those rights set out in the Bill of Rights.[133] The *Dred Scott* decision itself had held that since blacks were not citizens of the United States, they were not entitled to any of the "rights, and privileges, and immunities, guarantied by [the Constitution] to the citizen."[134] Later in the same opinion, Chief Justice Taney referred to guaranties of the Bill of Rights as the "rights and privileges of the citizen" and again as the "rights of person or rights of property."[135]

Radical abolitionism was only one strand of antislavery legal thought. At the other end of the spectrum was the constitutional thought of the Garrisonians. The ideas of William Lloyd Garrison, editor of the *Liberator*, developed over time. Originally, however, he accepted a philosophy that required secular change to await spiritual regeneration.

Garrison's practical political doctrines were an extreme departure from American political norms. They tended to repudiate politics and to label voting a sin.[136] In 1839, for example, Garrisonians opposed an antislavery resolution that proclaimed that voting "so as to promote the abolition of slavery is a high obligation."[137] Garrison condemned the Constitution as a proslavery document, a covenant with death. Many Garrisonians also rejected holding public office because of the oath office holders had to take to uphold the Constitution.[138]

Garrison's colleague, Wendell Phillips, argued that judges should be strictly bound by the intention of the framers of the Constitution. Slavery was a creature of state law, and the Constitution did not empower the government to interfere with the domestic institutions of the states.[139] In his belief that the Constitution did not sanction federal interference with slavery in the states, Phillips espoused views that were similar to those of most politically active opponents of slavery before the Civil War. But Phillips went farther. He thought that slaves were an exception to the Declaration of Independence. Furthermore, blacks were regarded as inferior beings at the time of the adoption of the Constitution. The Constitution did not "concede them any of its privileges."[140]

Such Garrisonian arguments were congruent, on a number of points, with the extreme southern interpretation of the Constitution. A leading southern politician suggested that, with a few deletions, Phillips's pamphlet *The Constitution as a Pro-Slavery Compact* could be used effectively as a proslavery tract.[141]

In rejecting any application of the Declaration to slavery and any protections for blacks under the Constitution, Garrison and Phillips rejected both moderate and radical antislavery constitutional thought. They abandoned as far as slavery was concerned the libertarian and natural law strands of the American constitutional tradition. As William Wiecek has noted, "The Garrisonians' postulates locked them into a legal status quo that could be changed only by a millennial and universal shift in public sentiment. In this way, as in others, the Garrisonian theory led functionally to de facto conservatism."[142]

Treating the Constitution simply as a proslavery document oversimplified it and overlooked cross-currents within the document. As Don Fehrenbacher has noted in his study of the *Dred Scott* decision, the striking fact about the clauses dealing with slavery is that the founders refused to use the word. "It is as though they were half consciously trying to frame two constitutions, one for their own time and the other for the ages, with slavery viewed bifocally—that is plainly visible at their feet but disappearing as they lifted their eyes."[143]

The political antislavery parties (the Liberty party, the Free Soil party, and finally the Republican party) occupied a middle position between radical political abolitionism, which held slavery unconstitutional even in the states, and the Garrisonian position, which denied any antislavery effect to the Constitution. For most antislavery politicians the Constitution made slavery illegal in the territories but did not protect slaves in the slave states. The Republican party followed this tradition. During the Civil War, however, a growing minority of Republicans endorsed the radical abolitionist doctrine that the Constitution outlawed slavery in the states.[144] Not surprisingly, the Garrisonian analysis had little appeal for Republicans. They were unlikely to embrace a theory that discouraged voting and officeholding by opponents of slavery.[145]

Radical political abolitionist thought differed from Republican constitutional doctrine mainly in its insistence on citizenship for slaves.

From this difference great theoretical consequences followed. In contrast to radical abolitionists, most Republicans admitted that slaves in the southern states were unprotected by the Constitution. But for most pre–Civil War Republicans, free blacks were entitled to constitutional protection. When the Civil War and the Thirteenth Amendment freed the slaves and, Republicans thought, made them citizens, many differences between Republican and radical abolitionist thought tended to disappear.

Republican Legal Theories—1866. By 1866, most Republicans accepted several unorthodox constitutional doctrines. Although the *Dred Scott* decision had held that free blacks were not citizens and therefore were not entitled to any constitutional rights or privileges, Republicans insisted that free blacks were indeed citizens.[146]

Republicans also relied on an unorthodox reading of the due process clause of the Fifth Amendment.[147] After the ratification of the Thirteenth Amendment, the question of slavery in the territories and District of Columbia was of no practical significance. Still, the debate on this question that raged before and during the Civil War highlights the Republican interpretation of the due process clause. In *Dred Scott* Chief Justice Taney insisted that slaveholders' rights to due process would be violated if they were denied the right to take their slaves into federal territories.[148] Republicans, on the other hand, believed that slavery in the territories—where the Fifth Amendment applied to all persons—would deprive slaves of due process of law. As Republicans read the clause, "citizens" in the states and "persons" within the exclusive jurisdiction of the federal government were to be deprived of their liberty only by appropriate legal process.[149] Since slaves had not been deprived of their liberty by the accepted process of trial in the courts, to hold them in slavery in the territories violated the Fifth Amendment. Where the clause applied in full force, it protected the rights to life, liberty, and property from illegal invasion from any quarter, even by private persons.[150] The Republican platform in 1856 had provided:

> Resolved: That, with our Republican fathers, we hold it to be a self-evident truth, that all men are endowed with the inalienable right to life, liberty and the pursuit of happiness, and that the primary object and ulterior design of our Federal Government were to secure these rights to all persons under its exclusive jurisdiction; that, as our Republican fathers, when they had abolished Slavery in all our National Territory ordained that no person shall be deprived of life, liberty, or property, without due process of law, it becomes our duty to maintain this provision of the Constitution against all

attempts to violate it for the purpose of establishing Slave
Territories of the United States by positive legislation, prohi
existence or extension therein. That we deny the autl
Congress, of a Territorial Legislation, of any individual, o. ̣ ̣ ̣ ̣ ̣ ̣ ̣ ̣
tion of individuals, to give legal existence to Slavery in any Territory
of the United States, while the present Constitution shall be
maintained.[151]

The 1860 Republican platform had a similar provision, as did the
Liberty platform of 1844 and the Free Soil platform of 1848.[152]

The Republican argument that slavery in the territories was unconstitutional was the mirror image of the southern proslavery argument
—which held the federal government lacked power to bar slavery
in the territories because the due process clause protected property in
slaves.[153] For southerners, slaves were property and the due process clause protected the rights of the owners. For Republicans,
slaves were persons whose liberty was protected by the due process
clause.

In 1862 during debate on emancipation in the District of Columbia,
Congressman Bingham used the due process clause of the Fifth
Amendment to support his argument for emancipation. Bingham
noted that the Bill of Rights protects "persons" while the Magna Carta
protected only "freemen."[154] To Bingham the question was simple and
compelling: "The Representative who refuses to provide the necessary
means, in accordance with the spirit of the Constitution, for the protection of every person in life, in liberty, in property, where ever our
jurisdiction is exclusive, trifles with his oath and breaks it."[155] Bingham
made clear, once again, that he read the due process clause of the
Fifth Amendment to require the federal government to grant persons
in its exclusive jurisdiction protection of the laws. "I would have the
declaration made here now . . . that no man shall ever . . . where our
power of legislation is supreme, be deprived of his life, of his liberty, or
of his property without due process of law; and that slavery or involuntary servitude shall never be tolerated here in all the hereafter, except
as punishment for crime upon due conviction."[156]

In addition to believing that free blacks were citizens and that the
due process clause had banned slavery in federal territories, leading
Republicans in the Thirty-ninth Congress relied on a reading of
the privileges and immunities clause of article IV, section 2 that is
unorthodox, at least by current legal standards. That clause provides:
"The Citizens of each State shall be entitled to all Privileges and
Immunities of Citizens in the several states." Leading Republicans
read the clause to protect the fundamental rights of American citi-

zens against hostile state action.[157] The clause had a twofold effect
—protecting substantive liberties of United States citizens and protecting equality in basic rights with other citizens of a state. But, in *Dred
Scott*, the Court had said that the clause applied only to temporary
visitors from other states. A state could still restrict the rights of its
own citizens and of citizens from other states who took up permanent
residence.[158] Republicans, however, believed in a body of national rights
that states were required to respect.[159]

Finally, Republicans who expressed their views on the subject
rejected the ruling in *Barron v. Baltimore*[160] that the guaranties of the
Bill of Rights did not limit the states. To these Republicans, section 1 of
the Fourteenth Amendment merely declared existing constitutional
law, properly understood.

For leading Republicans, the Civil War and the Thirteenth Amendment transformed American constitutional law. Slavery had subverted
the guaranties of the Constitution and the libertarian character of
American government. With the end of slavery, however, the situation
changed. "Hitherto," Wisconsin Radical Senator Timothy Howe noted,
"we have taken the Constitution in a solution of the spirit of State
rights. Let us now take it as it is sublimed and crystallized in the flames
of the most gigantic war in history."[161] Congressman George Anderson,
a conservative Republican from Missouri, came to a similar conclusion:
"We are today interpreting the Constitution from a freedom and not
from a slavery standpoint."[162]

To these Republicans, the Thirteenth Amendment had a broad
libertarian effect. It provided:

> Section 1. Neither slavery nor involuntary servitude, except as a
> punishment for crime whereof the party shall have been duly
> convicted, shall exist within the United States, or any place subject to
> their jurisdiction.
> Section 2. Congress shall have the power to enforce this article by
> appropriate legislation.[163]

Republicans believed that the Thirteenth Amendment effectively overruled *Dred Scott* so that blacks were entitled to all rights of citizens. As
Senator Richard Yates put it, "by the amendment to the Constitution
. . . the freedman becomes a free man, entitled to the same rights and
privileges as any other citizen of the United States."[164] According to
Congressman Thomas Eliot, "The slave becomes freedman, and the
freedman man, and the man citizen, and the citizen must be endowed
with all the rights which other men possess."[165] "They are free by the
constitutional amendment lately enacted," said Senator James Lane,
"and entitled to all the privileges and immunities of other free citizens

of the United States."[166] According to Senator Trumbull, blacks were made citizens by the Thirteenth Amendment and so were entitled to the great fundamental rights of citizens.[167] Trumbull believed that the Thirteenth Amendment authorized Congress to pass laws to secure freedom. Although it was "difficult to draw the precise line, to say where freedom ceases and slavery begins," a "law that does not allow a colored person to hold property, does not allow him to teach, does not allow him to preach, is certainly a law in violation of the rights of a freeman, and being so may properly be declared void."[168]

A resolution of the New York legislature expressed a similar idea. The Thirteenth Amendment, it said,

> conferred upon Congress all the constitutional powers needful to establish and enforce universal freedom in practice and in fact; so the nation is pledged . . . that in all lawful ways the liberty and civil rights of every human being, subject to the Government of the United States, shall be protected and enforced, regardless of race, color, or condition, against every wrongful, opposing law, ordinance, regulation, custom or prejudice.[169]

The Rights of Citizens: The Republican View. With the end of slavery, Republicans considered blacks to be citizens entitled to all the rights, privileges, and immunities of citizens of the United States.[170] What, then, did Republicans see as the rights, privileges, and immunities of citizens? And what was the scope of these protected rights?

First, Republicans believed that the rights of citizens established by the Constitution limited both state and federal governments. Second, they believed that these rights, privileges, and immunities included the rights in the Bill of Rights. Several Republicans recognized that Supreme Court decisions were contrary to their view and needed correction.[171]

In the Thirty-eighth Congress, Congressman James Wilson, the influential chairman of the House Judiciary Committee, said that he might enumerate "many . . . constitutional rights of the citizen which slavery had disregarded and practically destroyed."[172] He discussed specifically "freedom of religious opinion, freedom of speech and press, and the right of assemblage for the purpose of petition." These rights belonged "to every American citizen, high or low, rich or poor, wherever he may be within the jurisdiction of the United States. With these rights no State may interfere."[173] Although Wilson spoke of denial of First Amendment rights, it is clear that his concern involved other fundamental rights as well. "Sir, I might enumerate many other constitutional rights of the citizen, which slavery has disregarded and practically destroyed, but I have enough to illustrate my proposition: that slavery disregards the supremacy of the Constitution and denies to the citizens of each State the privileges and immunities of citizens in the several States."[174] Other congressmen complained of denials of the "constitutional rights of our citizens in the South," including freedom of speech and of the press,[175] and of violations of protection against unreasonable searches and seizures.[176] The latter complaint was made by Congressman Owen Lovejoy, a longtime political abolitionist and also a close friend and strong supporter of Abraham Lincoln.

Lovejoy's brother Elijah had been a minister and publisher of the antislavery *Observer* located in Alton, Illinois. Elijah Lovejoy's press had been destroyed repeatedly by Illinois mobs determined to silence dissent on the slavery question. Confronted with such opposition, Elijah Lovejoy had stood squarely on his right of free speech. He was killed in 1837 defending his fourth press from a mob.[177]

Congressman Owen Lovejoy had worked in antislavery politics since the 1840s, when he became active in the Liberty party.[178] Throughout his career he repeatedly insisted that Bill of Rights liberties including free speech applied to Americans throughout the country, even in the southern states.[179]

In the Thirty-eighth Congress, Congressman Arnold complained that the Constitution had disappeared in slave states. He cited state denial of liberty of speech, freedom of the press, and trial by jury,[180] all secured by the Bill of Rights. Congressman Glenni Scofield also referred to rights secured by the Bill of Rights. Slavery, he said, "suspends the great writ of liberty in time of peace, tramples down the trial by jury when found in its way, contracts freedom of speech to the right to advocate its unchristian cause, revives constructive treason, and . . . indicts of that high crime respectable citizens who spoke too rudely of its traffic in men."[181] Scofield grew up in Chautauqua County, New York, long a center of reform activity. He moved to Pennsylvania and had been a state legislator and judge before his election to the Thirty-eighth Congress, where he was a Radical.[182]

In discussing the proposed Thirteenth Amendment and the claim that it would interfere with the reserved rights of the states, Congressman William Higby expressed his views on the Bill of Rights:

> Rights reserved. Why, just look at these amendments which have already been made, and you will find that they were all for the purpose of securing liberties to the people, and not for the purpose of giving them power of oppression and despotism. Rights were reserved, fearing that the General Government might be too strong or too weak; if too strong, that it might trample underfoot the liberties of the people, might establish despotism; rights were

reserved, if it proved too weak, for the purpose of keeping vitality in the General Government, that it should be administered for the purpose of securing liberties to the people.[183]

Republicans in the Thirty-ninth Congress also interpreted the guaranties of the Bill of Rights to limit the states as well as the federal government. Early in the session Senator Henry Wilson of Massachusetts, like many of his colleagues, complained that the South enacted laws that discriminated against blacks.[184] Senator Edgar Cowan, a Republican legislator who later abandoned the party to support Andrew Johnson, interrupted:

> The Constitution of the United States make provision by which the rights of no free man, no man not a slave, can be infringed insofar as regards any of the great principles of the English and American liberty; and if these things are done by the authority of any of the southern States, there is ample remedy now. Under the fifth amendment of the Constitution, no man can be deprived of his rights without the ordinary process of law; and if he is, he has his remedy.[185]

Although he believed that Bill of Rights liberties limited the states, Cowan voted with the most conservative Democrats in the Thirty-ninth Congress.[186]

Wilson might have cited *Barron v. Baltimore* to show that Cowan was wrong, and that the Bill of Rights did not limit the states. Instead, he agreed that the Constitution protected blacks "so far as the Constitution can do it; and the [thirteenth] amendment to the Constitution empowers us to pass the necessary legislation to make them free indeed."[187]

Congressman James A. Garfield also believed that the Bill of Rights limited the states.

> In reference to *persons*, we must see to it, that hereafter, personal liberty and personal rights are placed in the keeping of the nation; that the right to life, liberty, and property shall be guarantied to the citizen in reality as they are now in the words of the Constitution, and no longer left to the caprice of mobs or the contingencies of local legislation. If our Constitution does not now afford all the powers necessary to that end, we must ask the people to add them. We must give full force and effect to the provision that "no citizen shall be deprived of life, liberty, or property without due process of law." We must make it as true in fact as it is in law, that "the citizens of each State shall be entitled to all the privileges and immunities of

citizens in the several States." We must make American citizenship
the shield that protects every citizen, on every foot of our soil.[188]

Garfield later became president. In 1866 he represented a district in
northeastern Ohio, long a bastion of antislavery radicalism. He was
already influential in the Thirty-ninth Congress, where he fought for
suffrage for newly freed blacks. He was a Radical in the Thirty-ninth
Congress and a conservative or centrist thereafter.[189]

Radical Senator Samuel Pomeroy of Kansas was a veteran of antislavery struggles. He joined the Liberty party and later became an agent
for the New England Immigrant Aid Society. The society was dedi-
cated to encouraging opponents of slavery to settle in Kansas. Pomeroy
went to Kansas with the society's second party of settlers and was a
delegate to the first Republican convention in 1856. He became one of
Kansas's first senators.[190]

Senator Pomeroy believed that the Thirteenth Amendment "secured
the freedom of all men wherever the old flag floats" and provided for
the protection of freedom by appropriate legislation.[191] Such legislation,
he said, "can be nothing less than throwing about all men the essential
safeguards of the Constitution."[192] One of the safeguards that he
mentioned was the right to bear arms, secured by the Second
Amendment.[193]

Some Republicans frankly recognized that their constitutional views
were unorthodox. Still, they insisted that the government had the
power to protect individuals from state abuses.

Congressman John Broomall was a Pennsylvania lawyer who had
been a presidential elector for Lincoln in 1860. Benedict rates him as a
radical in 1866.[194] Broomall noted that the government had been
considered powerless to guard a citizen of Pennsylvania from illegal
arrest in Virginia, or to protect the liberty of an agent of the state of
Massachusetts in the city of Charleston. He insisted that the Constitution should be read in light of its preamble. Broomall considered
illegal arrests and denials of due process, together with denials of the
rights of speech, petition, habeas corpus, and transit, to be denials of
the privileges and immunities of citizens secured by article IV, section
2.[195]

Congressman Roswell Hart, of New York, a lawyer and a Radical,
noted that before the war southern states had denied that the Constitution contained any guaranties of freedom worth respecting. "Within
their own borders they assumed to be beyond constitutional control."
Those who dared question slavery were silenced.

In 1866 Hart insisted that the rebellious southern states should not
be restored to full relations with the Union "until the bondsmen we

have set free shall stand erect in all the rights of citizenship, protected in person, property, and liberty and burdened by no restriction imposed because of race or color."[196] Hart demanded that the rebellious states provide "a government whose citizens shall be entitled to all privileges and immunities of other citizens," where the guaranties of the First, Second, Fourth, and Fifth Amendments should be respected.[197]

Republican speakers approached the subject of Reconstruction with remarkable awareness of the historical significance of their actions. The results would be, as Radical Congressman Sidney Clarke of Kansas noted, "momentous to the interest of civil liberty."[198] Clarke sought "a more perfect freedom and a grander nationality" and "an enlarged liberty to the citizen." He said that the Constitution provided that "'the right of the people to keep and bear arms shall not be infringed.'" Alabama and other rebellious states had denied blacks the right to bear arms, a right Clarke insisted should be respected.[199]

Senator Nye of Nevada made one of the most comprehensive analyses of the Constitution's protection of the rights of citizens. Nye came to the Republican party from the Van Buren wing of the New York Democratic party. In New York he had served as a state judge. Nye had been a close political ally of Abraham Lincoln, who appointed him governor of the Nevada territory. When Nevada became a state, he was one of its first senators.[200] His view that the Bill of Rights limited the states was consistent with the views of other Republicans. According to Nye,

> the enumeration of personal rights in the Constitution to be protected, prescribes the kind and quality of the governments that are to be established and maintained in the States.
>
> . . . .
>
> In the enumeration of natural and personal rights to be protected, the framers of the Constitution apparently specified everything they could think of—"life," "liberty," "property," "freedom of speech," "freedom of the press," "freedom in the exercise of religion," "security of person" . . . and then, lest something essential in the specifications should have been overlooked, it was provided in the ninth amendment that "the enumeration in the Constitution of certain rights should not be construed to deny or disparage other rights not enumerated."
>
> Will it be contended, sir, at this day, that any State has the power to subvert or impair the natural and personal rights of the citizen? Will it be contended that the doctrine of "State sovereignty" has so far survived the wreck of its progenitor, slavery, that we are yet aloof from the true construction of the Constitution?

While slavery existed as a political power, it was not possible to adopt a true construction of the fundamental law.[201]

Later in the same speech Nye summarized his understanding of the Constitution as it affected the rights of citizens. Congress could "give effect by the enactment and enforcement of laws to all the protective provisions of the Constitution." In addition, both Congress and the legislatures of the states were prohibited from subverting or impairing "the natural or personal rights enumerated or implied in the Constitution." Finally, Congress could enforce the guaranty of republican government, "making the enumeration of personal and natural rights and the protective features of the Constitution the definition and test of what is republican government."[202]

Republican Goals for Reconstruction. So far, I have examined the Fourteenth Amendment in light of the Republican view of history, Republican political philosophy, and Republican legal thought. Another way to understand the amendment is to look at the goals Republicans sought to achieve. Almost invariably, these goals were stated in broad, libertarian terms. To Republicans the great objects of the Civil War and Reconstruction were securing liberty and protecting the rights of citizens of the United States. As Speaker Schuyler Colfax saw it, the goal was to protect men in their inalienable rights.[203] Senator Henry Wilson sought "security of the liberties of all men, and the security of equal, universal, and impartial liberty."[204] Congressman Farnsworth insisted on "security for the protection of the rights of men."[205] Congressman John L. Thomas, like a number of his colleagues, sought to ensure for blacks the rights to acquire and dispose of personal and real property, to testify, and to have their life, liberty, and property protected by the same laws that protected whites.[206]

Several senators wanted to "carry out and give effect to every single guarantee of the Constitution."[207] Other congressmen insisted on protection for the rights and privileges of citizens,[208] for the personal and natural rights of citizens,[209] for the fundamental rights of citizens,[210] for the civil rights of citizens,[211] and for the natural and personal rights enumerated in the Constitution.[212]

Like Garfield, many Republicans wanted personal liberty and personal rights placed in the keeping of the nation and protected from local legislation.[213] According to Senator Lot M. Morrill, the government should ensure that states did not deny equal rights to their citizens. In this respect it "should protect its citizens against state authority and state interpretations of their rights, privileges, and immunities as citizens of the United States."[214] Many Republicans believed that authority to protect those rights already existed and needed, at most, clarification.

Senator Richard Yates of Illinois was a lawyer who had been governor of Illinois during the Civil War, a moderate, and a strong Lincoln supporter. By 1866 he was an advocate of black suffrage and a Radical.[215] Yates was surprised at suggestions that the federal government lacked the power to protect its citizens:

> I had in the simplicity of my heart, supposed that "State rights" being the issue of the war, had been decided. I had supposed that we had established the proposition that there is a living Federal Government and a Congress of the United States. I do not mean a consolidated Government, but a central Federal Government which, while it allows the States the exercise of all their appropriate functions as local State governments, can hold the States well poised in their appropriate spheres, can secure the enforcement of the constitutional guarantees of republican government, the rights and immunities of citizens in the several States, and carry out all the objects provided for in the preamble of the Constitution . . . "establish justice," and "secure the blessings of liberty to ourselves and our posterity."[216]

While Republican congressmen emphasized the need to protect the basic rights of blacks, they also expressed concern for the protection of rights of white unionists and for rights in the Bill of Rights.[217] Senator B. Gratz Brown suggested an amendment "so as to declare with greater certainty the power of Congress to enforce and determine by appropriate legislation all the guarantees contained in that instrument," including the clause guarantying a republican form of government and that securing privileges and immunities of citizens in every state.[218]

Brown had a long history in the antislavery cause. He had edited the *Missouri Democrat*, a Free Soil and later Republican paper, and was one of the organizers of the Republican party in Missouri. His consistent devotion to black suffrage made him, along with Senators Charles Sumner and Benjamin Franklin Wade, an extreme Radical in 1866. He also supported women's suffrage, the eight-hour day for government workers, and other "radical" causes.[219]

Congressman Ignatius Donnelly of Minnesota was a farmer trained in law. In the 1850s he was an active Republican. By 1859 he became lieutenant governor of Minnesota. Donnelly spent three terms in the House from 1863 to 1869. On the conservative-to-radical continuum, Benedict found him impossible to scale.[220] Donnelly also advocated an amendment that provided for congressional power to enforce all the guaranties of the Constitution. He listed specifically its "sacred pledges of life, liberty, and property."[221]

Congress itself, in passing a resolution proposed by Congressman

Joseph McClurg, indicated its belief that it was enforcing the guaranties of the Bill of Rights in the southern states. The resolution asserted that Congress was forced by the "continued contumacy in the seceding states" to legislate "to give the loyal citizens of those states protection in their natural and personal rights enumerated in the Constitution."[222]

Often, Republican goals were stated in general but comprehensive terms. Republican congressmen typically insisted on protection of individual liberty for blacks and white unionists within the southern states. Congressman John Baldwin insisted on protection for the rights of loyal people—white and black—in the South. They had been persecuted during the war and were still "intensively hated." Government was obligated to protect those from whom it demanded allegiance.[223]

Congressman Sidney Holmes insisted on the rights of the newly freed slaves to "life, liberty, and the pursuit of happiness, to protection of person and property, to equal and exact justice and privileges before the law." These he insisted must be amply guarantied. The great truths of the Declaration of Independence and the blessings of free government needed to be recognized and enforced by the rebellious states.[224]

Congressman Ralph Buckland insisted that the government was bound to provide for future protection of the lives, the liberty, and the rights of property of the loyal whites and blacks of the rebellious states.[225] The government needed to "insist on such measures as will secure to every American citizen the natural rights of life, liberty, and property in all the states."[226]

Petitions presented to Congress by Republican lawmakers on behalf of private citizens demanded protection for rights in the Bill of Rights, as well as equality before the law. Senator Sumner presented a petition "from the colored citizens of the State of South Carolina" asking for "constitutional protection in keeping arms, in holding public assemblies, and in complete liberty of speech and of the press."[227] Senator Trumbull submitted a petition from citizens of Quincy, Illinois, demanding absolute equality of political as well as civil rights and "free speech, free press, free assembly, and free instruction."[228] A similar petition from Detroit Germans presented by Senator Jacob Merritt Howard sought "prohibition of all restrictions on free speech, free press, free assemblage and free instruction."[229]

Chapter 3

The Framing of the Fourteenth Amendment

Chronological Overview of the Debates

When Congress opened on December 4, 1865, southern congressmen were excluded.[1] Congress then appointed a joint committee of fifteen to investigate the condition of the southern states and to decide if they should be readmitted.[2] Meanwhile, the Congress and the committee proceeded to consider what conditions should be required of the southern states prior to their full readmission.[3] One requirement that Congress eventually passed was, of course, the Fourteenth Amendment.

As early as December 6, 1865, Congressman Bingham had introduced a resolution for a proposed constitutional amendment.[4] It authorized Congress to pass all laws necessary to secure all persons in every state of the Union equal protection in their rights to life, liberty, and property.[5] On December 19, 1865, Senator Trumbull announced that he would introduce a bill to modify the Freedman's Bureau bill and to make personal rights more secure.[6] Later this measure was split into two parts, one of which was the Civil Rights bill.[7] Debate on the Civil Rights bill stretched from January through March 1866.

Meanwhile, in January and February 1866 the Joint Committee considered various proposed constitutional amendments, including a number of variations on what later became the first section of the Fourteenth Amendment. On February 3, 1866, the committee agreed by a vote of 9 to 4 on a proposed amendment drafted by Bingham.[8] It provided: "The Congress shall have power to make all laws which shall be necessary and proper to secure to the citizens of each state all privileges and immunities of citizens in the several states (Art. 4, Sec. 2); and to all persons in the several states equal protection in the rights of life, liberty, and property (5th Amendment)."[9]

The amendment was reported in the Senate on February 13, 1866, and was debated and then postponed in the House on February 26, 27, and 28, 1866.[10] On March 27, 1866, the president vetoed the Civil Rights bill.[11] The veto was based in part on a claim that Congress lacked power to pass it. On April 9 the bill was passed over his veto.[12]

In April the Joint Committee continued to work on versions of what would become the Fourteenth Amendment. On April 28, 1866, it passed another Bingham proposal by a vote of 10 to 3.[13] This amendment was a modification of Bingham's amendment, which had been debated and postponed by the House. The new proposal provided: "Sec.1. No State shall make or enforce any law which shall abridge the privileges or immunities of citizens of the United States; nor shall any State deprive any person of life, liberty, or property, without due process of law, nor deny to any person within its jurisdiction the equal protection of the laws."[14]

The Fourteenth Amendment was reported to the House on April 30, 1866. It was debated and passed the House with the first section intact on May 10, 1866. The provision making all persons born or naturalized in the United States citizens of the United States and of the state wherein they reside was added by the Senate. The amendment passed the Senate in final form on June 8, 1866, and passed the House on June 13, 1866.[15]

Bingham's Prototype

President Johnson's message to Congress in December 1865 emphasized limitation of government, both state and national, in the interest of protecting the rights of man. These included the "equal right of every man to life, liberty, and the pursuit of happiness [and] to freedom of conscience." "As a consequence," Johnson noted, "the State government is limited, as to the General Government in the interests of union [and] as to the individual citizen in the interest of freedom."[16] Johnson specifically mentioned separation of church and state and free speech. "Here," he noted, "toleration is extended to every opinion, in the quiet certainty that truth needs only a fair field to secure the victory."[17]

Congressman Bingham, a member of the Joint Committee and the future author of section 1 of the Fourteenth Amendment, was a veteran antislavery congressman from Ohio. Bingham was a lawyer and a former prosecutor. Elected to Congress as a Republican in 1855, he served until 1863. He was defeated in 1862 and reelected in 1864. The *New York Times* described Bingham as one of the most "learned and talented members of the House."

In the Thirty-ninth Congress, Bingham was a congressman with preeminent influence. Benedict rates him as a centrist Republican in the first session of the Thirty-ninth Congress and as a conservative in the second session. Another student of Reconstruction considered Bingham one of the most conservative Republicans in the House.[18] Bingham's case shows, once again, that by 1866 antislavery legal thought was simply not an issue that divided Republican conservatives from Radicals.

Like many opponents of slavery, Bingham had a deep and emotional respect for the Bill of Rights.[19] On December 6, 1865, Bingham introduced a resolution proposing a constitutional amendment authorizing Congress to pass all laws necessary to secure all persons in every state of the Union equal protection in their rights to life, liberty, and property.[20]

When Bingham spoke on January 9, 1866, he hailed the president's message. Equal and exact justice had been denied to white and black alike, Bingham explained, so it had been unsafe for advocates of equality to be found in Richmond or Charleston:

> It was not because the Constitution of the United States sanctioned any infringement of his rights in that behalf, but because in defiance of the Constitution its very guarantees were disregarded. . . . [I]n view of the fact that many of the States—I might say, in some sense, all the States of the Union—have flagrantly violated the absolute guarantees of the Constitution of the United States to all its citizens, it is time that we take security for the future, so that like occurrences may not again arise to distract our people and finally dismember the Republic.
>
> When you come to weigh these words, "equal and exact justice to all men," go read, if you please, the words of the Constitution itself: "The citizens of each State (being *ipso facto* citizens of the United States) shall be entitled to all the privileges and immunities of citizens (supplying the ellipsis "of the United States") in the several States."[21]

In proposing his amendment, Bingham wanted to ensure that the provisions of article IV, section 2, were respected in each state. Therefore, his understanding of the section is of crucial importance.

Bingham had spoken in Congress in 1859 against the admission of Oregon to the Union as a "free" (nonslave) state. Oregon, like some other northern states, had provided in its constitution that no free Negro or mulatto could come into the state after the adoption of the constitution. No free Negro or mulatto migrant could hold real estate, make contracts, or sue in the courts of the state. The constitution also provided for the removal of "all such free negroes or mulattoes."[22] Bingham, together with a number of his fellow Republicans, opposed Oregon's admission because of these provisions. The Republican press had denounced the Oregon constitution as tyrannical, disgraceful, and barbaric. Seventy-three of eighty-eight Republican representatives had voted against the admission of Oregon under the proposed constitution, even as a "free" state.[23]

Bingham considered the proposed provisions of the Oregon constitution both unconstitutional and "an infamous atrocity."[24] He felt obligated to oppose them by his oath to uphold the Constitution.

> In my judgment, sir, this constitution framed by the people of Oregon is repugnant to the Federal Constitution, and violative of the rights of citizens of the United States. I know, sir, that some gentlemen have a short and easy method of disposing of such objections as these, by assuming that the people of the State, after admission, may, by changing their constitution, insert therein every objectionable feature which, before admission, they were constrained to omit in order to secure the favorable action of Congress.[25]

Bingham denied that states had the right to infringe rights of citizens of the United States but admitted they might arrogate to themselves the power to do so. His answer to the argument that once a territory became a state it could pass all the restrictions on liberty it desired was simple and direct. He did not agree "that the States are not limited by the Constitution of the United States, in respect of the personal or political rights of citizens of the United States." "To the right understanding of the limitations of the Constitution of the United States upon the several States, it ought not to be overlooked that, whenever the Constitution guaranties its citizens a right, either natural or conventional, such guarantee is in itself a limitation upon the States."[26]

Contrary to *Dred Scott*, Bingham believed free blacks to be citizens of the United States. "All free persons born and domiciled within the jurisdiction of the United States, are citizens of the United States from birth."[27] As citizens, they are entitled to protection under the privileges and immunities clause of the original Constitution, which Bingham construed to say exactly what the privileges and immunities clause of the Fourteenth Amendment later said.

> The citizens of each State, all the citizens of each State, being citizens of the United States, shall be entitled to "all privileges and immunities of citizens in the several States." Not to the rights and immunities of the several States; not to those constitutional rights and immunities which result exclusively from State authority or

State legislation; but to "all privileges and immunities" of citizens of the United States in the several States. There is an ellipsis in the language employed in the Constitution, but its meaning is self-evident that it is "the privileges and immunities of citizens of the United States in the several States" that it guaranties.[28]

Bingham found the provisions of the Oregon constitution a violation of the privileges and immunities clause and, therefore, of the Fifth Amendment.

The persons thus excluded from the State by this section of the Oregon constitution, are citizens by birth of the several States, and therefore are citizens of the United States, and as such are entitled to all the privileges and immunities of citizens of the United States, amongst which are the rights of life and liberty and property and their due protection in the enjoyment thereof by law.[29]

Here we see Bingham's constitutional theory: the privileges and immunities of citizens, including the rights set out in the Bill of Rights, may not be abridged by any state. Consequently, the provisions of the Oregon constitution violated the Fifth Amendment.

That Bingham considered the guaranties of the Fifth Amendment binding on the states also is demonstrated by another portion of his speech. After pointing out that natural rights are guarantied by the Constitution to persons "as in the fifth article of amendments . . . that 'no person shall be deprived of life, liberty, or property but by due process of law, nor shall private property be taken without just compensation,'" Bingham notes, "And this guarantee applies to all citizens within the United States."[30] In short, the Fifth Amendment protects all persons in connection with the federal government and all citizens against the states. After citing the supremacy clause, Bingham says, "There, sir, is the limitation upon State sovereignty—simple, clear, and strong. No State may rightfully, by constitution or statute law, impair any of these guaranteed rights, either political or natural. They may not rightfully or lawfully declare that the strong citizens may deprive the weak citizens of their rights."[31]

Bingham believed that the rights in the Bill of Rights were protected from state infringement by the privileges and immunities clause of article IV, section 2. Still, he was aware of decisions like *Barron v. Baltimore* to the contrary.[32] Moreover, unlike Tiffany, Bingham denied that the rights could be enforced by congressional legislation. Indeed, in Bingham's view, the only enforcement method was the oath state officials took to obey the Constitution.[33]

When Bingham spoke again on January 25, 1866, he warned his

colleagues that a constitutional amendment was required before Congress would have the power to enforce all the guaranties of the Constitution. "In what I have said upon the limitations of power," Bingham said, "I do not express my own opinion, but the opinions of others and the uniform construction."[34] Bingham thought that the question "whether the Constitution shall be so amended as to give Congress the power by statute to enforce all its guarantees" was the most important issue that would come before the Congress.[35] With such powers, Congress could legislate "that hereafter no state shall make it a crime for a man, whether he be black or white, a citizen of the Republic, to learn the alphabet of his native tongue and his rights and duties."[36] Southern states, of course, had made it a crime to teach slaves to read.[37]

On February 1, 1866, Congressman Donnelly spoke in favor of Bingham's proposed amendment. It provided "in effect that Congress shall have the power to enforce by appropriate legislation all the guarantees of the Constitution." Donnelly asked, "Why should this not pass? Are the promises of the Constitution mere verbiage? Are its sacred pledges of life, liberty, and property to fall to the ground through lack of power to enforce them? . . . Or shall that great Constitution be what its founders meant it to be, a shield and a protection over the head of the lowliest and poorest citizen in the remotest region of the nation?"[38]

Since January, the Joint Committee had been considering proposed amendments to the Constitution. On February 3, 1866, the committee agreed to report favorably on one drafted by Bingham.[39] It provided: "The Congress shall have power to make all laws which shall be necessary and proper to secure to the citizens of each State all privileges and immunities of citizens in the several States (Art. 4, Sec. 2); and to all persons in the several States equal protection in the rights of life, liberty and property (5th Amendment)."[40] On February 13, 1866, Bingham reported the amendment to the House. Shortly thereafter, Bingham and Congressman James Brooks, a Democrat, argued over when the amendment would be considered. Brooks said he wanted the country to know "how these things are managed." Bingham shot back, "And I want it understood who are opposed to enforcing the written guarantees of the Constitution."[41]

On February 26, 1866, Bingham presented his proposal to the House. It gave Congress power to secure privileges and immunities to citizens and equal protection in the rights of life, liberty, and property to persons.[42] The proposal contained several defects. First, it was not self-executing, but depended upon congressional legislation. The rights Bingham wanted to secure were left to a majority of Congress, vulner-

able to the shifting winds of the political process. Second, it was written on the assumption that Bingham's views and those of a number of
his colleagues, not the decisions of the Supreme Court, accurately
stated the law.[43] The proposal assumed, without providing explicitly,
that contrary to *Dred Scott* free blacks were citizens of the United
States. And it assumed that the Republican reading of the privileges
and immunities clause of article IV, section 2,[44] not the dictum in *Dred
Scott*, was correct. Many other Republicans held similar views.[45]

When Bingham introduced his resolution, he spoke briefly in its
support. He said that the due process clause required equal protection,
and that the provisions of the proposed amendment were already in
the Constitution, except for the enforcement power.[46] All state officers
took an oath to support the Constitution as the supreme law of the
land. And, Bingham observed, "it is equally clear by every construction of the Constitution . . . legislative, executive, and judicial, that
these great provisions of the Constitution, this immortal Bill of Rights
embodied in the Constitution, rested for its execution and enforcement hitherto on the fidelity of the States."[47]

Bingham's understanding of how article IV, section 2 made the Bill
of Rights a limit on the states is analogous to Chief Justice Taney's
interpretation of another clause of article IV, section 2 in the case of
Kentucky v. Dennison.[48] William Lago, a free Negro, had helped a fugitive slave escape in Kentucky. When Lago was indicted for this crime
by the state of Kentucky, he fled to Ohio to avoid trial. The governor of
Kentucky presented a request to return Lago, and the governor of
Ohio refused. Kentucky brought suit, relying on a command of article
IV, section 2: "A Person charged in any State with Treason, Felony, or
other Crime, who shall flee from Justice, and be found in another
State, shall on demand of the executive Authority of the State from
which he fled, be delivered up, to be removed to the State having
Jurisdiction of the Crime." Chief Justice Taney, speaking for the Court,
held that the constitutional duty to return the fugitive was indisputable,
but the national government could not coerce a state official. The
provisions of article IV, section 2 represented an unenforceable legal
obligation.[49]

The idea of unenforceable constitutional requirements was not new
to opponents of slavery. In addition to the privileges or immunities
clause and the clause providing for the return of fugitives from justice,
article IV contained the fugitive slave clause. Before the Civil War,
Salmon P. Chase of Ohio had argued that Congress lacked power to
enforce the clause because no such power was delegated in article IV.
The clause was in the nature of a compact between the states.[50]

Bingham's position was similar to that taken by the Court in *Kentucky*

v. Dennison. He thought the provisions of the Bill of Rights were binding on state officers by their oath and by the privileges and immunities
clause of article IV, section 2, but he denied that the requirements of
the Bill of Rights were enforceable by the national government.

Bingham, like other leading Republicans, read article IV, section 2
as protecting the privileges and immunities of citizens of the United
States, including those in the Bill of Rights, from state infringement.[51]
As Bingham said on January 25, 1866, "I believe that the free citizens
of each State were guarantied, and intended to be guarantied by the
terms of the Constitution, all—not some, 'all'—the privileges of citizens of the United States in every state."[52]

Both in his prototype and in his final version of the Fourteenth
Amendment, Bingham used the words *privileges* and *immunities* as a
shorthand description of fundamental or constitutional rights. Use of
the words in this way had a long and distinguished heritage. Blackstone's
Commentaries on the Laws of England, published in the colonies on the
eve of the Revolution, had divided the rights and liberties of Englishmen into those "immunities" that were the residuum of natural liberties and those "privileges" that society had provided in lieu of natural
rights.[53]

By the time of the Revolution most basic liberties later set out in the
American Bill of Rights had been asserted by Parliament as liberties
of Englishmen. Set out in a series of British constitutional documents
ranging from the Magna Carta to the Petition of Right and the English
Bill of Rights, these rights were treated by Blackstone as "privileges"
and "immunities" of the people of England.[54]

American colonists had, from early times, relied on these basic
declarations of the rights of Englishmen. William Penn, the Quaker
founder of Pennsylvania, wrote a commentary on English liberties for
Americans, *The Excellent Priviledge of Liberty & Property Being the Birth-
Right of Free-Born Subjects of England.*[55] For Penn, jury trial was one of
the fundamental privileges of English subjects.

Before the Revolution the American colonists claimed the right to
all "Liberties, Privileges, Franchises, and Immunities of the People of
Britain." The words were adopted by the Virginia House shortly after
it listened to Patrick Henry's famous "give me liberty or give me
death" speech.[56] The Massachusetts assembly claimed all "essential
Rights, Liberties, Privileges and Immunities of the People of Great
Britain."[57] The rights colonists generally asserted included basic guaranties of English liberty later included in the federal Bill of Rights,
including the right to petition, to protection against unreasonable
searches and seizures, and to jury trials.[58]

The words *rights, liberties, privileges,* and *immunities,* seem to have been used interchangeably. A 1774 resolution from Georgia insisted that Americans were entitled to "the same rights, privileges, and immunities with their fellow subjects in Great Britain."[59] In 1774 the "freeholders and inhabitants" of Fairfax County, Virginia, met under the chairmanship of George Washington. They claimed "all the privileges, immunities, and advantages" of the people of Great Britain.[60] Resolves of the First Continental Congress also claimed "all the rights, liberties, and immunities of free" English subjects. Among these was "the great and inestimable privilege of being tried by their peers of the vicinage," according to the due course of law.[61]

The words *privileges* and *immunities* reappeared in the Articles of Confederation. Article IV provided:

> The better to secure and perpetuate mutual friendship and intercourse among the people of the different states in this union, the free inhabitants of each of these states, paupers, vagabonds, and fugitives from justice, excepted, shall be entitled to all privileges and immunities of free citizens in the several states; and the people of each state shall have free ingress and regress to and from any other state, and shall enjoy therein all the privileges of trade and commerce, subject to the same duties, impositions and restrictions as the inhabitants thereof respectively.[62]

When the Constitution replaced the Articles of Confederation, it also contained a privileges and immunities clause: "The citizens of each State shall be entitled to all Privileges and Immunities of Citizens in the several States."

What these clauses mean has ever since been a source of controversy. Leading Republicans read the privileges and immunities clause of article IV, section 2 to protect fundamental constitutional rights of American citizens against state action.

In *Paul v. Virginia*, decided in 1869, the Supreme Court restricted the clause of the original Constitution to providing the citizens of one state sojourning in another with only certain of those rights given to its people by law of the second state.[63] Two contemporary scholars argue that the Republicans were right and the court in *Paul* was wrong in limiting the clause to equality of certain rights under state law. Chester Antieau argues that the purpose of article IV, section 2 was to secure basic, natural, fundamental rights to citizens of the United States. These rights were to be the same throughout the nation, and the states were prohibited from violating them.[64] Indeed, Antieau argues that early judicial decisions were consistent with his reading of the clause and were abruptly departed from in *Paul*.[65]

Michael Conant examines the privileges and immunities clause of article IV from the point of view of historical linguistics and reaches a similar conclusion as to the intended scope of the clause. Conant also concludes that the privileges and immunities clause of article IV established a uniform set of privileges or immunities that included the basic liberties of Englishmen that the states must respect. References to fundamental rights, according to Conant, referred to constitutional rights.[66]

Many of the early decisions on the privileges or immunities clause of article IV are ambiguous. They do not clearly address or do not clearly answer the question of whether the privileges or immunities guarantied by the original Constitution went beyond a right to equal protection in certain rights under state law to secure basic, absolute, national rights.[67] At least some of the early decisions, especially Justice Bushrod Washington's 1823 decision in *Corfield v. Coryell*,[68] seem to support a reading of the clause to recognize a body of national rights.

> The next question is, whether this act infringes that section of the Constitution which declares that "the citizens of each shall be entitled to all the privileges and immunities of citizens in the several states"? The inquiry is, what are the privileges and immunities of citizens in the several states? We feel no hesitation in confining these expressions to those privileges and immunities which are, in their nature, fundamental; which belong, of right, to the citizens of all free governments; and which have, at all times, been enjoyed by the citizens of the several states which compose this Union, from the time of their becoming free, independent, and sovereign. What these fundamental principles are, it would perhaps be more tedious than difficult to enumerate. They may, however be all comprehended under the following general heads: Protection by the government; the enjoyment of life and liberty, with the right to acquire and possess property of every kind, and to pursue and obtain happiness and safety; subject, nevertheless, to such restraints as the government may justly prescribe for the general good of the whole. The right of a citizen of one state to pass through, or to reside in any other state, for purposes of trade, agriculture, professional pursuits, or otherwise; to claim the benefit of the writ of habeas corpus; to institute and maintain actions of any kind in the courts of the state; to take, hold and dispose of property, either real or personal; and an exception from higher taxes or impositions than are paid by the other citizens of the state; may be mentioned as some of the particular privileges and immunities of citizens, which are clearly embraced by the general description of privileges deemed to be fundamental; to which may be added, the elective franchise, as regulated and

established by the laws or constitution of the state in which it is to be exercised. These, and many others which might be mentioned, are, strictly speaking, privileges and immunities, and the enjoyment of them by the citizens of each state, in every other state, was manifestly calculated (to use the expressions of the preamble of the corresponding provision in the old Articles of Confederation) "the better to secure and perpetuate mutual friendship and intercourse among the people of the different states of the Union." But we cannot accede to the proposition which was insisted on by the counsel, that, under this provision of the Constitution, the citizens of the several states are permitted to participate in all the rights which belong exclusively to the citizens of any other particular state, merely upon the ground that they are enjoyed by those citizens; much less, that in regulating the use of the common property of the citizens of such state, the legislature is bound to extend to the citizens of all other states the same advantages as are secured to their own citizens.[69]

Justice Washington's reference to rights that belonged to citizens of all free governments seems to some modern minds to be quite a different thing from the guaranties of the Bill of Rights. But of course it is anachronistic to see the Republican understanding of rights essential to freedom in the light of fashionable modern ideas.

Justice David J. Brewer was an antislavery activist in the years before the Civil War.[70] In an 1871 state court opinion written before his appointment to the high court, Brewer described bills of rights as "those essential truths, those axioms of civil and political liberty on which all free governments are founded."[71]

The idea that *Corfield* recognized article IV as protecting a set of basic national liberties was accepted by Justice Owen J. Roberts, speaking for the Court in *Hague v. CIO*.[72] "It was thought," Roberts wrote ". . . that the purpose of the section was to create rights of citizens of the United States guaranteeing the citizens of every State the recognition of this group of rights by every State. Such was the view of Justice Washington."[73]

Despite a tradition supporting the way Bingham and leading Republicans read the original privileges and immunities clause, the clause clearly had a mixed heritage. Some commentators and courts seemed to read it only to provide temporary visitors with equality in certain rights with the citizens of the states they were visiting. Justice Joseph Story, for example, wrote that the clause "was to confer on [the citizens of each state] a general citizenship; and to communicate all the privileges and immunities which citizens of the same state would be entitled to under the like circumstances."[74] The prevailing view of the

whether the Bill of Rights should apply as a limitation on the states[94] and believe that such a change would be regarded as an intolerable interference with state sovereignty.[95] Such a reading is mistaken, however, because Hale already considered the Bill of Rights as a limitation on the states.[96] As Hale said, "If he claims that those provisions of the constitution or the laws of Oregon are inconsistent with the bill of rights contained in the Constitution of the United States, then I answer that his remedy is perfect and ample, and the courts may be appealed to to vindicate the rights of the citizens, both under civil and criminal procedure."[97]

Hale cannot reasonably be cited for the proposition that application of the Bill of Rights to the states would violate state sovereignty, because he thought that the states were already obligated to obey the Bill of Rights. Hale shows, once again, that such belief was held by Republicans of all persuasions.

In addition to Hale, Senator William Morris Stewart of Nevada opposed Bingham's prototype on the ground that it would "obviate the necessity of any more State legislatures." Stewart thought the first, or privileges or immunities provision, "not very material." A law abridging privileges or immunities would be declared unconstitutional by the courts. Stewart thought that state laws that kept free blacks from entering the state violated article IV, section 2 and would fall.[98] The clause that upset Stewart was the equal protection provision. Stewart read it as allowing Congress to make all laws affecting life, liberty, and property precisely equal.[99]

Bingham spoke again in support of his amendment on February 28, 1866. By this point Bingham was getting exasperated: "The proposition pending before the House is simply a proposition to arm the Congress of the United States, by the consent of the people of the United States, with the power to enforce the bill of rights as it stands in the Constitution today."[100] Although, Bingham said, "gentlemen [admitted] the force of the provisions in the bill of rights, that the citizens of the United States shall be entitled to all the privileges and immunities of citizens of the United States in the several States, and that no person shall be deprived of life, liberty, or property without due process of law," still they insisted that "enforcement of the bill of rights, as proposed" would "interfere with the reserved rights of the States." Who had ever before heard, Bingham asked, "that any State had reserved to itself the right, under the Constitution of the United States, to withhold from any citizen of the United States within its limits, under any pretext whatever, any of the privileges of a citizen of the United States?"[101]

In the same speech, Bingham cited *Barron v. Baltimore*[102] and

Livingston v. Moore[103] to show "that the power of the Federal Government to enforce in the United States courts the bill of rights under the articles of amendment to the Constitution had been denied."[104] Those who opposed the amendment, Bingham insisted, opposed federal authority to enforce the Bill of Rights.[105]

Despite Bingham's appeal, many were not convinced. Congressman Giles W. Hotchkiss, a New York Radical, wanted "to secure every privilege and every right to every citizen in the United States" that Bingham wanted to secure.[106] He objected, however, to the equal protection provision because he believed it would allow Congress to legislate directly on all subjects that might be included within the phrase "life, liberty, or property"—in short, on all imaginable subjects.[107] Hotchkiss said that he understood Bingham's object was to prevent discrimination in rights among citizens. He believed the privileges or immunities section was identical to the guaranty already in the Constitution. Hotchkiss concluded, "Now I desire that the very privileges for which the gentleman is contending shall be secured to the citizens; but I want them secured by a constitutional amendment that legislation cannot override."[108]

Bingham's amendment was tabled.

Debate on the Civil Rights Bill

Both before and after its discussion of Bingham's prototype of the Fourteenth Amendment, Congress debated the Civil Rights bill. As enacted, the Civil Rights bill provided that "all persons born in the United States and not subject to any foreign power, excluding Indians not taxed" were "citizens of the United States." "Such citizens," the act continued,

> of every race and color, without regard to any previous condition of slavery . . . shall have the same right, in every State and Territory in the United States, to make and enforce contracts, to sue, be parties, and give evidence, to inherit, purchase, lease, sell, hold, and convey real and personal property, and *to full and equal benefit of all laws and proceedings for the security of person and property, as is enjoyed by white citizens.*[109]

Scholars who argue that the Fourteenth Amendment was not intended to make the Bill of Rights a limit on the states have relied on statements made by some congressmen that the amendment incorporated the substantial protections of the Civil Rights bill—such as rights to contract and to testify at trials and to full and equal benefit of all laws for security of person and property. They assume that these rights exclude those in the Bill of Rights.[110] The problem with this analysis is that provisions of the Bill of Rights are, by ordinary use of language, "laws for security of person and property." For example, Joel Tiffany described the rights in the Bill of Rights as "guarantys" for "personal security and liberty."[111]

In *Dred Scott v. Sandford* Justice Taney noted that Congress could make no law respecting the establishment of religion or prohibiting the free exercise thereof, or abridging the freedom of speech and the press, or the right to bear arms. These provisions limited the power of the federal government over the "person or property" of the citizen.[112]

> These powers, and others, in relation to rights of person . . . are, in express and positive terms, denied to the General Government; and the rights of private property have been guarded with equal care. Thus the rights of property are united with the rights of person, and placed on the same ground by the fifth amendment to the Constitution, which provides that no person shall be deprived of life, liberty, and property, without due process of law.[113]

In 1886, in *Boyd v. United States*,[114] the Court again referred to the rights in the Bill of Rights in the same way. In a case that turned on Fourth and Fifth Amendment rights, the Court noted that "constitutional provisions for the security of person and property" should be liberally construed.[115]

The most telling evidence that the "full and equal benefit of all laws and proceedings for the security of person and property" could be read to include constitutional rights in the Bill of Rights comes from Republicans in the Thirty-ninth Congress themselves. When they passed the Freedman's Bureau bill, they provided that blacks should have, among other things, "full and equal benefit of all laws and proceedings for the security of person and estate, *including the constitutional right of bearing arms*."[116]

Virtually all Republicans who spoke on the subject believed that the rights in the Bill of Rights were rights of citizens that limited or should limit the powers of the states as well as the federal government.[117] Once blacks became citizens, they were entitled, like other citizens, to all the rights, privileges, and immunities of citizens of the United States.[118] Consequently, the Republicans reasonably may have read the Civil Rights bill as protecting the rights in the Bill of Rights from state infringement. At the very least, statements that the Fourteenth Amendment embodied the provisions of the Civil Rights bill do not prove that the speaker believed that the amendment did not apply the Bill of Rights to the states. Bingham himself had referred to the Civil Rights bill as a bill providing for enforcement of the Bill of Rights.[119]

Senator Trumbull managed the Civil Rights bill in the Senate. He was a Republican leader of preeminent influence.[120] He had served in the state legislature, as a justice of the Illinois Supreme Court, and as a senator for Illinois from 1865 to 1873.[121] He was chairman of the Senate Judiciary Committee in 1866. Benedict found him impossible to categorize in the first session of the Thirty-ninth Congress. Throughout Reconstruction as a whole he tended to be conservative.[122]

Trumbull considered the provision of the Civil Rights bill making people born in the United States citizens "declaratory of what in my judgment, the law now is."[123] The Civil Rights bill was "a bill providing that all people shall enjoy equal rights."[124] Trumbull's language is ambiguous. *Dred Scott* held that blacks were not citizens and not entitled to any of the rights, immunities, or privileges secured by the Constitution to citizens. So a bill that secured, among other things, the rights in the Bill of Rights to all citizens would secure equal rights.

Trumbull said the bill "declares that all persons in the United States shall be entitled to the same civil rights, the right to the fruit of their own labor, the right to make contracts, the right to buy and sell, *and enjoy liberty* and happiness."[125] At times Trumbull suggested that the bill would have no operation in a state that did not discriminate in civil rights among its citizens.[126] But at other times he was more precise: *"Each state, so that it does not abridge the great fundamental rights belonging under the Constitution, to all citizens,* may grant or withhold such civil rights as it pleases; all that is required is that, in this respect, its laws shall be impartial."[127] Citizenship, Trumbull insisted, carried with it some rights, "those inherent, fundamental rights which belong to free citizens or free men in all countries, such as the rights enumerated in this bill, and they belong to them in all the States of the Union."[128] He quoted Chancellor Kent to establish that the inalienable rights of citizens included equality of rights and the "absolute rights of individuals" to personal security, personal liberty, and the acquisition and enjoyment of property.[129]

In short, Trumbull accepted the Republican view that there were certain fundamental rights of citizens of the United States that no state could abridge, and he identified these rights with the privileges and immunities secured by article IV, section 2.[130] For Trumbull, these privileges and immunities seem to have had a dual aspect: protecting the fundamental rights that belong to all free persons and providing the privileges and immunities the citizen of the same state would get under like circumstances—for example, the same right to hold property enjoyed by other citizens of the state.[131] To support his fundamental rights reading of article IV, Trumbull and other prominent Republicans relied on Justice Washington's dictum in *Corfield v. Coryell*[132] that the privileges and immunities protected by article IV, section 2 were those "which are, in their nature, fundamental; which belong, of right, to the citizens of all free governments."[133] These included broad categories of rights such as protection by government, the enjoyment of life and liberty, and the right to acquire and possess property.[134]

Congressman James F. Wilson, chairman of the House Judiciary Committee, managed the Civil Rights bill in the House. Wilson was also a Republican of preeminent influence. He was thirty-eight years old in 1866 and had served in the Iowa House and later as president pro tempore of the Iowa Senate. In December 1861 he was elected to the House of Representatives. He had opposed use of federal troops to return fugitive slaves, favored enfranchisement of blacks in the District of Columbia, and introduced the original resolution to abolish slavery.[135] Benedict rates him as Radical in the Thirty-ninth Congress but overall as erratic.[136]

Like Trumbull, Wilson also relied on the broad references to liberty in Blackstone, Kent, and *Corfield*.

> I have already said, "If citizens of the United States, as such, are entitled to possess and enjoy the great fundamental civil rights which it is the true office of Government to protect, *and* to equality in the exemptions of the law, we must of necessity be clothed with the power to insure each and every citizen these things which belong to him as a constituent member of the great national family."[137]

"What are these rights?" Wilson asked. "Certainly they must be as comprehensive as those which belong to Englishmen." He then quoted Blackstone and Kent to show that English and American authorities agreed that these fundamental rights were rights to personal security and personal liberty, and the right to acquire and enjoy property.[138]

> Thus, sir, we have English and American doctrine harmonizing. The great fundamental rights are the inalienable possession of both Englishmen and Americans; and I will not admit that the British constitution excels the American Constitution in the amplitude of its provision for the protection of these rights. *Our Constitution is not a mockery; it is the never-failing fountain of power from whence we may draw our justification for the passage of this bill; for there is no right enumerated in it by general terms or by specific designation which is not definitely embodied in one of the rights I have mentioned, or results as an incident necessary to complete defense and enjoyment of the specific right.*[139]

Wilson had argued that the great fundamental rights of citizens "must be as comprehensive as those which belong to Englishmen." He cited Blackstone.

Blackstone classifies them under three articles, as follows: 1. The right of personal security; which he says,

> "Consists in a person's legal and uninterrupted enjoyment of his life, his limbs, his body, his health and his reputation."

2. The right of personal liberty; and this, he says,

> "Consists in the power of locomotion, of changing situation, or moving one's person to whatever place one's own inclination may direct, without imprisonment or restraint, unless by due course of law."

3. The right of personal property; which he defines to be,

> "The free use, enjoyment, and disposal of all his acquisitions, without any control or diminution save only by the laws of the land."[140]

Since Wilson referred to Blackstone on the absolute rights of an individual—the right to personal security, personal liberty, and the right to acquire and enjoy property—a careful examination of Blackstone is in order. Blackstone's *Commentaries* notes:

> The absolute rights of every Englishman (which, taken in a political and extensive sense are usually called their liberties) as they are founded on nature and reason, so they are co-eval with our form of government. . . . [T]he ballance of our rights and liberties has settled to its proper level; *and their fundamental articles have been from time to time asserted in Parliament, as often as they were thought to be in danger.*[141]

Blackstone then cites the Magna Carta, the Petition of Right, the Habeas Corpus Act, the English Bill of Rights, and the Act of Settlement.[142] The Magna Carta, of course, was the origin of our due process clause and was read to secure a jury trial. The Petition of Right lists rights such as due process, the right to habeas corpus, and the right not to have troops quartered in private homes.[143] The English Bill of Rights provides that "excessive bail ought not to be required, nor excessive fines imposed, nor cruel or unusual punishments inflicted," that jurors should be duly impanelled, that subjects had the right to petition the king for redress of grievances and that all commitments and prosecutions for such petitionings are illegal, and that "Protestants" had a right to have arms for their defense as allowed by law.[144]

After listing such things as the Magna Carta, the Habeas Corpus Act, the Petition of Right, and the Bill of Rights, Blackstone says:

> Thus much for the *declaration* of our rights and liberties. The rights themselves, thus defined by these several statutes, consist in a number of private immunities; which will appear, from what has been premised, to be indeed no other, than either that *residuum* of natural liberty, which is not required by the laws of society to be sacrificed to public convenience; or else those civil privileges, which society hath engaged to provide, in lieu of the natural liberties so given up by individuals. These, therefore, were formerly, either by inheritance or purchase, the rights of all mankind; but . . . they at present may be said to remain, in a peculiar and emphatical manner, the right of people of England. *These may be reduced to three principal or primary articles; the right of personal security, the right of personal liberty; and the right of private property: because, as there is no other known method of compulsion, or abridging man's natural free will, but by infringement, or diminution of one or other of these important rights, the preservation of these, inviolate, may justly be said to include the preservation of our civil immunities in their largest and most extensive sense.*[145]

So Blackstone says that there are absolute rights of Englishmen and that their fundamental articles have from time to time been asserted in Parliament. He then lists some of the great acts of Parliament that were precursors to the American Bill of Rights and that represent the declaration of rights and liberties of Englishmen. These he says consist of "immunities" and "privileges" of British subjects. These various immunities and privileges can be reduced to three primary articles: personal security, personal liberty, and the right to private property —because an infringement of any of the important rights set out in any of the great acts of Parliament could not be accomplished without some invasion of one of the three fundamental rights. For Blackstone, the absolute rights of Englishmen encompass all their liberties. The Blackstonian heritage tends to support the idea that the Fourteenth Amendment was designed to apply basic liberties in the Bill of Rights to the states.

In addition to Wilson, other leading Republicans also relied on absolute constitutional rights that limited the power of the states. One of these was centrist William Lawrence of Ohio, a widely respected lawyer and formerly a prosecuting attorney, a member of the Ohio legislature, a reporter for the Ohio Supreme Court, editor of the *Western Law Monthly*, and a judge.[146]

According to Lawrence, questions of contracting, suing, and being parties in court, and property rights were left to the states "subject only to the limitation that there are some inherent and unalienable rights, pertaining to every citizen, which cannot be abolished or abridged by State constitutions or laws."[147] Under article IV, section 2 citizens removing from one state to another were "'entitled to the privileges that persons of the same description are entitled to in the State to which the removal is made.'" Although distinctions of age, sex and mental capacity were recognized, those of color were not.[148]

In his defense of the Civil Rights bill, Lawrence noted that there was a national citizenship. And "citizenship implies certain rights which are to be protected, and imposes the duty of allegiance and obedience to the laws." He noted that the Continental Congress of 1774 in the Declaration of Rights declared

> That the inhabitants of the English colonies of North America, by the immutable laws of nature, the principles of the English Constitution, and the several charters or compacts, have the following rights:
> "*Resolved* that they are entitled to life, liberty, and property, and that they have never ceded any sovereign Power whatever right to dispose of either without their consent."[149]

Lawrence noted that citizens have certain absolute rights including personal security, personal property, and liberty and that the Bill of Rights of the national Constitution declared that no person should be deprived of life, liberty, or property without just compensation.[150]

> Without further authority I may assume, then, that there are certain absolute rights which pertain to every citizen, which are inherent, *and of which a state cannot constitutionally deprive him.*
> . . . .
> Every citizen, therefore, has the absolute right to live, the right of personal security, personal liberty, and the right to acquire and enjoy property. These are rights of citizenship. As necessary incidents of these absolute rights, there are others, as the right to make and enforce contracts, to purchase,. hold, enjoy property, and to share the *benefit of laws for the security of person and property.*[151]
> . . . .
> I maintain that Congress may by law secure the citizens of the nation in the enjoyment of their inherent right of life, liberty, and property and the means essential to that end, by penal enactments to enforce the observance of the provisions of the Constitution, article four, section two, and the equal civil rights which it recog-

nizes or by implication affirms to exist among citizens of the same
state.
. . . .
     Congress has the incidental power to enforce and protect the
equal enjoyment in the States of civil rights which are inherent in
national citizenship. The Constitution declares these civil rights to
be inherent in every citizen, and Congress has the power to enforce
the declaration. If it has not, then the Declaration of Rights is in
vain, and we have a Government powerless to secure or protect
rights which the Constitution solemnly declares every citizen shall
have.[152]

Lawrence concluded "that 'the citizens of each state' if they remove
from one state to another 'shall be entitled to all privileges and immunities of citizens' of the United States 'in the' State to which they
remove." There was one kind of fundamental civil privilege equal for
all citizens. So all citizens were entitled to privileges and immunities
of United States citizens whether they were migrants or not. The
privileges referred to in the Constitution were "such as are fundamental civil rights, not political rights, nor those dependent upon local
law."[153]
     Sometimes a congressman or senator seems to describe the Civil
Rights bill as securing equal rights to blacks and not limiting state law
in any other way—as if it merely encompassed equal protection. On
examination, such remarks are often qualified and ambiguous. Ohio
Radical Congressman Samuel Shellabarger, for example, said: *"But
sir, except so far as it [the Civil Rights bill] confers citizenship it neither confers
nor defines nor regulates any right whatever.* Its whole effect is not to
confer or regulate rights, but to require that whatever of these enumerated rights and obligations are imposed by State law shall be for and
upon all citizens alike without distinctions based on race or former
condition in slavery."[154] The Civil Rights Act, of course, made all persons born in the United States and subject to its jurisdiction citizens of
the United States and gave such citizens the full and equal benefit of
all laws and provisions for the security of person and property as
enjoyed by white citizens. Shellabarger seems to have felt that states
could continue to refuse to allow married women to testify after the
passage of the bill. Such a rule of law seems to be the very sort of
denial of due process forbidden by the Civil Rights bill in the case of
blacks and by the Fourteenth Amendment in the case of *all* "persons."[155]
     Exactly what Shellabarger thought on the relation between the Four-
teenth Amendment and the Civil Rights bill is hard to fathom. But to
use his remarks on the Civil Rights bill to disprove application of the

Bill of Rights to the states by the amendment, one must assume that the bill and the amendment were identical, a statement Shellabarger never made. Indeed, Shellabarger, speaking years later, indicated he thought a reading of the Fourteenth Amendment that limited it to securing equality was incorrect.[156]

Congressman M. Russell Thayer of Pennsylvania was a respected lawyer who would later become a distinguished jurist. He was a centrist Republican in 1866.[157] Thayer insisted that Congress had power to pass the Civil Rights bill. The sole purpose of the bill, according to him, was to secure "the fundamental rights of citizenship; those rights which constitute the essence of freedom. . . . [T]hose rights which secure life, liberty, and property, and which make all men equal before the law."[158] The fundamental rights of citizenship were stated in the bill.[159]

Thayer found power to pass the bill in the Thirteenth Amendment and also in the Fifth Amendment. It would be extraordinary, Thayer argued, if the framers had made a "Constitution which was powerless to protect the citizens of the United States in their fundamental civil rights, their rights of life, liberty, and property."[160]

Thayer said that the rights enumerated in the Civil Rights bill "preclude[d]" extension of the general words "beyond the particulars which [have] been enumerated."[161] Thayer's remarks (which have sometimes been quoted to disprove application of the Bill of Rights to the states) were made in response to assertions that Civil Rights bill protection for "civil rights and immunities" included the state law right to vote. Thayer denied the claim. He noted that the words were "civil rights and immunities," not political privileges. The matter was "put beyond all doubt by the subsequent particular definition of the general language which has been just used." "Enumeration precludes any possibility that the general words which have been used [can be extended] beyond the particulars which have been enumerated."[162] The general words referred to were the words *civil rights* or *immunities*. After arguing again that suffrage was not included, Thayer said:

> Why should not these fundamental rights and immunities which are common to the humblest citizen of every free State, be extended to these citizens? Why should they be deprived of the right to make and enforce contracts, of the right to sue, of the right to be parties and give evidence in courts of justice, of the right to inherit, purchase, lease, hold, and convey real and personal property? *And why should they not have full and equal benefit of all laws and proceedings for the security of person and property?*[163]

A reading of Thayer's remarks makes clear that the general phrase he spoke about was "civil rights and immunities" and that the particular rights he believed limited the general phrase included "the full and equal benefit of laws and proceedings for the security of person and property." Thayer believed that Congress had power to pass the Civil Rights bill because of its power to enforce guaranties contained in the Bill of Rights.

> If, then, the freedmen are now citizens, or if we have the constitutional power to make them such, they are clearly entitled to those guarantees of the Constitution of the United States which are intended for the protection of all citizens. They are entitled to the benefit of that guarantee of the Constitution which secures to every citizen the enjoyment of life, liberty, and property, and no just reason exists why they should not enjoy the protection of that guarantee of the Constitution.[164]

Later, Thayer's argument was characterized as meaning that the provisions of the first eleven amendments "contain guarantees which it is the right and duty of Congress to secure and enforce in the States," and Thayer accepted the characterization as correct.[165]

John Bingham was one of only a handful of Republicans who thought Congress lacked power to pass the Civil Rights bill. James Wilson rejected Bingham's argument. Citizens of the United States, Wilson insisted, were entitled "to certain rights," and "being entitled to those rights it is the duty of the Government to protect citizens in the perfect enjoyment of them."[166] Wilson also rejected Bingham's argument that the oath taken by state officers was the sole enforcement mechanism.[167] Government that could "draw the citizen by the strong bond of allegiance to the battlefield" had to have the power to give protection to the citizen's rights. If Bingham's assertion were correct, it meant "that at the mercy of the States lie all the rights of the citizen of the United States . . . that revolted South Carolina may put under lock and key the great fundamental rights belonging to the citizen."[168]

According to Wilson, the Bill of Rights gave Congress the authority to pass the Civil Rights bill. He relied specifically on the due process clause.

> [Bingham] says that we cannot interpose in this way for the protection of rights. Can we not? . . . I find in the bill of rights which the gentleman desires to have enforced by an amendment to the Constitution that "no person shall be deprived of life, liberty, or property without due process of law."
>
> I understand that these constitute the civil rights belonging to the

citizens in connection with those which are necessary for the protection and maintenance and perfect enjoyment of the rights thus specifically named, and these are the rights to which this bill relates.[169]

Wilson then cited *Prigg v. Pennsylvania*[170] to support the idea that the existence of the rights in the Bill of Rights necessarily implied congressional power to enforce them. *Prigg* had held that the existence of a right to have fugitive slaves "delivered up" necessarily implied congressional power to enforce that right.[171] Wilson's argument is nearly identical to that made by Tiffany in his *Treatise on the Unconstitutionality of American Slavery*.[172] Wilson concluded, "Now, sir, in relation to the great fundamental rights embraced in the bill of rights, the citizen being possessed of them is entitled to a remedy. . . . The possession of the rights by the citizen raises by implication the power in Congress to provide appropriate means for their protection."[173]

Democrats were not convinced. In addition to making frequent and blatant appeals to racism,[174] most insisted that Congress has no power to pass the Civil Rights bill.[175] Republicans relied on the Thirteenth Amendment, the privileges and immunities clause of article IV, section 2, and the Bill of Rights, but most Democrats denied that any of these provisions supplied the power needed. Free blacks in the North had been denied the rights set out in the Civil Rights bill, so Democrats found it clear that the bill could not be authorized by an amendment prohibiting slavery.[176] The privileges and immunities clause, Democrats insisted, merely protected the citizens of each state "while *temporarily* sojourning in any other State," and it prohibited discrimination against citizens of any other state merely for that reason. But Texas could deny to "paupers, vagabonds, or negroes of New England privileges and immunities which it denies, on grounds of local public policy" to the same classes from other states and within the state of Texas itself.[177]

Resort to the Bill of Rights as a basis for power to secure privileges of citizens was also rejected by the Democrats. Michael C. Kerr of Indiana noted that the Supreme Court had held the amendments only limitations of power, not grants of legislative power, and that the limitations applied only to the national government, not the states. To support this argument Kerr cited *Barron v. Baltimore*, the same case relied on by Bingham to show the necessity of his proposed constitutional amendment.[178] Republican speakers supported the bill on grounds of a paramount national citizenship and a national body of fundamental privileges and immunities; the Democratic doctrine was more in keeping with accepted Supreme Court doctrine.

The Democratic argument of unconstitutionality was supported by Congressman Bingham. Bingham said that he did not oppose the bill's purpose; he only doubted that it was authorized by the Constitution.[179] He did not "oppose any legislation which is authorized by the Constitution of my country to enforce in its letter and its spirit the bill of rights as embodied in that Constitution. I know that the enforcement of the bill of rights is the want of the Republic."[180] Bingham agreed with Wilson "in an earnest desire to have the bill of rights in your Constitution enforced everywhere." But the enforcement of the Bill of Rights was, in view of past interpretation and the text of the Constitution, left to state officials and tribunals, subject to the requirements of an oath they took to support, protect, and defend the Constitution as supreme law.[181] Bingham said, "I have advocated here an amendment which would arm Congress with the power to compel obedience to the oath, and punish all violations by State officers of the bill of rights, but leaving those officers to discharge the duties enjoined upon them as citizens of the United States by that oath and by that Constitution."[182]

As originally proposed, the Civil Rights bill provided that "there shall be no discrimination in civil rights or immunities among citizens of the United States in any State or Territory of the United States on account of race, color, or previous condition of slavery."[183] Bingham objected that the phrase embraced every right, state or federal, belonging to any citizen, and urged that it be deleted.[184] Even with its deletion, he insisted that a constitutional amendment would be required to empower Congress to pass the Civil Rights bill.[185]

Wilson denied that the phrase encompassed rights belonging to citizens of the United States *and* all rights conferred on any citizen of a state. "He knows, as every man knows, that this bill refers to those rights which belong to men as citizens of the United States and none other; and when he talks of setting aside the school laws and jury laws and franchise laws of the States by the bill now under consideration, he steps beyond what he must know to be the rule of construction."[186] Wilson then said that the rights of citizens of the United States that Congress would require the states to respect included rights in the Bill of Rights.[187]

In the final version of the Civil Rights bill the phrase prohibiting discrimination in "civil rights or immunities" was omitted.[188] In the final version of the Fourteenth Amendment the states were prohibited from abridging "privileges or immunities of citizens of the United States," a phrase that Bingham read as applying only to those rights provided for in the Constitution. Although many Republicans believed that "fundamental" rights not explicitly listed in the Constitution were included, there was no consensus on what these rights were.[189]

Republicans believed that rights in the Bill of Rights did, or should, limit the states, and they explicitly criticized Court decisions to the contrary. Republicans thought that slavery had perverted constitutional law and produced Court decisions that restricted liberties of the citizen. In discussing the Civil Rights bill, Congressman Wilson said the courts had drifted from the "old moorings of equality and human rights."[190] Senator Nye insisted that the rights in the Bill of Rights limited the states (and provided a basis for legislative power to secure the rights of citizens), and he noted that slavery had made true interpretation of the Constitution impossible.[191] Slavery, as Congressman William A. Newell said, had a "contaminating influence" on the principles on which the Constitution was founded. It "gave the lie direct to its declaration of rights."[192] Other Republican congressmen believed that slavery had "polluted" or "defiled"[193] the judiciary. Republicans believed that the Bill of Rights limited the states and therefore rejected decisions like *Barron v. Baltimore*, but Democrats generally embraced these decisions and used them as a text from which to lecture the Republicans.[194]

The Amendment in Committee

Back in the Joint Committee the proposed amendment to the Constitution underwent a curious development. On April 21, 1866, the committee was considering an amendment that provided: "Section 1. No discrimination should be made by any state, nor by the United States, as to the civil rights of persons because of race, color, or previous condition of servitude."[195]

Bingham moved to amend the provision by adding to it "nor shall any state deny any person within its jurisdiction the equal protection of the laws, nor take private property for public use without just compensation." The proposed addition to section 1 was defeated. Later, Bingham persuaded the committee to add a new section 5 to the amendment to provide as follows: "Section 5. No state shall make or enforce any law which shall abridge the privileges or immunities of citizens of the United States; nor shall any state deprive any person of life, liberty or property without due process of law, nor deny to any person within its jurisdiction the equal protection of the laws."[196] Subsequently, the committee agreed to strike the fifth section. Still later, Bingham's section 5, which had been struck, became section 1.[197]

One could argue that the Joint Committee's rejection of Bingham's proposal to add the Fifth Amendment phrase "nor shall private property be taken for public use without just compensation" is incompatible with incorporation of the Bill of Rights.[198] Basically, the argument would be that rejection of the proposal is incompatible with subsequent acceptance.

To understand this argument we need to recall the chronology. On February 3, 1866, the Joint Committee approved Bingham's prototype of the Fourteenth Amendment—the one that gave Congress the power to secure privileges and immunities and equal protection in the rights of life, liberty, and property. The amendment was postponed by the House on February 28, 1866.

On April 21, 1866, the Joint Committee considered a totally new amendment, section 1 of which prohibited discrimination in civil rights by any state or by the United States on account of race, color, or previous condition of slavery. Its general language failed to take account of and overrule the doctrine of *Barron v. Baltimore* that the Bill of Rights did not limit the states. It also contained no equal protection clause.

Bingham's proposal to amend this new proposal by adding "nor shall any state deny to any person within its jurisdiction the equal protection of the laws, nor take private property for public use without just compensation" was rejected by a vote of 7 to 5. Subsequently, Bingham's proposal to add a new section 5 to the new amendment (prohibiting states from abridging privileges or immunities of citizens of the United States, due process, or equal protection) was accepted.[199] After further developments, Bingham's proposal became section 1 of the Fourteenth Amendment and was reported to Congress.

Suppose the committee had added only one of the narrow guaranties of the Bill of Rights to the proposed section 1 and had provided in section 1 of the proposed amendment only that no state could discriminate in civil rights based on race or take private property for public use without just compensation. And suppose (as was the case in the April 21 proposal) that the amendment had contained no general language that could be read as broad enough to cover other Bill of Rights liberties. Then, no doubt, critics would have argued that the proposal was designed to incorporate only one provision from the Bill of Rights and no others. The critics' argument, logically developed, tells us that if Bingham's April 21 amendment had passed, it would have disproved incorporation; and also tells us that the defeat of the proposal disproves incorporation—an absurd result.

On April 21, 1866, the committee rejected a proposal providing for equal protection and just compensation. It subsequently passed one providing for equal protection, due process, and privileges or immunities. In short, the April 21 rejection proves nothing except that at the time it was submitted the committee found the form of Bingham's proposal deficient.[200] In fact, when Senator Howard presented the Fourteenth Amendment to the Senate, he implied that it would overturn court decisions holding that states could take private property for public use without just compensation. Finally, American courts prior to the passage of the Fourteenth Amendment had held that the law of the land clauses or due process clauses of state constitutions prohibited taking without just compensation.[201]

Final Debates
on the Fourteenth Amendment

On April 30, 1866, the Joint Committee reported a revised resolution for a constitutional amendment.[202] Section 1 of the proposed amendment provided: "No State shall make or enforce any law which shall abridge the privileges or immunities of citizens of the United States; nor shall any State deprive any person of life, liberty, or property without due process of law; nor deny to any person within the jurisdiction the equal protection of the laws."[203] A fifth section gave Congress enforcement power.

The amendment still did not declare that all persons born in the United States and subject to its jurisdiction were citizens. In other respects, however, it was substantially improved from Bingham's earlier proposal. The rights secured by the amendment no longer depended upon the will of Congress. And the Republican view, that the fundamental privileges and immunities secured by the Constitution to citizens of the United States could not be abridged by any state, was incorporated explicitly in the amendment. Persons, whether citizens or not, were protected from state denial of due process or equal protection.

Congressman Thaddeus Stevens was the first to speak in favor of the amendment. He was a preeminent Republican in 1866, chairman of the Ways and Means Committee, and a consistent Radical.[204] He had studied law and emigrated from Vermont to Pennsylvania. By 1821 he was an outstanding and successful lawyer. Stevens had defended fugitive slaves without fee and with considerable success. He had been in the state legislature and in Congress. He took a leading role in the formation of the Republican party. He spoke with eloquence and simplicity on behalf of blacks. His farsighted project to provide freed slaves with forty acres and a mule failed, but showed he had a clearer grasp of the economic plight of blacks than most of his colleagues. By his own wish he was buried in a black cemetery.[205]

Stevens supported the Fourteenth Amendment as the best measure that could be passed. He considered section 2, which reduced the representation in Congress of states that excluded adult males from the franchise, as the most important part. After summarizing section 1, he said,

> I can hardly believe that any person can be found who will not admit that every one of these provisions is just. They are all asserted, in some form or other, in our DECLARATION or organic law. But the Constitution limits only the action of Congress, and is not a limitation on the States. This amendment supplies that defect, and allows Congress to correct the unjust legislation of the States, so far that the law which operates upon one man shall operate equally upon all.[206]

Stevens said that it was "partly true" that the Civil Rights bill secured the same things, but, he noted, "a law is repealable by a majority."[207]

Congressman Thayer claimed that the amendment added to the Constitution "what is found in the bill of rights of every State of the Union." The amendment "incorporat[ed] in the Constitution of the United States the principle of the civil rights bill which has lately become a law . . . in order . . . that that provision so necessary for the equal administration of the law, so just in its operation, so necessary for the protection of the fundamental rights of citizenship, shall be forever incorporated in the Constitution of the United States."[208] Thayer believed that Congress had the constitutional power to pass the Civil Rights bill because it could legislate to enforce the rights in the Bill of Rights. Indeed, when Thayer advocated the Civil Rights bill in March 1866, he said it simply declared that "all men born upon the soil of the United States shall enjoy the fundamental rights of citizenship" that were "stated in the bill."[209] Power to pass it could be found in the Fifth Amendment, which guarantied "to all the citizens of the United States their right to life, liberty, and property."[210]

Several congressmen observed that the amendment would eliminate any question about the power of Congress to pass the Civil Rights bill.[211] Others considered the amendment a reiteration of the Civil Rights bill.[212] Several other congressmen suggested that the Constitution already effectively contained the provisions of the amendment.[213] Implicit in such remarks, of course, was the view that the due process clause of the Fifth Amendment applied to the states even prior to the passage of the Fourteenth Amendment—that the guaranties of the Bill of Rights already limited the states and that the amendment was declaratory of existing law.

Bingham was one of the last speakers to support the amendment the first time it passed the House.

There was a want hitherto, and there remains a want now, in the Constitution of our country, which the proposed amendment will supply. . . . It is the power in the people, the whole people of the United States, by express authority of the Constitution to do that by congressional enactment which hitherto they have not had the power to do, and have never even attempted to do; that is, to protect by national law the privileges and immunities of all the citizens of the Republic and the inborn rights of every person within its jurisdiction whenever the same shall be abridged or denied by the unconstitutional acts of any State.[214]

Although states had no right to deny privileges or immunities or equal protection, they had exercised the power to do so and no remedy was available.[215]

Bingham insisted that the section was necessary even though it did not confer suffrage. "Many instances of State injustice and oppression have already occurred in the State legislation of this Union, of flagrant violations of the guarantied privileges of citizens of the 'United States' for which the national Government" could furnish no remedy. As an example, Bingham explained that "contrary to the express letter of your Constitution, 'cruel and unusual punishments' have been inflicted under State laws within this Union upon citizens."[216]

Senate consideration of the amendment was delayed by the illness of Senator William Pitt Fessenden, chairman of the Joint Committee. Finally, on May 23, 1866, with Fessenden present but still ill,[217] Senator Howard presented the amendment on behalf of the committee.

By 1866, Senator Howard had enjoyed a long and distinguished career. He had come to Michigan from Vermont. By 1854 he had served in the state legislature and in Congress. In that year he led the movement to organize the Republican party in Michigan. From 1854 to 1861 he was attorney general of the state and from 1862 to 1871 United States senator from Michigan. Howard was a consistent Radical. But Howard, unlike Sumner, had the confidence of more conservative Republican senators.[218] After quoting section 1, Howard noted:

It will be observed that this is a general prohibition upon all the States, as such, from abridging the privileges and immunities of the citizens of the United States. That is its first clause, and I regard it as very important. . . .

The first clause of this section relates to the privileges and immunities of citizens of the United States as such, and as distinguished from all other persons not citizens of the United States. It is not, perhaps, very easy to define with accuracy what is meant by the expression, "citizen of the United States."[219]

Howard discussed citizenship and cited *Corfield v. Coryell* to identify some of the privileges and immunities secured by article IV, section 2. He continued:

> Such is the character of the privileges and immunities spoken of in the second section of the fourth article of the Constitution. To these privileges and immunities, whatever they may be—for they are not and cannot be fully defined in their entire extent and precise nature—to these should be added the personal rights guarantied and secured by the first eight amendments of the Constitution; such as the freedom of speech and of the press; the right of the people peaceably to assemble and petition the Government for a redress of grievances, a right appertaining to each and all the people; the right to keep and to bear arms; the right to be exempted from the quartering of soldiers in a house without the consent of the owner; the right to be exempt from unreasonable searches and seizures, and from any search or seizure except by virtue of a warrant issued upon a formal oath or affidavit; the right of an accused person to be informed of the nature of the accusation against him; and his right to be tried by an impartial jury of the vicinage; and also the right to be secure against excessive bail and against cruel and unusual punishments.
>
> Now, sir, here is a mass of privileges, immunities, and rights, some of them secured by the second section of the fourth article of the Constitution, which I have recited, some by the first eight amendments of the Constitution; and it is a fact well worthy of attention that the course of decision of our courts and the present settled doctrine is, that all these immunities, privileges, rights, thus guarantied by the Constitution or recognized by it, are secured to the citizen solely as a citizen of the United States and as a party in their courts. They do not operate in the slightest degree as a restraint or prohibition upon State legislation. States are not affected by them, and it has been repeatedly held that the restriction contained in the Constitution against the taking of private property for public use without just compensation is not a restriction upon State legislation, but applies only to the legislation of Congress.
>
> Now, sir, there is no power given in the Constitution to enforce and to carry out any of these guaranties. They are not powers granted by the Constitution to Congress, and of course do not come within the sweeping clause of the Constitution authorizing Con-

gress to pass all laws necessary and proper for carrying out the foregoing or granted powers, but they stand simply as a bill of rights in the Constitution, without power on the part of Congress to give them full effect; while at the same time the States are not restrained from violating the principles embraced in them except by their own local constitutions, which may be altered from year to year. The great object of the first section of this amendment is, therefore, to restrain the power of the States and compel them at all times to respect these great fundamental guarantees.[220]

After Howard spoke, Senator Benjamin F. Wade suggested an amendment to identify those whose privileges and immunities were protected, and it subsequently became the definition of citizenship contained in the first sentence of section 1.[221]

There was no extended discussion of section 1 in the Senate after Howard spoke. Senator John Brooks Henderson's remarks on section 1 were brief but consistent with Howard's speech. He discussed the first section "only so far as citizenship is involved in it. . . . It makes plain only what has been rendered doubtful by the past action of the Government." The remaining provisions of section 1, Henderson said, "merely secure the rights that attach to citizenship in all free Governments."[222]

Today, some scholars have difficulty with the idea that all the rights in the Bill of Rights are essential to liberty.[223] Framers of the Bill of Rights, however, described them as "essential and unalienable rights of the people" and as "essential to secure the liberty of the people."[224]

Several congressmen and senators construed section 1 to mean that the rights of citizens of the United States should not be abridged by any state, a reading consistent with Senator Howard's interpretation. For example, Radical Republican Senator Richard Yates, a lawyer who had been wartime governor of Illinois and a close ally of Lincoln,[225] noted: "But above all there is in the first section a clause that I particularly favor. It is this: All persons born in the United States, and subject to the jurisdiction thereof, are citizens of the United States and of the States where they reside. And then it goes on to provide that their rights shall not be abridged by any State."[226]

Congressman William Windom, a Radical from Minnesota, supported the amendment by citing the South's reluctance to accept the full consequences of its defeat. Initially, "they understood well the principles of liberty and equal rights for which the nation had contended, and they anticipated such terms and conditions as would forever guaranty them." Yet, because of President Johnson's encouragement, they were recalcitrant.[227] "Has the Government," Windom asked, "a right to demand of traitors, as a condition precedent to their full restoration to political power, such guarantees as will insure its own safety, guard its honor, and protect its humblest defender in all the rights of citizenship? Congress asserts that right. The rebels deny it."[228] Congressman Godlove S. Orth read the amendment in the same way. Section 1, he said, secures "to all persons born or naturalized in the United States the rights of American citizenship."[229] For Congressman Hezekiah S. Bundy, section 1 protected "the security and defense of the personal and property rights of the citizen in all the States."[230]

Republican discussion of section 1 of the amendment was typically brief. According to Congressman George F. Miller, its provisions that no state could deny any person "life, liberty, or property without due process" and its guaranty of equal protection were "clearly within the spirit of the Declaration of Independence."[231] Senator Stewart read the amendment as declaring that "all men are entitled to life, liberty, and property" and as imposing "upon the Government the duty of discharging these solemn obligations."[232] Congressman Henry Jarvis Raymond, who supported President Johnson, described the amendment as "giving to the freedman of the South all the rights of citizens in the courts of law and elsewhere" and as "protecting him in their enjoyment."[233]

Senator Luke P. Poland of Vermont said the amendment had been so elaborately and ably discussed that he would not discuss it at length or in detail. He thought that the privileges or immunities clause secured "nothing beyond what was *intended*" by the similar provision of article IV, section 2. Slavery had led "to a practical repudiation of the existing provision on this subject, and it was disregarded in many of the states. State legislation was allowed to override it." It became "really a dead letter." Finally, Poland believed that legislative power to pass the Civil Rights bill was clearly provided by the due process clause of the Fourteenth Amendment.[234]

Congressman Jehu Baker of Illinois, a lawyer and a former judge, discussed the amendment on July 9, 1866. Baker recalled that slavery had gone "about overthrowing the great landmarks of liberty." The proposed amendment, Baker said, was most valuable "for the security and future growth of liberty." He apparently regarded section 1 as a declaration of existing constitutional law, properly understood. After quoting it, he said, "This section I regard as more valuable for clearing away bad interpretations and bad uses of the Constitution as it is than for any positive grant of new power which it contains."[235] Since the amendment expressed existing law, Baker must have believed that the states already were prohibited from denying due process, that is, that the guaranties of the Bill of Rights already applied to them. After quoting the privileges and immunities clause, Baker asked, "What business is it of any State to do the things here forbidden? To rob the American citizen of rights thrown around him by the supreme law of the land? When we remember to what an extent this has been done in the past, we can appreciate the need of putting a stop to it in the future."[236]

In summary, debates in the Thirty-seventh, Thirty-eighth, and Thirty-ninth Congresses show that Republicans were unhappy with the protection individual liberties had received from the states. Concern for individual liberty together with increased concern for the rights of blacks shaped the Fourteenth Amendment. Leading framers of the Fourteenth Amendment and most Republicans who spoke on the subject in 1866 believed that the states were already required to obey the Bill of Rights. For them, the Fourteenth Amendment was an affirmation of their own deeply held legal theories. Even those who did not accept the unorthodox Republican doctrines could agree that the rights in the Bill of Rights were privileges and immunities of citizens of the United States that should be shielded from hostile state action.

So for Republicans the amendment was simply declaratory of existing constitutional law, properly understood. They rejected *Dred Scott* and instead believed that all free persons born in the United States were citizens of the United States. Still, they explicitly wrote into the Fourteenth Amendment national citizenship for all persons born in the United States. Some believed, contrary to *Barron v. Baltimore*, that states could not deprive persons of due process. Still, they wrote this limitation into the Fourteenth Amendment. Finally, leading Republicans believed that no state could abridge the privileges and immunities of citizens of the United States—including those privileges and immunities secured by the Bill of Rights. This idea also was written into the Fourteenth Amendment.

The Fourteenth Amendment debates show that Republicans were willing to criticize what they considered its shortcomings. The failure to give blacks the right to vote produced protests and laments that lasted to the very end of the debates.

John Bingham, the author of the amendment, and Senator Howard, who managed it for the Joint Committee in the Senate, clearly said that the amendment would require the states to obey the Bill of Rights. *Not a single senator or congressman contradicted them.* No one complained that the amendment would allow the states to continue to deprive citizens of rights secured by the Bill of Rights. Today, the idea that states should obey the Bill of Rights is controversial. It was not controversial for Republicans in the Thirty-ninth Congress.

Chapter 4

In Which

Some Arguments Against Application

of the Bill of Rights to the States

Are Analyzed

Professor Fairman's Fourteenth Amendment

In December 1949 Charles Fairman published his article entitled "Does the Fourteenth Amendment Incorporate the Bill of Rights?"[1] It was an historical examination of the subject. Fairman's timing was excellent. Four members of the Supreme Court had very recently indicated their belief that the amendment did apply the Bill of Rights to the states. Their spokesman, Justice Black, had based his analysis on history.[2]

Fairman's article was 139 pages long and contained 381 footnotes. He believed that he had uncovered a "mountain of evidence" that the framers of the Fourteenth Amendment did not intend to apply the Bill of Rights to the states.[3] Fairman's assessment was shared by others. Years later, Justices John Marshall Harlan and Potter Stewart would rely on the "overwhelming evidence" against total application of the Bill of Rights to the states marshaled by Fairman.[4] In the historical dispute between the professor and the justice, many academic commentators came down on the side of the professor.[5]

When Professor Fairman wrote in 1949, he lacked help available to later students. Although historians had written about the crusade against slavery, legal historians had not yet started to view Republican legal thought from that perspective. The studies of Jacobus tenBroek and Howard Graham would not appear until the 1950s.[6]

Fairman began his consideration of the Fourteenth Amendment with a brief overview of article IV, section 2. He looked at Justice Washington's opinion in *Corfield v. Coryell,* and at a few other cases cited by Republicans. Fairman thought Washington's discussion was "badly confused." Washington was thinking "subconsciously at least" of a national standard of rights that were fundamental and that belonged to citizens of all free governments. Fairman wondered whether "all free governments" was more than a "careless phrase." Washington had referred to the writ of habeas corpus, but where, Fairman asked, did that writ exist except in Anglo-American law?[7]

Fairman contrasted Justice Washington's confusion with the clarity of the analysis of article IV by Joseph Story in his *Commentaries on the Constitution*. For Story, the measure of rights under article IV was purely local; the standard was a protection against discrimination.[8]

With that preface, Professor Fairman launched into the debates in the Thirty-ninth Congress. He started with the debates on the Civil Rights bill. As Fairman's article would unfold, the Civil Rights bill would become the main reference point for the meaning of the Fourteenth Amendment. Fairman would later show that some congressmen said that the object of the amendment was to constitutionalize the bill and that a few said that the amendment and the bill were identical.[9] The bill, Fairman explained, "made these provisions: (1) no discrimination in civil rights on account of race; and (2) inhabitants of every race should have the same right to contract, sue, take and dispose of property, and to equal benefit of all laws for the security of person and property."[10] Fairman understood the Civil Rights bill to provide for equality under *state* or local law. As he put it in his later massive study of the Supreme Court during Reconstruction, the bill "declared that in every State *all* citizens would thenceforth have the same right to contract, to sue, to testify, to hold property, and to enjoy the equal benefit of the laws, as the State allowed to white citizens."[11]

Professor Fairman set out some of Senator Trumbull's comments on the Civil Rights bill. The bill was to secure practical freedom. To Fairman's dismay, Trumbull quoted both *Corfield* and Story as to privileges or immunities, as though the two were consistent.[12] After looking at some comments by Democrats, Fairman moved on to the action in the Joint Committee. The committee, as Fairman noted, produced Bingham's prototype of the Fourteenth Amendment.

Before looking at the debates, Fairman made his own "independent analysis of the problem." He wrote, "So far as civil rights were concerned, the mischief to be remedied was, first of all, discrimination against the Negro by the government of the state wherein he resided—notably in the 'black codes.' This was an evil against which Article IV, Section 2 had nothing to say." "Far less important, though frequently mentioned as a subsidiary point, was the mistreatment that at times had been meted out in Southern states to visitors from out of state."[13]

From this vantage point, Fairman began to look at the debates.

Bingham's prototype had provided: "The Congress shall have power to make all laws which shall be necessary and proper to secure the citizens of each state all privileges and immunities of citizens in the several states (Art. 4, Sec. 2); and to all persons in the several states equal protection in the rights of life, liberty and property (5th Amendment)."

Fairman listed Bingham's main points. It had been the want of the Republic that Congress lacked express power to enforce the provisions of Bingham's prototype. If such power had been available and used, there would have been no rebellion.[14] The amendment did not impose on any state any duty not already required by the Constitution. The Constitution was supreme law. But "these provisions of the Constitution, this immortal bill of rights embodied in the Constitution, rested for its execution and enforcement hitherto upon the fidelity of the States."[15] If a state legislator or officer made or enforced a law that would have violated the federal Bill of Rights if done in the federal system, Fairman noted, by Bingham's view "that state officer or legislator thereby violated his oath to observe the Constitution of the United States!"[16] The exclamation mark indicates Fairman's exasperation with the argument.

To Professor Fairman, Bingham's presentation made little sense. It revealed a "novel" and "befuddled" construction of the Constitution.[17] Fairman attempted to explain Bingham's reference to "these great provisions of the Constitution, this immortal bill of rights embodied in the Constitution." The antecedent to "this immortal bill of rights," Professor Fairman believed, was "evidently" the privileges and immunities clause of article IV and the due process clause of the Fifth Amendment. "The bill of rights" was on this occasion, he said, "a fine literary phrase, not referring precisely to the first eight amendments."[18]

Fairman found a welcome contrast to Bingham's confusion in the clarity of his Democratic critics. Andrew Jackson Rogers, Fairman noted, pointed out that the Supreme Court had decided that the Bill of Rights limited the federal government only, not the states.[19]

Fairman then quoted Representative Higby, a Republican. Bingham's proposal would only "have the effect to give vitality and life to portions of the Constitution that probably were intended from the beginning to have life and vitality but which have received such a construction that they have been entirely ignored and have become as dead matter in that instrument." The proposal, Fairman explained, was "a sort of elixir calculated to give a general toning up to the Constitution."[20] After citing another Republican who believed the powers conferred in the amendment were already in the Constitution, Fairman moved on to a detailed consideration of remarks by New York Congressman Robert S. Hale, whom he identified as a former state judge. Fairman cited long excerpts from Hale. Hale thought the amendment allowed Congress to pass laws covering virtually every subject previously covered by state law. Part of Bingham's answer was that the amendment would apply to all states that "have in their constitutions and laws" provisions "in direct violation of every principle of our Constitution." This was so in Oregon. Fairman commented, "Of course a state law could hardly violate *every* provision of the Constitution. Bingham's answers simply did not meet the issue."[21]

Fairman next cited a speech by Congressman Woodbridge of Vermont: The amendment would enable Congress to give a citizen "those privileges and immunities which are guaranteed to him under the Constitution of the United States. It is intended to enable Congress to give to all citizens the inalienable rights of life and liberty, and to every citizen in whatever State he may be that protection to his property which is extended to other citizens of the State."[22] Fairman concluded that the explanation was "rather hazy."[23]

Fairman then turned to Bingham's last speech in favor of his prototype, and he cited portions of it.

> I repel [Bingham said] the suggestion made here in the heat of debate, that the committee or any of its members who favor this proposition seek in any form to . . . take away from any State any right that belongs to it. . . . The proposition pending before the House is simply a proposition to arm the Congress . . . with the power to enforce the bill of rights as it stands in the Constitution today. It "hath that extent—no more."
>
> . . . .
>
> Gentlemen admit the force of the provisions in the bill of rights, that the citizens of the United States shall be entitled to all the privileges and immunities of citizens of the United States in the several States, and that no person shall be deprived of life, liberty, or property without due process of law; but they say, "We are opposed to its enforcement by act of Congress under an amended Constitution, as proposed." That is the sum and substance of all the argument that we have heard on this subject. Why are gentlemen opposed to the enforcement of the bill of rights, as proposed? Because they aver it would interfere with the reserved rights of the States! Who ever before heard that any State had reserved to itself the right, under the Constitution of the United States, to withhold from any citizen of the United States within its limits, under any pretext whatever, any of the privileges of a citizen of the United States, or to impose upon him, no matter from what State he may have come, any burden contrary to that provision of the Constitu-

tion which declares that the citizen shall be entitled in the several States to all the immunities of a citizen of the United States?

What does the word immunity in your Constitution mean? Exemption from unequal burdens. Ah! say gentlemen who oppose this amendment, we are not opposed to equal rights; we are not opposed to the bill of rights that all shall be protected alike in life, liberty, and property; we are only opposed to enforcing it by national authority, even by the consent of the loyal people of all the States.[24]

After citing Bingham at some length, Fairman attempted again to sort out what Bingham was saying:

Bingham certainly says that the effect of his proposal is to arm Congress with power to enforce the bill of rights: it will do this and nothing more. What bill of rights? Once more he makes it clear by the context: The bill of rights that says that the citizens of the United States shall be entitled to the privileges and immunities of citizens of the United States in the several states (which refers to, but misquotes, Art. IV, section 2) and that no person shall be deprived of life, liberty, or property without due process of law (which is one of the Fifth Amendment's limitations upon the Federal Government). And this measure would take from the state no authority it now enjoys under the Constitution.[25]

Fairman noted with some astonishment that Bingham cited *Barron v. Baltimore* in defense of the need for his proposal. The citation to *Barron* was, Fairman thought, beside the point. Fairman seemed to conclude that Bingham could not possibly have been talking about the first eight amendments for a second reason.

This we know, the rights that Congress was to be empowered to *compel* the state and its officers to respect were only the rights that they were already obligated to respect. . . . No matter, then, what his personal views may have been as to the duty of the state and its officers to respect "the immortal bill of rights": the law had been clearly established in *Barron v. Baltimore*, to the effect that the first eight Amendments did not bind the states.[26]

Fairman noted that Bingham's proposed amendment was returned to committee and then turned his attention to the Civil Rights bill. Civil rights were explained by Wilson, chairman of the Judiciary Committee, to include the absolute rights of individuals to personal security, personal liberty, and the right to enjoy property.[27] Fairman noted that "the power to forbid discrimination in these matters" was,

Wilson believed, derived from the Thirteenth Amendment[28] and also, as he fails to note, from article IV, section 2.[29]

Fairman then moved on to Congressman Thayer. Fairman quoted Thayer's assertion that the power to pass the bill could be found, among other places, in the power to enforce the Fifth Amendment's due process clause.[30] Thayer was a Republican. Once again, Fairman found clarity from the Democrats. Michael C. Kerr, Indiana Democrat, "found Thayer an easy target."[31] Kerr noted that the amendments limited only the federal government, not the states, and cited *Barron v. Baltimore*.[32]

Fairman then quoted briefly from the speech Bingham gave against the Civil Rights bill. Bingham indicated that his proposed amendment was designed to allow Congress to enforce the oath that state officers took to uphold the Constitution. But it was not designed to take over all subjects to state legislation. Without the amendment, Bingham thought, Congress lacked power to pass the Civil Rights bill.[33]

After noting developments in the Joint Committee,[34] Fairman turned his attention to the amendment finally produced. The amendment provided that no state should abridge the privileges or immunities of citizens of the United States, or deny due process or equal protection to any person.[35]

The first speech in the House on the proposal was given by Thaddeus Stevens. The provisions of section 1 were set forth in some form or another in the Declaration or in organic law, "but the Constitution limits only the action of Congress and is not a limitation of the states. This amendment supplies that defect, and allows Congress to correct the unjust legislation of the States, so far that the law which operates upon one man shall operate equally and upon all."[36] "As Stevens saw it," Fairman concluded, "*discrimination* was a great evil, *equal* protection was the dominant purpose of Section 1."[37]

Fairman summarized several other speeches about section 1 of the amendment. Congressman Garfield said that section 1 would "hold over every American Citizen without regard to color, the protecting shield of law." It would put the Civil Rights bill "above the reach of political strife . . . and fix it in the serene sky, in the eternal firmament of the Constitution."[38]

Fairman quoted Congressman Broomall: "we propose, first, to give power to the Government to protect its own citizens within the States, within its own jurisdiction." Those who voted for the Fourteenth Amendment had voted for "this proposition in another shape in the Civil Rights Bill."[39] Fairman noted that "over and over in this debate, the correspondence between Section 1 of the Amendment and Civil

Rights Act is noted. The provisions of one are treated as though they were essentially identical with those of the other."[40] But Fairman insisted that the rights established by the act were the rights to contract, to testify, and to sell, to enjoy the full and equal benefits of laws for the security of person and property. "Never, even once, does advocate or opponent say 'first eight amendments.'" Fairman overlooked Bingham's references to "all the guaranties of the constitution."[41]

Fairman also cited a speech from Henry Raymond. Bingham's prototype of the Fourteenth Amendment had been designed to give Congress "power to secure an absolute equality of civil rights in every state of the Union." Now an amendment was proposed to make the constitutional power to do that clear. Since Raymond was in favor "of securing an equality of rights to all citizens of the United States, and of all persons within their jurisdiction," he favored the amendment. The principle of the first section secured an equality of rights among all citizens of the United States.[42]

Generally, the more Professor Fairman thought that a speech tended to disprove application of the Bill of Rights to the states, the better introduction the speaker got.[43] John F. Farnsworth was "an important member of the Republican delegation from Illinois and a professional lawyer." Farnsworth said there was only one clause in the amendment that was not already in the Constitution—the equal protection section—"but a reaffirmation of a good principle will do no harm, and I shall not therefore oppose it on account of what I may regard as surplusage." From this speech, Fairman concluded that "to Farnsworth Section 1 means equal protection, expressed with harmless surplusage."[44]

Bingham's final speech to the Congress about the amendment was presented at some length. Congress will be given the power to protect the privileges and immunities of citizens of the Republic and inborn rights of man. Cruel and unusual punishments have been inflicted by the states in the past and this would be corrected. Section 1 would provide protection by national law from unconstitutional state enactments.

Fairman's conclusion about the speech was framed in the form of rhetorical question. "Can it possibly be said that in this final utterance he was putting the House on notice that, at least to him, Section 1 meant the provisions of the first eight Amendments. The answers seem obvious."[45]

Senator Howard's speech presented an even greater problem for Fairman. Fairman conceded that it was a full statement of an intent to apply the Bill of Rights to the states.

Still, Fairman thought incorporation was disproved by a redundancy.

If the privileges or immunities clause incorporated the Bill of Rights, the due process clause would be found both in the privileges or immunities clause and in the due process clause for the Fourteenth Amendment. "How can this be maintained?"[46]

Finally, Fairman cited a speech by Senator Henderson of Missouri. The provisions of section 1 "secure rights that attach to citizenship in all free governments."[47] Fairman concluded, "Unless the first eight amendments enumerated 'rights that attach to citizenship in all free governments,' Henderson's understanding is to be counted as opposed to that of Howard."[48]

Looking back at the debates, Fairman concluded that "Bingham . . . did a good bit of talking about 'this immortal bill of rights,' and once spoke of 'cruel and unusual punishments.' Senator Howard, explaining the new privileges or immunities clause, said that it included . . . 'the personal rights guaranteed and secured by the first eight amendments. . . .' That is all. The rest of the evidence bore in the opposite direction, or was indifferent."[49]

Fairman looked at the campaign of 1866. He found some speakers who said, "the first clause in that Constitutional Amendment is simply a reaffirmation of the first clause in the Civil Rights bill, declaring the citizenship of all men born in the United States, without regard to race or color."[50] This is true but is a somewhat unenlightening observation. Several congressmen noted the correspondence between the bill and the amendment.[51] A senator is quoted as saying that the amendment would allow Congress to ensure equal justice when the states refuse to enforce it.[52] Several representatives, including Bingham, talked about the protection for freedom of speech,[53] leading Fairman to wonder whether a selective incorporation was intended.[54] Still, he suggested that perhaps the freedom of speech protected was speech limited to federal matters.[55]

This account summarizes the evidence presented by Professor Fairman from the Thirty-ninth Congress and the campaign of 1866. Fairman also looked at ratification proceedings in the states and construction of the amendment in Congress after 1866. Looking at these items, he found little evidence of an intent to apply the Bill of Rights to the states under the Fourteenth Amendment.[56] These matters will be discussed in subsequent chapters, where I will show that Professor Fairman overlooked significant evidence.

Fairman's conclusion is puzzling. After much analysis that seems designed to show that basic rights in the Bill of Rights were not to be applied to the states, Fairman opted for selective incorporation. Republican thinking was "hazy," making it hard to catch the "vague aspirations" Republicans had for the privileges or immunities clause.

But the amendment "undoubtedly" proposed to establish a standard below which state action must not fall.[57]

Professor Fairman's Analysis:
A Critical Appraisal

The major fault with Professor Fairman's effort to understand the Fourteenth Amendment is that it overlooked the antislavery origins of the amendment. Much of what Republicans had to say does seem confused if read without an understanding of the antislavery background, and in light of modern legal ideas.

Read in light of antislavery legal thought, Bingham's remarks are fairly clear. Bingham and other leading Republicans read article IV, section 2 to protect fundamental rights of citizens of the United States from violation by the states. Bingham recognized that the Supreme Court had held otherwise, but he thought that the states *were* obligated to obey the Bill of Rights. Still, he found the obligation legally unenforceable—just as the Court had treated other obligations of article IV, section 2 as unenforceable.

Fairman's analysis should alert the reader that something is askew. The Fourteenth Amendment was a Republican amendment. It was opposed by the mass of Democrats. But Fairman regularly found the Democrats to be the people who had a clear understanding of the Bill of Rights question.[58] Republicans, he said, were confused.[59]

In fact, of course, the Republicans and Democrats adhered to different legal philosophies. The Republican philosophy emphasized protection of the rights of the individual under the Bill of Rights from hostile acts of states. Democrats left the question to the states themselves. In a large section of the country before the Civil War the states had done an excellent job of suppressing Republican ideas. A whole section of the country had been out of bounds for Republican campaigners. It is not surprising that the two parties saw the issue differently.

Much of Fairman's mountain of evidence is simply beside the point. For example, Fairman used Hale's attack on the prototype of Bingham's amendment—the one that gave Congress power to secure privileges and immunities and equal protection in the rights of life, liberty, and property—to disprove incorporation of the Bill of Rights. What concerned Hale, however, was another issue—the power of Congress to secure equal protection in the rights of life, liberty, or property. Hale was afraid that the amendment would give Congress power to legislate generally on matters of state law —such as the status of married women. Hale thought that the states were already required to obey the Bill of Rights and that in any case the issue was a side issue.[60]

In responding to Hale, Bingham explicitly noted the case of *Barron v. Baltimore* to show why his amendment was required.[61] Another Republican noted that Bingham had not gone far enough. Because Bingham assumed that the states were already bound to obey the Bill of Rights under a proper reading of the law, he had failed to write an explicit limitation on the states into the amendment.[62] The final draft corrects his mistake.

Bingham claimed that if the grant of power in his prototype had been in the Constitution and had been enforced by legislation, the rebellion would have been impossible. Fairman found that claim "difficult to square . . . with *any* reading of the amendment."[63] But if one takes Bingham's argument seriously and reads it in light of the antislavery heritage, it makes perfect sense.

In reply to Hale, Bingham had cited *Barron v. Baltimore* and *Livingston v. Moore*, noting, "By the decisions read the people are without remedy." "Is the Bill of Rights," Bingham asked, "to stand in our Constitution . . . a mere dead letter?"[64] He answered with his view of the proper construction of the Constitution. "As the whole Constitution was to be the supreme law in every State, it therefore results that the citizens of each State, being citizens of the United States, should be entitled to all the privileges and immunities of citizens of the United States in every State and all persons, now that slavery has forever perished, should be entitled to equal protection in the rights of life, liberty, and property."[65]

A grant of power such as that sought by Bingham was not inserted in the original Constitution, he said, because such a grant "would have been utterly incompatible with the existence of slavery in any State: for although slaves might not have been admitted to be citizens, they must have been admitted to be persons." Slaves, and here Bingham was apparently referring to slaves in the slave states, "were not protected by the Constitution."[66] But, in Bingham's view, the guaranties of the Bill of Rights applied to the states under the privileges and immunities clause, which protected *citizens* of the United States.[67] Consequently, he asserted, "there might be some color of excuse for the slave States in their disregard for the requirement of the bill of rights as to slaves and refusing them protection in life or property."[68] But there never was any excuse, he continued, "for any man North or South claiming that any state Legislature or State court, or State Executive, has any right to deny protection to any free citizen of the United States within their limits in the rights of life, liberty, or property."[69] In fact, however, free blacks—considered citizens by Bingham—had been denied by racist laws equal access to the courts to protect their rights, even in the North.[70]

Bingham thought slavery was incompatible with the Bill of Rights. If the due process clause (read by Bingham to require equal protection in the right of life, liberty, and property) had applied to all persons (including slaves in the states) and if it had been enforced, slavery would have been impossible. Slavery was the cause of the war. To Bingham it was as simple as that.

Unlike Professor Fairman, Congressman Hale took Bingham's argument seriously and treated it respectfully. Hale noted:

> But the gentleman says there is, and there has been first to last, a violation of the provisions of this bill of rights by the very existence of slavery itself; that the institution of slavery itself has existed in defiance of the provisions of the bill of rights; that all the anomalies and all the enormities that have grown out of that institution have been equally in violation of it. I concede there is much force in that reasoning.[71]

Fairman attempted to explain Bingham's repeated references to "the Bill of Rights." Since Bingham referred to this immortal bill of rights, Fairman said, his reference must have had an antecedent. The antecedent, Fairman claimed, was article IV, section 2 and the due process clause. Before and after in American history, the phrase "bill of rights" had referred to the first eight or ten amendments to the Constitution. On this occasion, according to Fairman, it had a specialized meaning, never given to it before or since. When Bingham answered Hale by showing the need for his amendment, he referred to cases "showing that the power of the Federal Government to enforce in the United States courts *the Bill of Rights* under *the articles of amendment* to the Constitution had been denied."[72]

Finally, a reading of the debates shows that Bingham's colleagues understood "the bill of rights" to refer to the amendments to the Constitution. During the debate on the Civil Rights bill, Representative Wilson noted, "I find in the bill of rights which the gentleman desires to have enforced by an amendment to the Constitution that 'no person shall be deprived of life, liberty, or property without due process of law.'"[73] Obviously, Wilson understood the Bill of Rights to be a document containing various guaranties, of which the due process clause was only one.

One of Fairman's major arguments centers on the Civil Rights bill. Fairman read the bill as securing equality under state law. Some congressmen indicated that the bill was incorporated in the amendment or equivalent to it. The inference the reader is apparently expected to draw is that the amendment excluded Bill of Rights liberties because the Civil Rights bill excluded them. There are a number of problems with this argument.

Before looking at the problems, however, it is important to note that Professor Fairman's reading is plausible. The Civil Rights Act listed certain specific rights, such as the right to testify and to hold property. These are rights under local law. It is natural to read the general words in the act in light of the specific ones.

Although some speakers suggested that the Civil Rights bill and the Fourteenth Amendment were identical,[74] Thaddeus Stevens, manager of the Fourteenth Amendment in the House, denied that the amendment and the Civil Rights bill were identical. That was, as he said, only partly true.[75]

Several congressmen noted an equivalence between the amendment and the Civil Rights bill. Most of the statements by congressmen indicated that the amendment provided power for Congress to pass the bill and that the principles of the bill were protected by the amendment.[76] And, of course, both statements are clearly true. It is clear that the amendment incorporated the principles of the bill. What is not clear is that the bill, *if read so narrowly as to provide only equality under state law*, encompassed the entire amendment. The evidence shows that Republicans did not read the bill so narrowly.

Leading supporters of the Civil Rights bill had argued that its enactment could be justified because Congress had power to enforce the Bill of Rights, specifically the Fifth Amendment. Bingham had insisted that an amendment allowing enforcement would be required.[77] Bingham got his amendment, and there is no doubt that Congress got the power to pass the Civil Rights bill, if, as Bingham believed (probably correctly), it did not already have it.

Both the amendment and the bill made all persons born and naturalized in the United States citizens of the United States. Earlier in the session several congressmen noted that making blacks citizens would solve the entire problem, since they would have all rights of citizens of the United States.[78] For most Republicans who spoke on the subject, rights in the Bill of Rights (protected from invasion by the states as well as by the federal government) were rights of citizens in the United States.[79] For example, Representative Thayer argued that the due process clause provided the constitutional power necessary to pass the Civil Rights bill.

If, then, the freedmen are now citizens, or if we have the power to make them such, they are clearly entitled to those guarantees of the Constitution of the United States which are intended for the protection of all citizens.

They are entitled to the benefit of that guarantee of the Constitution which secures to every citizen the enjoyment of life, liberty, and property.[80]

Among the rights that Republicans in the Thirty-ninth Congress relied on as absolute rights of the citizens of the United States were the right to freedom of speech, the right to due process of law, and the right to bear arms.[81]

In addition, the Civil Rights bill gave all United States citizens "full and equal benefit of all laws and proceedings for security of person and property, as is enjoyed by white citizens." Rights in the Bill of Rights could be, and have been, read as provisions for security of person and property. The Freedman's Bureau bill, passed by Republicans in the Thirty-ninth Congress, provided that blacks should be protected in, among other things, "the full and equal benefit of all laws and proceedings for the security of person and estate, including the constitutional right of bearing arms."[82] The phrase "including the constitutional right of bearing arms" was added by an amendment in the House. In explaining the amendment to the Senate, Senator Trumbull said that it did not change the meaning of the bill.[83]

Suppose the amendment and the Bill were "identical." If they were, it follows that the Civil Rights bill included a federal standard of due process. If a federal standard of due process was included in the language of the Civil Rights bill, it might be included in several ways. First, since the bill made all persons born in the United States citizens, they would have all the rights of citizens, rights that most Republicans who spoke on the subject believed included the protection of Bill of Rights liberties against infringement by the states.[84]

One such right would have been the Fifth Amendment's guaranty of due process. The Court in *Dred Scott v. Sandford*,[85] of course, had held that blacks were not citizens of the United States and consequently had deprived them of the protection of the rights in the Bill of Rights, as well as other basic rights.[86] Second, the due process clause—and other provisions of the Bill of Rights—could also be comprehended in the phrase "full and equal benefit of all laws and provisions for security of person and property, as is enjoyed by white citizens."[87]

The inescapable implication of the assertion that the Civil Rights bill and section 1 of the Fourteenth Amendment are identical is that at least some rights in the Bill of Rights applied to the states prior to the passage of the Fourteenth Amendment. In short, that some Republicans considered the amendment identical to the Civil Rights bill provides no proof that incorporation of the Bill of Rights was not intended by the framers.

In all of Fairman's examination of the evidence, both in Congress and in the campaign of 1866, he found no congressman or senator who said explicitly that the amendment would *not* require the states to obey the Bill of Rights. He overlooked a number of cases where senators and representatives said the amendment would protect all rights of citizens or all constitutional rights.[88] He found that the manager of the proposal in the Senate and the author of the proposal in the House did indicate that the amendment would apply the Bill of Rights to the states. But he discounted their statements as unsupported in or contradicted by the rest of the record. On careful analysis most (but not all) of Fairman's contradictory evidence tends to dissolve, and in some cases it even supports full application of the Bill of Rights to the states.

Other Arguments Against Incorporation

Scholars opposing full incorporation have insisted that the country would not have tolerated having the "federal provisions on grand jury, criminal jury, and civil jury . . . fastened upon them in 1868."[89] Fairman described the Seventh Amendment's requirement of a civil jury as such a waste of time as to be an "atrocity."[90]

This argument ignores the realities of the political process. The campaign of 1866 dealt with gut issues: the rights of blacks, the political power of the rebellious southern states, racism, and protection for loyalists in the South. These were issues that could and did defeat politicians. No politician, then or since, is likely to be defeated for advocating grand juries, criminal juries of twelve, or the right to jury trial in civil cases where the damages exceed twenty dollars. The argument assumes that Republicans in state legislatures would allow the South a dramatic increase of political power by counting disfranchised blacks for purposes of representation rather than provide for jury trials in civil cases where the damages exceed twenty dollars. Politicians do not behave in this fashion.

In any case, it is unlikely that Republicans would have shared the view that the Seventh Amendment jury trial requirement was an atrocity. Republicans were familiar with real atrocities. Slavery was anathema to them. Even worse, however, were provisions of fugitive slave laws that had extended the grasp of slavery into the North. Northern opponents of slavery watched with horror the spectacle of people being captured in their states and hauled into slavery. To Republicans, northern blacks—free as well as escaped slaves—faced capture and enslavement.[91]

Opponents of slavery responded by arguing that all people in their states were presumed free and by insisting on procedural guaranties secured to free persons.[92] Among the most important of these guaranties were trial by jury, the writ of habeas corpus, and the writ de homine replegiando, an ancient writ designed to test the question of freedom, which secured trial by jury.[93]

Trial by jury was an issue on which both abolitionists and more moderate politicians agreed. Benjamin Lundy, a veteran abolitionist, had warned in 1837 that free blacks were being seized and sold into slavery. Lundy's solution was "trial by jury in all cases of claims to service, that the acknowledged rights, privileges, and immunities of our own citizens may be duly guarded and protected."[94] Several states, through personal liberty laws, provided for trial by jury in the case of alleged fugitive slaves and secured other procedural rights to alleged slaves.[95]

These protections were crippled by the Supreme Court's decision in *Prigg v. Pennsylvania* and by the Fugitive Slave Act of 1850.[96] *Prigg* held the federal power over fugitive slaves to be exclusive, permitting the seizure of blacks in the free states without any of the guaranties prescribed by personal liberty laws.[97] The Fugitive Slave Act of 1850 explicitly provided that blacks could be denied the right to testify, to cross-examine, and to receive a jury trial before they were delivered to those claiming them as slaves.[98]

These restrictions on liberty produced protests from northerners, who insisted that fugitive slave laws violated the Fourth, Fifth, and Seventh amendments.[99] Supporters of the laws replied that such guaranties applied only to citizens, not to slaves. But that, as opponents of slavery noted, was the very matter to be resolved.[100]

The Fugitive Slave Act of 1850 was vigorously attacked by antislavery legislators. Congressman Horace Mann of Massachusetts argued that a claim for a fugitive was a suit at common law that, under the Seventh Amendment, required a jury trial.[101] He believed that the Fugitive Slave Act also violated the due process clause, which required a jury trial, and the Fourth Amendment. "What 'seizure' can be more 'unreasonable,'" he asked, "than one whose object is, not an ultimate trial, but bondage forever, without trial?"[102] When the Fugitive Slave Act was finally repealed in 1864 by a Republican Congress, its repeal was justified as securing trial by jury "in accordance with the Constitution of the United States and the laws of the State where such person is found."[103] To leading Republicans, "trial by jury in civil cases where the amount in controversy exceeds twenty dollars" was one of the precious guaranties of the Bill of Rights designed to prevent atrocities.

The second problem with Fairman's argument is that the due process clause of the Fourteenth Amendment would likely have been read to include the right to trial by jury. American statesmen from John Adams to John C. Calhoun had assumed that due process, or its ancestor the law of the land clause of the Magna Carta, protected the right to trial by jury.[104] There was substantial seventeenth- and eighteenth-century historical support for such a reading.[105]

Another argument asserting that section 1 did not apply the Bill of Rights to the states is that the due process clause would appear in the amendment twice, once as a privilege or immunity of citizens, and again in the due process clause as a protection for all persons. Fairman suggested that one might attribute to the committee "a design to give the citizen the protection of the entire Bill of Rights, and then" extend due process to aliens as well. But, Fairman tells us, no particular interest in aliens was expressed, so such an interpretation must be rejected.[106]

This argument overlooks the effect of the struggle against slavery on the amendment. Republicans had believed and announced in their party platforms that the due process clause prohibited slavery in national territories. As to the states, however, most Republicans believed that due process guaranties were limited to citizens.[107] The amendment contained conscious duplication to prevent any person from ever again suffering atrocities like slavery. Indeed, Bingham explained that a grant of power such as that sought in his prototype of section 1 had not been included in the Constitution because such power "would have been utterly incompatible with the existence of slavery in any State; for although slaves might not have been admitted to be citizens they must have been admitted to be persons."[108]

Shaped, no doubt, by the law's treatment of slaves, concern for the rights of aliens was also expressed in the debate on the Civil Rights bill. Congressman Wilson believed that Congress could not protect inhabitants who were not citizens under the Civil Rights bill. Since Wilson justified the bill by citing Congress's power to enforce the Bill of Rights in the states, he apparently believed such power was limited to citizens.[109]

Congressman Bingham was convinced that Congress lacked the power to pass the Civil Rights bill. Beyond that, he objected to the bill because it did not follow the scope of the Fifth Amendment and protect "strangers" as well. The bill, Bingham complained, would permit the states to deny aliens their due process rights.[110] The Fourteenth Amendment's duplication in the case of persons was consciously designed to protect those who were not citizens and to prevent denials of due process such as those that had characterized slavery.

Professor Fairman's article on incorporation of the Bill of Rights by the Fourteenth Amendment ignored antislavery legal thought. The oversight was corrected in Fairman's massive and thoughtful study of the Supreme Court during Reconstruction and reunion. But Fairman's later study tended to confuse radical abolitionist and moderate anti-slavery legal thought and so to assume that antislavery ideas—such as the idea that the liberties in the Bill of Rights protect American citizens in the states—were held by only a small minority of wild thinkers.[111] In fact, such ideas were held by a wide range of Republicans, from conservative to radical, including some of the most influential Republicans—among them the chairman of the House Judiciary Committee[112] and the author of section 1 of the amendment.[113]

Fairman considered and rejected the thesis that the Thirteenth Amendment was designed to protect basic constitutional rights of whites as well as blacks, such as those in the Bill of Rights.[114] He cited the statement of James Wilson, chairman of the House Judiciary Committee, to the effect that the amendment "introduces no intricate question of constitutional law for discussion." Since that statement would "have been untruthful" if the abolitionists' "peculiar mode of interpretation" was to be imposed, Fairman concluded that the amendment was to have no such effect.[115] Wilson's major speech on the Thirteenth Amendment shows that he believed that the guaranties of the Bill of Rights protected American citizens against infringement by the states and did so prior to the passage of the Thirteenth Amendment. The Bill of Rights was a reference point for the rights or liberties or privileges of American citizens.

In short, Wilson, like other Republicans, thought that the Constitution already protected the basic Bill of Rights liberties of the citizen prior to the passage of the Thirteenth Amendment. Abolition of slavery eliminated an institution that had perverted the Constitution and caused violation of constitutional rights. By the Thirteenth Amendment, blacks were freed and given the right to liberty enjoyed by other Americans.

In his book, Fairman's account of the battle over the Civil Rights bill omitted several significant portions of the debates. Both Congressmen Wilson and Thayer indicated their belief that the due process clause of the Fifth Amendment limited the states and supplied legislative power to pass the Civil Rights bill. Congressman Bingham insisted that his amendment would provide the power needed to justify passage of the Civil Rights bill—power to enforce the Bill of Rights.[116] Fairman's belief that antislavery legal ideas were limited to "the most radical" Republicans was simply a mistake.[117]

Fairman cited congressmen who said that the amendment clearly conferred on Congress power to pass the Civil Rights bill. From these statements, Fairman concluded that nothing more specific was in their minds.[118] What this analysis leaves out is the fact that Wilson, Thayer, and Bingham all analyzed the bill as an attempt to enforce the Bill of Rights, specifically, the due process clause of the Fifth Amendment. The claim that the Fourteenth Amendment clearly supplied power to pass the bill, if anything, supports the conclusion that the amendment was designed to apply the Bill of Rights to the states.

Professor Fairman argued that there were only a few federal rights in 1866—the right to petition the *federal* government, to communicate through the post office, for example. When Congress in the Fourteenth Amendment undertook to secure the "enjoyment of federal rights against denial by a state, inherent problems were raised which members of Congress, in the main, failed accurately to perceive."[119] Although the analysis probably accurately reflects the state of constitutional law in 1866, it ignores a Republican consensus on the proper interpretation of the Constitution.

Professor Fairman's treatment of the amendment lacked balance. Robert Hale of New York, a critic of Bingham's prototype, is presented as a "discriminating lawyer." Hale, however, had never heard of *Barron v. Baltimore* and assumed the courts would require the states to obey the Bill of Rights.[120] Bingham was aware of the holding in *Barron* and insisted that a constitutional amendment was required to correct it. But Bingham was subjected by Fairman to a series of ad hominem attacks: Bingham is a man of "peculiar conceptions," not a man of "exact knowledge or clear conceptions or accurate language."[121] He "purport[ed] to explain" generally in "confused discourse" and "pluck[ed] a constitutional phrase and toss[ed] it in at some point to which it ha[d] no relevance." Many of his utterances "cannot be accepted as serious propositions."[122]

Fairman took a modest statement from Howard's speech and presented it in a way to suggest ignorance. He quoted Howard, accurately, as saying that he would present the views and motives of the committee "so far as I understand those views and motives." Fairman then implied that Howard did not understand Bingham's proposal because he had voted for provisions providing for black suffrage instead. "Howard, apparently, had not entered into the spirit of Bingham's drafting: three times in the committee he had voted against the author's work."[123] In fact, Howard's explanation closely paralleled Bingham's discussion of why his prototype was required—to overrule *Barron* and allow Congress to enforce guaranties of the Bill of Rights against the states.

The Influence
of Professor Fairman

It is a tribute to the influence of Fairman's Stanford article, and
perhaps also to the tendency of the human mind to seek agreement
with others, that students of the antislavery origins of the Fourteenth
Amendment have sought to make their conclusions more nearly congruent with Fairman's. The attempt is all the more remarkable since
Fairman wrote his article with little or no understanding of antislavery
constitutional theory.

Jacobus tenBroek in his pioneering work *Equal under Law*, for
example, accepted Fairman's reading of some of Bingham's statements about applying the Bill of Rights to the states. Bingham, as we
have seen, argued that those who opposed his prototype of the Fourteenth Amendment opposed enforcement of the "Bill of Rights as it
stands in the Constitution today":

> Gentlemen admit the force of the provisions in the Bill of Rights,
> that the citizens shall be entitled to all the privileges and immunities
> of citizens of the United States in the several states, and that no
> person shall be deprived of life, liberty, or property without due
> process of law; but they say, 'we are opposed to its enforcement by an
> act of Congress under amended Constitution as proposed.' Why are
> gentlemen opposed to the enforcement of the Bill of Rights, as
> proposed?

The Bill of Rights referred to by Bingham, tenBroek said, is "certainly
not the first eight amendments" but instead is the original privileges
and immunities clause, the due process clause, and a requirement of
equal protection.[124] No one has read the phrase "Bill of Rights" in this
fashion before or since.

Another problem with the argument that Bingham's reference to
the Bill of Rights did not mean *the* Bill of Rights is that it contradicts
Bingham's later statement that his amendment was designed to apply
the first eight amendments (and other privileges of citizenship) to the
states.[125] It is possible, of course, that Bingham's later statement was
not candid. But because Bingham's earlier and later statements are
apparently consistent, one should be slow to ascribe dishonest motives.
This is particularly so where the hypothesis to be salvaged by a charge
of dishonesty is as weak as the one in the present case.

TenBroek concluded that the Fourteenth Amendment was not
intended to apply the Bill of Rights to the states, only to apply natural
rights, some of which were mentioned in the first eight amendments.
These included the substantive rights to life, liberty, and property

protected by due process (certainly), and (perhaps) the procedural guaranties of the Fifth Amendment, the guaranties of the Fourth, and those of the First.[126] According to tenBroek, Bill of Rights liberties of a lesser order were not protected. The reason for doubt as to free speech and other basic rights is that they were rarely mentioned in the final stages of the debate.[127] But they were emphatically mentioned by Senator Howard speaking on behalf of the committee that reported the amendment. And other congressmen repeatedly said the "rights of citizens" of the United States would be protected by the amendment.

Careful study of the legal ideas held by Republican congressmen and expressed in the Thirty-eighth and Thirty-ninth Congresses provides content to their appeal to the rights of American citizens. Such rights were first and foremost those protected by the Constitution. These rights which they believed protected American citizens throughout the nation included rights to freedom of expression, religious liberty, the right to bear arms, the right to due process, to civil jury trials, together with those mentioned by tenBroek.[128] Since these rights were viewed as privileges and immunities of American citizens, it is difficult to understand the basis for excluding other fundamental constitutional rights listed in the Bill of Rights.

Howard Graham, like tenBroek, was another pioneer who has contributed much to our understanding of the antislavery origins of the Fourteenth Amendment.[129] He argued for a selective incorporation of rights in the Bill of Rights. Graham concluded tentatively that Howard's failure to list all guaranties in the Bill of Rights supported selective incorporation.[130] In fact, of course, Howard's speech militated strongly in the direction of full incorporation. Howard said that to the privileges listed by Justice Washington in *Corfield* "should be added the personal rights guaranteed and secured by the first eight amendments to the Constitution; *such as*" freedom of speech and press, the right to assemble, the right to bear arms, not to have troops quartered in private homes during peacetime, to be free from unreasonable searches and seizures and from unreasonable bail, to be tried by an impartial jury, to be informed of the nature of an accusation, and to be free from cruel and unusual punishments.[131] Howard's use of the words "such as" makes clear that the rights he cited were illustrative of those in the first eight amendments, and that he was referring to the entire list. Later in his speech Howard indicated that the amendment would protect against taking private property for public use without just compensation. That protection was not on Howard's illustrative list. Nor, as Graham noted, did Howard list the due process clause.[132]

Graham also pointed out that different amendments received different emphasis during the antislavery crusade. From this fact he concluded that full incorporation was probably not considered in 1866.[133] The problems with *Barron*, Graham noted, had been limited practically to cases involving freedom of speech and of the press, unreasonable seizures and searches, due process, just compensation, and criminal procedure. From this fact Graham seemed to conclude that these rights would be the ones as to which incorporation was intended. To Graham's list one needs to add the right to bear arms and the right to civil jury trial—both of which received strong emphasis from Republicans. Howard mentioned specifically the protection against quartering troops. When one adds all these guaranties together, little if anything is left to be selected out. Furthermore, it is difficult to see a logical basis for eliminating some guaranties but not others.

Judge Henry Friendly argued that the doctrine of selective incorporation of rights in the Bill of Rights has "no historical support."[134] This proposition, he insisted, is "undisputed."[135] Unless one is willing to disregard virtually all the evidence, however, the contest is between selective and full application of the provisions of the Bill of Rights to the states. The common description of the Fourteenth Amendment was that it would protect the rights of citizens of the United States from violation by the states. To the extent that Republicans gave content to these rights in the years from 1864 to 1866 they read them to protect Bill of Rights liberties from state violations. I have found over thirty examples of statements by Republicans during the Thirty-eighth and Thirty-ninth Congresses indicating that they believed that at least some Bill of Rights liberties limited the states. I looked only at the debates on the abolition of slavery, Reconstruction, the Civil Rights bill, and the Fourteenth Amendment. Since a number of Republicans did not speak about these issues at all, among those who did speak, the percentage who accepted the application of the Bill of Rights to the states is high. The statements are made by Republican conservatives, moderates, and Radicals in the years from 1864 to 1866. When one adds statements by Republicans in Congress in the years immediately after the passage of the amendment, the total is even higher. Conversely, I found no statements by Republicans indicating that the states were free under a proper understanding of the law to violate rights in the Bill of Rights.[136]

Leading Republicans believed that the Fourteenth Amendment protected fundamental rights from violation by the states and that in this sense, as in others, it was declaratory of constitutional law properly understood. The often expressed idea that the amendment protected fundamental rights could provide a basis for selective incorporation. But, as Michael Conant has shown, *fundamental* was often used as a synonym for *constitutional.*[137] Certainly Republicans often used the word in that sense. After listing Bill of Rights liberties, for example, Senator Howard said that the great object of the first section of the Fourteenth Amendment was to "restrain the power of the states and compel them at all times to respect these great fundamental guaranties."[138]

Raoul Berger—No Application

The most vigorous current critic of incorporation is Mr. Raoul Berger. Mr. Berger rejects any incorporation. Because his work on the Fourteenth Amendment and the Bill of Rights has been accepted by a number of scholars and judges as historically accurate and because it has had growing influence, it requires careful examination. Moreover, because Berger's arguments often summarize those made by others, his work is representative of a broadly held scholarly view.

Raoul Berger and those who have accepted his arguments about application of the Bill of Rights to the states have treated their claims as generally accepted in the scholarly community. For example, Mr. Berger said, the theory that the Fourteenth Amendment was designed to make the states obey the commands of the Bill of Rights has been "discredited by Professor Charles Fairman in a study in which even activists" agree.[139] In fact, however, there is no solid wall of scholarly opinion on the subject. Among scholars who have actually studied the question at length, probably a majority have reached a view opposed to Berger's.[140]

Those who deny that any Bill of Rights liberties apply to the states have cited Fairman's[141] work as though it supported their thesis.[142] But Fairman himself seems to have concluded that the privileges or immunities clause of the Fourteenth Amendment was designed to apply many, but not all, of the guaranties of the Bill of Rights to the states.[143]

Professor Fairman's article and Mr. Berger's *Government by Judiciary* suffer some common faults. Both fail to recognize the extent to which suppression of civil liberty in the South in the thirty years before the Civil War molded the Fourteenth Amendment.[144] Both fail to recognize that Republicans operated from unorthodox legal premises.[145] Partly as a result of these shortcomings, Fairman and, to an even greater degree, Mr. Berger tended to misread the debates in significant ways.

Article IV, Section 2

Mr. Berger attempted to tie Republicans to an orthodox (or anti-discrimination) reading of the privileges and immunities clause of the original Constitution and then to equate the privileges or immunities clause of the Fourteenth Amendment with an orthodox reading of article IV, section 2.[146]

In the section of *Government by Judiciary* on privileges and immunities, Mr. Berger first discussed what he believed to be the conventional understanding of the clause in the original Constitution. The clause was, he asserted, not intended to control the powers of state governments over the rights of their citizens, but simply to ensure that a migrant citizen would enjoy the basic rights a state accorded to its own citizens.[147]

By conventional understanding as evidenced by *Dred Scott*,[148] the state could deprive migrants who became residents of rights that similar classes in the state were denied. Because blacks were not usually migrants, the clause, as conventionally understood, was of no help to them.[149]

Mr. Berger dealt with this problem by suggesting that the framers relied on an adaptation of article IV, section 2 to support the Civil Rights bill.[150] The debates show, however, that Bingham and others who framed the Fourteenth Amendment relied on a reading of the privileges and immunities clause of article IV, section 2 by which it protected a body of national privileges and immunities of citizens of the United States, including those in the Bill of Rights. This reading may have been incorrect.[151] It does not matter, however, because in the redrafting of Bingham's first proposal, the amendment was rewritten to secure privileges and immunities of *a citizen of the United States* from state abridgment.

One argument against application of the Bill of Rights to the states suggests that privileges and immunities in article IV, section 2 on which the Republicans relied were exhausted by the list of specific rights set out in *Corfield v. Coryell*[152] and by the list contained in the Civil Rights bill.[153] These specified rights, but no more, were incorporated as privileges and immunities of citizens of the United States.[154]

Some quotations that have been used to support this view instead refute it. Senator Trumbull, the bill's sponsor, said: "Citizens of the United States" have "fundamental rights . . . *such as* the rights enumerated in this bill."[155] In *Corfield* Justice Washington had said that the privileges and immunities protected by the original Constitution are those "which are, in their nature, fundamental; which belong, of right, to the citizens of free governments."[156] These fall under various headings, including protection by the government and the enjoyment of life and liberty, with the right to acquire and possess property of every kind.[157] The general categories, such as the "enjoyment of . . . liberty," are quite broad.[158] Particular privileges falling under the head-ing of those considered fundamental include the right to pass through or reside in a state; the benefit of the writ of habeas corpus; the right to institute and maintain court actions; and the right to take, hold, and dispose of property.

The reference to specific rights includes the following sentence: "These, and many others which might be mentioned, are strictly speaking, privileges and immunities."[159] Fairman conceded that the reference to fundamental rights in *Corfield* "cloud[s]" the simple antidiscrimination reading of article IV, section 2 that he advocated.[160]

In introducing the "prototype" of section 1 of the Fourteenth Amendment, Bingham said it had been patterned on article IV, section 2.[161] Bingham, however, had read article IV, section 2 to protect privileges and immunities of *citizens of the United States*, including rights in the Bill of Rights, from state interference. The final version of section 1 was rewritten to incorporate this understanding explicitly. Comments by a number of Bingham's colleagues show that they shared his reading of the original privileges and immunities clause.[162]

Senator Howard also referred to article IV, section 2 in discussing privileges and immunities.[163] But Howard, the member of the Joint Committee who had charge of the amendment in the Senate, said explicitly that privileges and immunities of citizens of the United States protected by the Fourteenth Amendment included those rights set out in the first eight amendments to the Constitution.[164]

By the Republican view of the privileges and immunities clause of the original Constitution, the clause protected residents as well as migrants and protected certain absolute rights—"the right of personal security," "personal liberty," and "the right to acquire and enjoy property."[165] According to Trumbull, "these are declared to be inalienable rights, belonging to every citizen of the United States . . . no matter where he may be."[166] Judge Washington referred to "fundamental rights," which "belong, of right, to the citizens of all free governments."[167]

One problem with arguing that the privileges or immunities clause is to be read as though it were a reiteration of an antidiscrimination understanding of article IV, section 2, is that then the clause of the Fourteenth Amendment would accomplish nothing beyond providing protection for temporary visitors. It would have been of no help to the mass of blacks in the South and of no help to southern unionists. All of the evidence indicates that these were the very people about whom Republicans were most concerned.

As some have read their remarks, the framers of the Fourteenth Amendment thought that the rights to liberty, security, and property were so inclusive that they included the right to testify, inherit, and

contract, but were so narrow that they excluded the rights in the Bill
of Rights. Senator Howard, however, described the rights in the Bill of
Rights as "great fundamental rights."[168]

Any attempt to define the Fourteenth Amendment privileges or
immunities clause by a rule of construction that gives it the orthodox
content of the privileges and immunities clause of article IV is not
legitimate. Even Mr. Berger attributed to Republicans an unorthodox
reading of the clause in the original Constitution (an adaptation, as he
put it) by which it protects residents as well as migrants.[169] "It cannot
too often be emphasized, the cardinal purpose of interpretation . . . is
to ascertain and effectuate, not defeat, the intention of the framers,"
Mr. Berger has written. "Once that purpose is ascertained, it may not
be thwarted by a rule of construction."[170]

Republicans suggested that the rights to make and enforce contracts,
to sue, to be parties, to give evidence, to inherit, and the like were
incidents of the absolute rights of individuals to "personal liberty,"
"personal security," and "private property" embraced by article IV.[171]
To define the "privileges or immunities of citizens of the United States,"
however, critics of incorporation choose to look at these *incidents*, not
the overarching principles from which they were derived.[172]

In an article defending his thesis, Berger sought to use an 1871
speech by Trumbull to prove that the Fourteenth Amendment privileges or immunities clause is equivalent to that of article IV (conventionally understood) and that the Fourteenth Amendment consequently does not include rights in the Bill of Rights.

> In 1871 Trumbull explained that the "privileges or immunities"
> clause is "a repetition of a provision [article IV] as it before exist-
> ed . . . The protection which the Government affords to American
> citizens under the Constitution as it was originally formed is *precisely*
> the protection it affords to American citizens under the Constitu-
> tion as it now exists. The fourteenth amendment *has not extended the
> rights and privileges of citizens one iota.*" As the draftsman of the ante-
> cedent "civil rights and immunities" in the Civil Rights Bill and
> chairman of the Senate Judiciary Committee who explained its
> meaning in unequivocal terms, Trumbull's views carry great weight.[173]

In the same speech Trumbull explained that the states were the deposi-
tories of the rights of the individual against encroachment.[174]

In *Government by Judiciary* Mr. Berger considered Trumbull's 1871
remarks, noted that the Supreme Court has attached little weight
to postenactment remarks, and concluded that remarks such as
Trumbull's should be treated with "special reserve," particularly "when
they contradict representations made by the speaker during the enact-

ment process."[175] Berger concluded that Trumbull's remarks were a "half truth" because Trumbull had adapted article IV to protect residents in the same way a migrant would be protected. Trumbull's remarks, he said, were "a repudiation of his own explanation to the framers, his enumeration of specific rights in the Bill that were to belong to 'citizens of the United States.'"[176] Since Trumbull's 1871 speech relied on so heavily by Mr. Berger was, by Mr. Berger's own prior analysis (though an analysis for different purposes), entitled to little weight, was a repudiation of Trumbull's prior statements, and was a half-truth, it seems to me it offers little or no support to Berger on the Bill of Rights question.[177]

Finally, there is a puzzling quality to Trumbull's remarks. If the Fourteenth Amendment had not extended the rights and privileges of citizens "one iota," then all of the rights it provides—including equal protection and due process—must have limited the states prior to its passage.

In a speech in the Thirty-ninth Congress Trumbull said that the "great fundamental rights, *which are set forth in the Civil Rights Bill,*" are "the right to come and go at pleasure, the right to enforce rights in the courts, to make contracts, and to inherit and dispose of property."[178] One might rely on this quotation to prove there was not room left in the privileges and immunities clause of the Fourteenth Amendment for the Bill of Rights liberties.[179]

At other times during the Thirty-ninth Congress, however, Trumbull gave other descriptions of rights in the Civil Rights bill, among them the right to "enjoy liberty and happiness."[180] Being a citizen, Trumbull insisted, carried with it some rights, "those inherent, fundamental rights which belong to free citizens or free men in all countries, such as the rights enumerated in this bill."[181] Another time, speaking of congressional power under the Thirteenth Amendment, he described laws that prohibit men from speaking or preaching as being laws inconsistent with the status of a free person.[182] Describing the effect of the Civil Rights bill, Trumbull said that "each State, *so that it does not abridge the great fundamental rights belonging under the Constitution, to all citizens,* may grant or withhold such rights as it pleases."[183] Clearly, in 1866 Trumbull had in mind some absolute rights seen as belonging to citizens under the Constitution.

Equal National Rights
or Equal Rights within a State

Professor Fairman's analysis of the intent of the framers of the Fourteenth Amendment has a somewhat schizophrenic quality. He concluded that the amendment in general and the privileges and immunities clause in particular were not intended to make all of the Bill of Rights applicable to the states.[184] In support of this argument, Fairman read most of the evidence to show that the framers of the Fourteenth Amendment understood it simply to incorporate the Civil Rights bill, a bill Fairman seems to have read as not including Bill of Rights liberties.[185] Still, and somewhat inconsistently, Fairman concluded that the framers intended selective incorporation of rights in the Bill of Rights.[186] By focusing on this issue and by taking one branch of Fairman's argument to its logical conclusion, Raoul Berger has illuminated the fallacy implicit in the argument based on the Civil Rights bill.

Mr. Berger said that a Republican centrist-conservative coalition was in control of the Thirty-ninth Congress and that abolitionist ideas were an anathema to these men.[187] Not only were these congressmen hostile to abolitionist ideas, Mr. Berger asserted, but also they were influenced by "Negrophobia,"[188] and they cherished states' rights.[189] Still, they were willing to invade states' rights, as conventionally understood, to protect blacks whom they supposedly disliked.[190] But they were not willing to interfere with states' rights by requiring the states to obey the Bill of Rights, guaranties that protect whites and blacks alike. Abolitionists had many ideas and most Republicans did not share them all. Certainly, the central idea of the abolitionists was that slavery should be abolished. If abolitionist ideas were an anathema to most Republican congressmen, why, in the previous session of Congress, had they abolished slavery in the states—the main goal of the radical political abolitionists?

In fact, leading Republicans gave the states' rights argument short shrift. As Representative William Lawrence put it, "I answer that it is better to invade the judicial power of the State than permit it to invade, strike down, and destroy the civil rights of citizens. A judicial power perverted to such uses should be speedily invaded."[191]

By one argument, the Civil Rights bill was merely designed to protect blacks by granting them equal protection in certain narrow rights secured by state law—the right to contract, own property, and the like. The Fourteenth Amendment, in turn, merely incorporated by the Civil Rights bill, read narrowly. The whole object, according to this view, was to grant certain rights to blacks—basically, the rights to contract, sell, testify, and to equal protection of certain state laws.[192] Fairman also seems to have read the Civil Rights bill only as providing for equal treatment under state law.[193]

The argument claims that the Fourteenth Amendment is absolutely the same as the Civil Rights bill.[194] Since the "act was merely to secure blacks against discrimination and not to displace nondiscriminatory state law,"[195] by this view the Fourteenth Amendment does not protect Bill of Rights liberties or any other absolute rights that states cannot abridge.

The argument is absolutely inconsistent with the language of the Fourteenth Amendment. If the amendment had been designed merely to prohibit discrimination in certain rights that states chose to accord their own citizens, then the due process and privileges and immunities clauses would have been superfluous. To say that "no state shall make or enforce any law which shall abridge the privileges or immunities of citizens of the United States, nor shall any state deprive any person of life, liberty, or property without due process of law" is a very odd way of saying that the state is prohibited only from discriminating in certain rights it gives its citizens.

In addition to being inconsistent with the language of the Fourteenth Amendment, the attempt to read the amendment as no more than a ban on discrimination collides with the way leading proponents of the amendment and the Civil Rights bill described the amendment and the overarching principles from which they derived the power to pass the bill—the absolute rights of "personal security," "personal liberty," and "the right to acquire and enjoy property."[196] These statements about power to pass the Civil Rights bill are significant because one purpose of the Fourteenth Amendment was to place the power to pass the bill in the Constitution if it was not there already.

As Senator Trumbull noted in arguing for the Civil Rights bill, the rights to personal liberty, personal security, and private property "are declared to be inalienable rights, belonging to every citizen of the United States . . . no matter where he may be."[197] If the states could eliminate such rights so long as they did it for all of their citizens, the rights would not be inalienable. Further, Congressman Wilson, chairman of the Judiciary Committee and manager of the Civil Rights bill in the House, noted that the rights of personal security, personal liberty, and the right to acquire property are "inalienable."[198] Wilson described "the right to personal security, the right to personal liberty, and the right to acquire and enjoy property" as absolute rights.[199] Bingham also referred to "absolute" rights.[200] Representative Lawrence noted "that there are certain absolute rights which pertain to every citizen, which are inherent, and of which a state cannot constitutionally deprive him."[201] Senator Howard, as we know, believed that the Fourteenth Amendment embodied the fundamental rights in the Bill of Rights and that states were not free to deny them.[202] The views of Congressman Bingham were the same.[203] If one treats the chairman of the Judiciary Committee and manager of the Civil Rights bill in the

Senate, the chairman of the Judiciary Committee and the manager of the Civil Rights bill in the House, the author of section 1 of the Fourteenth Amendment, and the senator who presented it on behalf of the Joint Committee to the Senate as leading proponents of these measures, then four of the five leading proponents of either the Civil Rights bill or the Fourteenth Amendment clearly adhered to the concept of absolute rights of citizens of the United States that no state could abridge. For that reason, attempts to use the Civil Rights bill to prove that no absolute rights are guarantied by the Fourteenth Amendment must fail. If absolute rights are guarantied by the Fourteenth Amendment, then a few statements that the Civil Rights bill and the Fourteenth Amendment are the same cannot be taken to disprove protection of Bill of Rights liberties.

If it is conceded that the Fourteenth Amendment was designed to secure absolute and fundamental rights of citizens of the United States, then the inquiry moves to what Republicans considered those rights to be. The overwhelming evidence from the Thirty-eighth and Thirty-ninth Congresses is that Republicans viewed rights in the Bill of Rights as rights of the citizens of the United States that states could not (or in a few cases should not) deny.[204] And there is evidence that leading Republicans read article IV, section 2 to embody such rights.[205]

Attacks on Bingham and Howard

John Bingham wrote section 1 of the Fourteenth Amendment (except for the citizenship clause) and was a member of the Joint Committee on Reconstruction, which reported the amendment. Jacob Howard, senator from Michigan, was a member of the Joint Committee and spoke for the committee in presenting the amendment to the Senate. The views of Bingham and Howard, leading proponents of the amendment, are entitled to very great weight. Indeed, some say that the intention of the legislature "may be evidenced by the statements of leading proponents."[206] The intent, once found, "is to be regarded as good as written into the enactment."[207] Since Bingham's and Howard's remarks are entitled to the greatest weight in determining the intent of the framers of the amendment and since what they said is extremely damaging to the thesis that the amendment does not apply the Bill of Rights to the states, both men have been subjected to personal attacks.

For example, Mr. Berger set out to prove that Bingham was a legal moron. Specifically, he said Bingham was "muddled,"[208] "inept,"[209] "veer[ed]" as "crazily as a rudderless ship,"[210] and was unable to "understand what he read."[211] Bingham was not viewed in this light by his contemporaries. The *New York Times*, for example, referred to

Bingham and Wilson as "among the most learned and talented" members of the House.[212] Bingham's reputation as a lawyer was excellent.[213] Professor Fairman took a similar, if milder, approach to Bingham. For Fairman, Bingham was a man of "peculiar conceptions,"[214] an "ardent rhetorician, not a man of exact knowledge or clear conceptions or accurate language."[215] Indeed, Fairman concluded that much of what Bingham had to say cannot be taken seriously.[216]

Mr. Berger said that Bingham was "utterly at sea as to the role of the Bill of Rights."[217] First, "he considered it to be binding on the States."[218] Then he noted *Barron v. Baltimore* had held the Bill of Rights was not applicable to the states.[219] Berger quoted other supposed "contradictions" in this vein.[220]

Bingham's remarks, however, show that he believed that the provisions of the Bill of Rights were in fact restrictions on the states by the privileges and immunities clause of article IV, section 2, but that the only enforcement mechanism was the oath state officials took to respect the Constitution as the supreme law of the land.[221] Bingham's remarks also show that Bingham was aware of Supreme Court decisions on the point but did not agree with them.[222] Wilson and Thayer held similar beliefs, but for them the rights in the Bill of Rights were privileges of citizenship secured against state interference, and Congress could legislate directly to secure the rights protected.[223]

In dealing with Bingham, Mr. Berger followed an analysis used by Professor Fairman in his article. In 1954 Fairman's article was subjected to a powerful critique by W. W. Crosskey. Interestingly, although Fairman's later book on the Supreme Court during Reconstruction and reunion did not cite Crosskey's article, it also did not repeat many of the arguments that Crosskey criticized in Fairman's original article.

Mr. Berger said that Bingham translated the provisions of "article IV that 'the citizens of *each state* shall be entitled to all privileges and immunities of citizens in the several States' as 'the provisions *in the Bill of Rights* that citizens *of the United States . . .*'"[224] Mr. Berger then commented, "the Bill of Rights contains no privileges and immunities provision."[225] Bingham never said it did. The argument indicates, it seems to me, a strained reading of what Bingham said. The quotation cited is an edited version of the following statement by Bingham:

> Gentlemen admit the force of the provisions in the bill of rights, that the citizens of the United States shall be entitled to all the privileges and immunities of citizens of the United States in the several states,[226] and that no person shall be deprived of life, liberty or property without due process of the law.[227]

Here, Bingham was supporting his contention that the amendment is in accordance with the Constitution. He seems to have been listing three items in a series. He wanted to enforce the Bill of Rights and equal protection. Why not? he said. We have the provisions of the Bill of Rights, the provisions of article IV, and the due process clause.

The second item in the series seems clearly to be Bingham's summary, not of the Bill of Rights, but of the privileges and immunities clause. Bingham interpreted section 2 of article IV as meaning that "the citizens of each State (being *ipso facto* citizens of the United States) shall be entitled to all the privileges and immunities of citizens (supplying the ellipsis 'of the United States') in the several states."[228]

Mr. Berger seems to have objected to Bingham's understanding of article IV, suggesting that Bingham's phrase "citizens of the United States shall be entitled to all privileges and immunities of citizens of the United States" shows that Bingham confused "the rights of citizens of a state with those of the United States." Bingham, the argument seems to suggest, read article IV to protect rights of citizens of the United States, not rights of a citizen of a state.[229]

Of course, the privileges or immunities clause of the Fourteenth Amendment that Berger equated with article IV does exactly that: "No state shall . . . abridge the privileges or immunities of citizens of the United States." As written, the Fourteenth Amendment was essentially equivalent to Bingham's reading of article IV, a reading that protects the rights of citizens of the United States.[230] *The privileges or immunities clause of the Fourteenth Amendment* was changed from Bingham's prototype, which gave Congress power to "secure to the citizens of each state all privileges and immunities of citizens in the several states." In the final draft, the Fourteenth Amendment provided that "no state shall make or enforce any law which shall abridge *the privileges or immunities of citizens of the United States.*"

Mr. Berger cited Bingham's March 9 speech on the Civil Rights bill to prove further "contradictions."[231] Bingham thought the states possessed the reserved power to control the property, life, and liberty of their citizens, that is, to legislate generally on these matters.[232] The power was subject to the limitations of the Bill of Rights enforced only by an oath to uphold the Constitution.[233] Here is how Berger showed Bingham to be so muddled that no one could understand him. First, Berger's edited version of what Bingham had to say:

> The care of the property, the liberty, and the life of the citizen . . . is *in the States*, and not in the Federal Government. I have sought to effect no change in that respect . . . I have advocated here an amendment which would arm Congress with the power to punish all viola-

tions of the bill of rights . . . I have always believed that *protection* . . . within the States of all the rights of person and citizen, was of the power *reserved to the States.*[234][*sic*]

"If the care of these rights," Berger asked, "'is in the states', how do state officers violate the Bill of Rights?"[235] Recall that Bingham believed that state officers were required to obey the Bill of Rights by their oath to support the Constitution, the decision of the Supreme Court in *Barron v. Baltimore* notwithstanding. At any rate, this is what Bingham actually said:

> The care of the property, the liberty, and the life of the citizen, *under the solemn sanction of an oath imposed by your Federal Constitution*, is in the States and not in the Federal Government. I have sought to effect no change in that respect in the Constitution of the country. I have advocated here an amendment which would arm congress with the power *to compel obedience to the oath*, and punish all violations by State officers of the Bill of Rights, *but leaving those officers to discharge the duties enjoined upon them as citizens of the United States by that oath and by that Constitution.*[236]

Mr. Berger's omissions produce a decidedly misleading effect. They leave out Bingham's qualification, which was, essentially, that the care of the property, life, and liberty of the citizen, *subject to constitutional limitations*, is in the states.[237]

The dangers of selective quotation (which haunt us all) are clear in Mr. Berger's quotations of Bingham's views. He quoted Bingham as saying, for example, that "'the bill of rights, as has been solemnly ruled by the Supreme Court of the United States, does not limit the power of the States.'"[238] The quotation is telling because it appears to be an endorsement of the Court's views by the man Berger considered to be a "rudderless ship." Actually, Bingham was complaining about the failure to include aliens in the Civil Rights bill. Here is what Bingham actually said: "*If* the Bill of Rights, as has been solemnly ruled by the Supreme Court of the United States, does not limit the powers of the States and prohibit such gross injustice by States, it does limit the powers of the Congress and prohibit any such legislation by Congress."[239] In the accurate quotation, Bingham's skepticism about the correctness of *Barron v. Baltimore* is clear. In the edited version that skepticism is eliminated.

Mr. Berger's analysis itself contains contradictions. First, he said that Bingham's references to the Bill of Rights meant and were understood to mean only the due process clause of the Fifth Amendment and article IV, section 2.[240] Later, Berger claimed, on the issue of incorporation of the Bill of Rights as a limitation on the states, "the fact that Bingham's amendment was shelved argues against the adoption of his view."[241] Finally, Berger said that Bingham's views were so confused and muddled that his colleagues could not understand what he meant.[242]

Berger vacillated among three very different views: that Bingham's remarks about the Bill of Rights were clearly understood but limited so as not to include the Bill of Rights; that his remarks were understood to include the Bill of Rights but were rejected; and that Bingham's ideas were so muddled no one could understand them. At times, Berger viewed the first version of Bingham's amendment, the one postponed by the House, as a prototype of the amendment finally adopted.[243] Where the Bill of Rights is concerned, however, the prototype becomes simply a rejected proposal.[244]

The truth, of course, is that the language of the "second" proposal was more effectively designed to make the Bill of Rights limit the states than was the prototype. The second version was an explicit limitation on the states and specifically secured all privileges and immunities of citizens of the United States against abridgment by a state. As the debates show, leading Republicans believed that the Bill of Rights were already binding on the states and enforceable.[245] The revised language of section 1 is clearly aimed to write such an understanding into law.

One might also argue that Bingham did not refer explicitly to the Bill of Rights in the final debate on the revised section 1,[246] presumably showing that Bingham's intent to enforce the Bill of Rights against the states was abandoned. But Congress had heard Bingham at length on the subject of the amendment and the Bill of Rights. His first proposal to arm Congress with power to enforce the Bill of Rights had been changed by explicitly protecting privileges and immunities of citizens of the United States and by providing that no state could abridge them.

In his final remarks Bingham pointed out that Congress had lacked power to protect privileges and immunities of citizens and basic rights of persons when they were abridged by the unconstitutional acts of states.[247] There had been no protection against flagrant state violations of guaranteed privileges of citizens of the United States.[248] For example, "contrary to the express letter of your Constitution 'cruel and unusual punishments' have been inflicted under State laws within this Union upon citizens."[249] Cruel and unusual punishments are forbidden by the Eighth Amendment, one of the Bill of Rights.

Critics point out that Bingham did not use the words "first eight amendments" in 1866.[250] However, Bingham did refer repeatedly to "the Bill of Rights." To paraphrase Crosskey, the phrase *Bill of Rights* is good enough to let readers of law review articles know that the author is talking about the first eight amendments to the Constitution. Still, opponents of incorporation have never considered the phrase adequate when Bingham uses it.[251]

Though Bingham seems not to have used the words *amendments one through eight* in 1866, he did use other phrases that are sufficiently broad in meaning to include the Bill of Rights. Early in the session Bingham said that the major question for Congress was whether the Constitution should be amended to allow Congress to enforce "all its guarantees."[252] On another occasion he referred to opponents of his prototype as "opposed to enforcing the written guarantees of the Constitution."[253] On January 25, 1866, in the same speech in which he had said he considered enforcement of all the guaranties of the Constitution the most important issue before Congress, Bingham explained, "I believe that the free citizens of each State were guarantied, and were . . . intended to be guarantied by the Constitution, all—not some, 'all'—the privileges of citizens of the United States in every State."[254]

One could ask why "the Bill of Rights" was not explicitly written into the Fourteenth Amendment, as due process and citizenship were.[255] The reason, of course, is that the rights in the Bill of Rights make up the most important, but not all, of the rights of citizens of the United States.

Another argument relies on Congressman Wilson's statement during the debate on the Civil Rights bill that "we are not making a general criminal code for the States."[256] The inference suggested is "that what was unpalatable in the Bill would be no more acceptable in the Amendment" so that "it becomes apparent that beyond due process the framers had no intention to adopt the Bill of Rights."[257] A code specifies offenses such as larceny and fornication. Although the Bill of Rights places some limits on state and federal criminal codes, it is not the same thing. Certainly the Bill of Rights was not viewed as a full criminal code in 1866, nor was the idea that states should obey its commands "unacceptable."

Like a number of his colleagues, Congressman Wilson thought the states were already required to obey the Bill of Rights.[258] All the evidence suggests that he considered this state of affairs desirable, not unacceptable. Although Wilson and the men who shared his views may have considered the amendment unnecessary, they would not have considered it undesirable. As Representative Farnsworth noted in the debate on the Fourteenth Amendment, "So far as this section [section 1] is concerned, there is but one clause in it which is not already in the constitution. . . . But a reaffirmation of a good principle will do no harm."[259] Apparently, for Farnsworth, in spite of *Barron v. Baltimore*,[260] states could not deprive any person of due process even before the passage of the Fourteenth Amendment.[261] Farnsworth, of course, was a radical abolitionist Republican. By 1864 he seems to have believed that the Constitution, properly construed, prohibited slavery in the states.[262]

Wilson believed that the Fifth Amendment provided all the legislative power necessary to pass the Civil Rights bill.[263] From that, one might conclude that "implicit in Wilson's formulation is the assumption that no more is needed."[264] Wilson's remarks, however, merely show that he thought Congress already had the power under article IV, section 2 and the Bill of Rights to pass the Civil Rights bill.[265] Bingham disagreed. To remove such doubt was one of the reasons the Fourteenth Amendment was passed.

The comments by senators and representatives suggesting that the provisions and powers of the amendment were already in the original Constitution[266] show that these men adhered to a radically unorthodox reading of the original Constitution.[267] These comments do not, however, prove that they thought the amendment did not make the Bill of Rights effective against the states.

Criticism of Senator Howard

After dismissing Congressman Bingham, Mr. Berger moved on to Senator Howard. Howard was a member of the Joint Committee and managed the amendment in the Senate. Because his views are also entitled to great weight, Howard, too, had to be attacked. We are told that Howard was a "reckless . . . radical," a "Negrophile" who held out for "black suffrage" to the end.[268] Because there was a considerable difference of opinion on the Joint Committee and because "non-radicals" outnumbered "radicals," Mr. Berger insisted that Howard's opinion must be taken "with 'a bushel of salts.'"[269] As the violence of the attack suggests, Howard's remarks are very damaging to the anti-incorporation thesis.

The argument is a non sequitur. The fact that Radicals and moderate Republicans were divided over black suffrage does not prove any similar division existed over the Bill of Rights. No such division surfaced in the debates. Speaker after speaker lamented that blacks had not been given the vote.[270] No one complained that the states would be permitted to continue to violate the guaranties of the Bill of Rights.

Mr. Berger took other steps to minimize Howard's speech. He said that the sum and substance of Howard's contribution to the incorporation debate was simply noting, after the privileges and immunities listed in *Corfield v. Coryell*,[271] that "to these privileges and immunities . . . should be added the personal rights guarantied and secured by the first eight amendments."[272] According to Berger, this "remark" by Howard was "casually tucked away in a long speech."[273]

The characterization is grossly inaccurate. In his speech Howard listed rights included in the Bill of Rights, pointed out that the courts had held that they did not operate as a restraint or prohibition on state legislation, summarized the holding in *Barron v. Baltimore*, and said that "the great object of the first section of this amendment is, therefore, to restrain the power of the States and to compel them at all times to respect these great fundamental guaranties."[274] Howard's statement on the Bill of Rights comprises about one-half of his entire discussion of the privileges or immunities clause of the Fourteenth Amendment and about one-ninth of his "long" speech. In short, treatment of it as a "remark casually tucked away in a long speech" is a serious misstatement.

To further denigrate Howard's speech, critics have cited Senator Poland as saying that the privileges or immunities provision of the Fourteenth Amendment secured nothing beyond what was intended by article IV.[275] Poland also said that article IV had become a dead letter because of the doctrine of states' rights, "induced mainly, as I believe, for the protection of the peculiar system of the South."[276] Even Berger believed that the privileges or immunities clause of the Fourteenth Amendment went beyond the conventional judicial interpretation of article IV. Either Poland gave the clause an unorthodox reading or, if Berger's book is correct in asserting that Republicans went beyond the conventional reading of article IV, section 2, then Poland's remarks did not reflect the intent of the framers. Once it is conceded that an unorthodox interpretation of article IV was held by Republicans, the question that remains is what exactly Poland thought the clause meant. On this subject, the critics provide us no guidance.

To discredit Howard's speech, Berger also cited Senator James R. Doolittle:

> Senator Doolittle stated that the Civil Rights Bill "was the forerunner of this constitutional amendment, and to give vitality to which this constitutional amendment is brought forward." Such reminders of known and limited objectives [excluding application of the Bill of Rights to the states] were designed to reassure those whose consent had thus far been won; and they rob Howard's remark of uncontroverted standing.[277]

Senator Doolittle, however, was an *opponent* of the measure.[278] His remarks obviously were not designed to "reassure" supporters.[279]

Furthermore, the claim that the Fourteenth Amendment was passed to give vitality to the Civil Rights bill is hardly inconsistent with the application of the Bill of Rights to the states. The amendment was passed in part to make clear the power of Congress to pass the Civil Rights bill, a power several leading Republicans had found under the power of Congress to enforce rights in the Bill of Rights.

One argument says that "no newspaper reported Howard's remarkable expansion of the privileges and immunities clause, notwithstanding that application of the Bill of Rights would cut a wide swath through State self rule."[280] In fact, Howard's speech was reported in detail on the front page of the *New York Times* of May 24, 1866, and elsewhere.[281] The *Times* report quoted verbatim the portion of the speech that stated that the privileges and immunities secured by the Fourteenth Amendment included the first eight amendments, Howard's listing of them, and his statement that the amendment would correct court rulings that the amendments did not bind the states.[282] Before that, the *Times* had reported Bingham's speech in which he said that the object of the "prototype" of section 1 was to enforce the Bill of Rights within the states.[283]

Mr. Berger argued that if the framers of the amendment intended to require the states to obey the Bill of Rights, "honesty required disclosure."[284] Why disclosure in the *Congressional Globe* and on page one of the *New York Times* was not adequate he did not explain.

The Power of the Courts

In a suggestion that would emasculate the Fourteenth Amendment, Mr. Berger argued that the amendment was to be enforced by Congress only, not the courts.[285] "Why," Berger asked, "did Hotchkiss protest that section five 'proposes to leave it to the caprice of Congress' whether or not to enforce antidiscrimination, if it was assumed that the courts could act in the face of congressional inaction?"[286]

There is a straightforward answer to Berger's rhetorical question. Hotchkiss did not make his protest about section 5 of the Fourteenth Amendment, as Berger believed when he wrote *Government by Judiciary*. He spoke on February 28, 1866. At that time, no section 5 was before the House or even existed. Instead, the remark quoted occurred in the debate on Bingham's prototype of the Fourteenth Amendment —the one that gave Congress the power to secure privileges and immunities and equal protection, which did not by its terms limit the states.[287]

When Hotchkiss spoke on February 28, 1866, he objected that Bingham's prototype was not self-executing and would depend on a majority of Congress.

Suppose that we should have an influx of rebels . . . ? What would become of this legislation? And what benefit would the black man or the white man derive from it? Place these guarantees in the Constitution in such a way that they cannot be stripped from us by any accident and I will go with the gentleman.

Why not provide by an amendment to the Constitution that no State shall discriminate against any class of its citizens; and let that amendment stand as part of the organic law of the land, subject only to be defeated by another congressional amendment. We may pass laws here today and the next Congress may wipe them out. Where is your guarantee then? . . .

I desire that the very privileges for which the gentleman is contending be secured to the citizens; but I want them secured by a constitutional amendment that legislation cannot override.[288]

Just as Hotchkiss suggested, the Fourteenth Amendment was recast in the form of a limitation on the states so that it could be enforced regardless of congressional action.[289] The final version of the Fourteenth Amendment broke the subject into two parts, with explicit restrictions on the states in section 1 and with congressional power to enforce in section 5. The amendment in this form was not approved by the Joint Committee until April 28, 1866.[290] It was not reported to the House until April 30, 1866.[291] Hotchkiss's speech, together with a change in the form of the amendment to meet his objection, proves that the amendment was to be enforced by courts as well as Congress.

Conclusion

The weight of the evidence from the Thirty-ninth Congress supports the conclusion that the Fourteenth Amendment was designed to require the states to respect all the guaranties of the Bill of Rights. The language of the amendment, which provides that no state could abridge the privileges or immunities of citizens of the United States, says as much. One natural place to look for the privileges and immunities of citizens of the United States is in the enumeration of rights in the Constitution. These certainly include the rights in the Bill of Rights, together with other rights secured to the citizen, such as the right to the writ of habeas corpus.

One of the most common contemporary descriptions of section 1 was that it protected the rights of citizens of the United States or all the rights the Constitution secured. Both Bingham and Howard described section 1 or its prototype as securing the rights in the Bill of Rights from state interference. Both said that a constitutional amend-

ment was needed to correct the doctrine set out in *Barron v. Baltimore*
that the Bill of Rights did not limit the states.[292] In addition, several
other congressmen who spoke in the Thirty-ninth Congress said that
they wanted a constitutional amendment to secure and enforce "all
the guaranties" of the Constitution,[293] a phrase that embraces the
rights in the Bill of Rights.

Most Republicans believed that the states were already required to
obey the Bill of Rights. They did not accept the "positivist" notion that
the Constitution was merely what the Supreme Court of the moment
said it was. For many Republicans, the amendment merely declared
constitutional law properly understood. Not a single Republican in the
Thirty-ninth Congress said in debate that states were not and should
not be required to obey the Bill of Rights. *Barron v. Baltimore* was
mentioned only when Republicans urged its repudiation.[294]

The privileges or immunities clause was the primary vehicle through
which Bingham, Howard, and their colleagues intended to force the
states to obey the commands of the Bill of Rights. The rights in the
Bill of Rights and all other privileges and immunities of citizens of the
United States were to be respected by the states. Read simply and
literally, the clause commands such a result.

Power to compel obedience was given to both Congress and the
courts. Republicans repeatedly said that the passage of the amendment put enforcement of its principles beyond the power of congressional majorities. These statements clearly presuppose judicial
enforcement.[295]

Some Republicans also read the due process clause to apply the Bill
of Rights to the states. The process required was the traditional one of
trial in the courts. So a number of Republicans read the clause to
mean that a person could be deprived of rights, including those guarantied by the Bill of Rights, only after conviction of a crime with all
the procedural protections inherent in such a trial, or after a trial with
all the safeguards that would protect a party in an action involving
property.[296] As Senator Sumner saw it, the due process clause "brief as
it is, it is in itself alone a whole Bill of Rights."[297] Finally, as Crosskey
noted, many of the guaranties in the Bill of Rights are "process"
guaranties. Prior to the framing of the Fourteenth Amendment,
the Court had suggested that procedural guaranties set out in the
Constitution were part of the process required by the due process
clause.[298]

In the years that followed congressional passage of the Fourteenth
Amendment, it would be debated in the election campaign of 1866,
ratified by the states, and would be tested first in Congress and finally
in the Courts.

Chapter 5

The Amendment Before the States

The Campaign of 1866

The election campaign that began in the summer of 1866, when Congress adjourned, was a referendum on the issue between President Johnson, who insisted that the rebellious states should be admitted at once with no further conditions, and Congress, which insisted on the conditions set out in the Fourteenth Amendment. Politically, the issue was whether the southern states, which had lost the war, would win the peace. Would the southern states be allowed to continue to deny blacks the right to vote but benefit from the substantial increase in representation in the House produced by the Thirteenth Amendment's repeal of the three-fifths clause? Most of the discussion of the Fourteenth Amendment centered on the political consequences of its rejection and on the merits of the contest between President Johnson and Congress. Still, there was much, albeit often cursory, discussion of section 1.

Many who advocated section 1 believed that it would protect the rights of American citizens from state interference. As the Republican National Committee observed in supporting the proposed amendment, "All persons born or naturalized in this country are henceforth citizens of the United States, and shall enjoy all the rights of citizens ever more; and no State shall have power to contravene this most righteous and necessary provision."[1]

A convention of pro-Republican soldiers and sailors chaired by Governor Jacob D. Cox of Ohio "resolved" that the constitutional amendment "clearly defines American citizenship, and guarantees all his rights to every citizen."[2] General John Alexander Logan, Republican candidate for congressman-at-large from Illinois, analyzed section 1 in a similar way. "The first article," he said, "is that all men born here, or who, being foreign born, take the oath of allegiance, shall have the rights of citizens, and be entitled to the protection of the Government."[3] He suggested that the rights of citizens include the right to own property, to sue, and to the protection of life, liberty, and property.[4]

An editorial in the *Dubuque Daily Times*, prompted by Alabama's rejection of the Fourteenth Amendment, also discussed the meaning of section 1. The paper noted that its definition of citizenship simply made clear who was entitled to the rights of citizenship:

> [A citizen has] a right to claim the privileges and protection of law. The right to "life, liberty, and the pursuit of happiness" is surely his; and the principle of a republican form of government cannot do less than secure to him those inherent rights which nature gives. This is the intent of the second clause of the condemned section above quoted. It prohibits any state from making laws to abridge the privileges rightly conferred on every citizen by the federal constitution, which instrument, before, only neglected to define who were entitled to the benefits it conferred.[5]

Many Republicans saw section 1 as a declaration of what the law was in any case.[6] A letter from a southern unionist published in the *New York Tribune* and reprinted in other northern papers typifies this view.

> For years before the war, almost everywhere in the South, northern born men were mobbed; some even put to death for uttering abolition sentiments. . . . The rights of American citizens, not only to enjoy their rights, but to protection in the full enjoyment of them, is now the dogma of the hour. At last it is to be asserted that it is the paramount duty of the government to protect its citizens in the full enjoyment of all constitutional rights, among which are the right to free speech, and to be secure in their personal property, as well as in redress of their grievances.
>
> This is what the Flag means. . . . [B]e assured that this great mass of free people, whose rights, whose hopes and destinies, are all wrapped up in and secured by this great chart of liberty, have studied it well, and most especially those clauses which relate to their right to migrate from one state to another, and to be secure in every place in all the high behests of an American citizen.[7]

"The right of the citizen to protection, by law, in and to all his Constitutional rights," the writer concluded, "is one which cannot be left out as a sequence to this war." The right was not a new one acquired by war, but one over which "the slave power had scattered so much dust that it took a war to upheave the incrustation."[8]

The idea that First Amendment rights, protected against state as well as federal invasion, are among the rights of all American citizens in every state was a recurring theme in the campaign. Although the idea was expressed by a number of the Republican speakers,[9] none emphasized it more than the southern unionists, who undertook it as a major campaign role. Their statements received wide attention from the Republican press.

The unionists convened in Philadelphia in September 1866. Their proceedings repeatedly emphasized the need to protect rights in the Bill of Rights. The call for the convention, issued in July and read again when the convention assembled in September, put the question squarely:

> *To the loyal unionists of the South*: The great issue is upon us. The majority in Congress, and its supporters, firmly declare that "the rights of the citizen enumerated in the Constitution, and established by the supreme law, must be maintained inviolate."
>
> Rebels and Rebel sympathizers assert that "the rights of the citizens must be left to the States alone, and under such regulations as the respective States choose voluntarily to prescribe."[10]

A letter accompanying the call asked for the appointment of delegates from southern states. "We had all hoped," the letter noted, "that when treason was beaten in the field . . . we of the South, who through four long years of untold suffering and horrors adhered to [the nation's] banners . . . would at least receive protection to all Constitutional rights of American citizens." The people of the country had resolved that "this shall be a government of freedom and equal rights for all." The signers recognized that attendance at the convention might be dangerous. Still, they urged, "let us do our duty and trust to God and our loyal countrymen for protection."[11] The southern loyalists had invited delegates from northern states to attend, and the convention was attended by a number of influential Republicans from the North, senators (including Senator Howard), governors, editors, and others. Former Attorney General James Speed of Kentucky was elected permanent president.[12]

At the convention, Governor Andrew Jackson Hamilton of Texas responded on behalf of the southern loyalists to the welcome to Philadelphia. Hamilton was a Texas unionist who had studied law and been admitted to the bar in 1841. He was an excellent stump speaker. By 1849 he was attorney general of Texas, and he later served in the state legislature. In 1859 he was elected to Congress. His election was part of the unionist victory that made Sam Houston governor.

Even as a freshman member in Congress, Hamilton received a

substantial vote as Speaker of the House. When other congressmen from Texas withdrew from Congress after secession, Hamilton remained. He returned to Texas in 1861, where he was elected to the state legislature as a unionist. With the outbreak of the Civil War, Hamilton was considered a traitor to his state. By 1862 he had fled the state, going to Washington by way of Mexico. Lincoln appointed him a brigadier general and provisional governor of Texas.

In 1865 President Johnson confirmed his appointment and Hamilton arrived in Galveston to begin his duties. By August 1866 he handed the government of Texas over to elected officials, most of whom turned out to be former Confederates. He was appointed to the Texas Supreme Court in 1866 by military authority. According to the *Dictionary of American Biography*, "his appointments were wise, his relations to the military officers were tactful . . . his courage, efficiency, and lack of rancor were generally recognized."[13]

Hamilton was a leader of the southern loyalists and one of three signers of a letter calling for the loyalist convention in Philadelphia in 1866. In 1866 he campaigned for Republican candidates throughout the North.[14] The administration, Hamilton insisted at the convention, refused to recognize that anything had been settled by the war. The government should be placed on the foundation of liberty and actual protection of the citizen. But Andrew Johnson, he said, was refusing to accept these principles. "The result was not to be the condition on which the Government was to be administered, but that we were left in the old condition to be remitted back to the tender mercy of the States which at their will and tender discretion might strike down the principles of human rights, and no protecting power to be found in them." The convention had been convened "to bring back the people of the Government to the primitive ideas of the Republic" and to bring the Republican party "back upon the old platform of the Constitutional rights of every citizen."[15]

While the southern loyalists were in Philadelphia, a Mr. Thomas Durant of Louisiana spoke at a reception for the loyalists at the Union League. Durant insisted that loyalists who were able to do so were fleeing the South to seek "freedom of voting and discussion here in the North." How long, Durant asked, would it be before the "Union will give the loyal people of the South a Government where opinion is free . . . ? Do you not know that the liberty of speech and the liberty of the press is dead in New Orleans?" American citizens were slaughtered there without provocation.[16]

The convention of southern loyalists produced "The Appeal of the Loyal Men of the South to their Fellow Citizens,"[17] which was reprinted in most of the Republican press. The "Appeal" assumed that universally applicable First Amendment rights were among the rights of citizens of the United States. "Seeds of oligarchy," the "Appeal" insisted, had been "planted in the constitution by its slavery feature" and had grown to be a monstrous power. The recognition of slavery

> wrung from the reluctant framers of that great instrument enabled these [slave] States to entrench themselves behind the perverted doctrine of State Rights. . . . The hand of the government was stayed for eighty years. The principles of constitutional liberty languished for want of government support. Oligarchy matured its power with subtle design. Its history for eighty years is replete with unparalleled injuries and usurpations. . . . It held four millions of human beings as chattels, yet made them the basis of unjust power for themselves in Federal and State Governments. . . . Statute books groaned under despotic laws against unlawful and insurrectionary assemblies aimed at the constitutional guarantees of the right to peaceably assemble and petition for redress of grievances; it proscribed democratic literature as incendiary; it nullified constitutional guarantees of freedom and free speech and a free press; it deprived citizens of other States of their privileges and immunities in the States—an injury and usurpation, alike unjust to Northern citizens, and destructive of the best interests of the States themselves.[18]

Judge Lorenzo Sherwood proposed an alternate address to the convention, differing from the one adopted in that Sherwood called for Negro suffrage. His proposal was rejected.[19] On the question of the Bill of Rights, however, Sherwood's address differed little from the call for the convention. It emphasized protection of "the Constitutional rights of the citizens . . . specified and enumerated in the [Constitution]," including "Security to Life, Person, and Property," free speech, press, exercise of religion, trial by jury, and the right to travel. "These rights being established by the supreme law of the land, there is no power, legislative, executive, or judicial, state or national, that has authority to transgress or invade them; and protection of these rights must be made coextensive with American Citizenship."[20]

The report to the convention of the Committee on Non-Reconstructed States[21] also concluded that black suffrage was necessary to protect the rights of unionists in the South.[22] In its recital of the sufferings of loyal men in the South the report cited violations of the Bill of Rights, violations that still occurred in the South after its defeat.

> The laws passed in the days of slavery for its protection are enforced with the same exactness today as ten years ago. Citizens have been arrested on the charge of having told negroes that they were right-

fully entitled to vote, thrown into prison, retained for months, tried by a judge without a jury, refused time to send for witnesses or counsel, convicted and sentenced to punishment in the penitentiary.[23]

The report also emphasized the denial of First Amendment rights in New Orleans. New Orleans had been occupied by federal troops during the war. With the evacuation of the troops, a reaction set in. Teachers accused of Union sympathies were fired; Union men on the police force were replaced with ex-Confederates; and the Southern Cross Association was formed to keep blacks in line. Meanwhile, at the state level resurgent Confederates were taking power from loyalists.[24]

The loyalists, with the cooperation of the Reconstruction governor, decided to try to salvage power for the Republicans by giving blacks the vote. Black suffrage would require constitutional sanction, so a group of white and black Republicans, with the support of the governor and a state supreme court justice, issued a call for a constitutional convention. About half the delegates to the previous constitutional convention agreed to attend. Elections were to be held to fill the vacancies. The convention was to frame a constitution enfranchising blacks, submit it to the people (white and black), and then to Congress.

Leading Democrats (including the Louisiana lieutenant governor, the attorney general, and the mayor of New Orleans) called a grand jury and indicted all members of the convention. But the commanding general in New Orleans refused to permit the arrests, taking the position that the legality of the convention could be tested in the courts.[25]

On the day of the convention, delegates and supporters gathered in Mechanics Institute. Meanwhile, state officials who wanted to suppress the meeting received a telegram from Andrew Johnson saying that he would expect the military to support arrests of members of the convention. The arrests were ordered. What happened next has been described by historian Michael Benedict.

> The police and white Louisianans, in a paroxysm of hatred and fear, mobbed the delegates. Ignoring white handkerchiefs that [delegates] ran up the flagpole and waved from the windows of the Institute, the mob fired into the building, shot loyalists as they emerged, and pursued them through the streets, clubbing, beating, and shooting all they caught. Forty of the delegates and their supporters were killed, another one hundred and thirty-six wounded.

When the military imposed martial law, President Johnson ordered the officers to support the civil authorities. General Sheridan wrote to General Grant, "It was not a riot. It was an absolute massacre by the police. . . . It was a MURDER which the Mayor and Police of the city perpetrated without the shadow of necessity. [I] believe it was premeditated."[26]

The New Orleans massacre had received detailed attention in the Republican press. As the report of the Committee on Non-Reconstructed States explained it, a loyal convention had been summoned to assemble in New Orleans in July.

> The Mayor of the city, by means of his police, put in circulation the report of his determination to suppress that body if it should attempt to meet in the city of New Orleans. The judge of the criminal court made a charge to the grand jury, in which he discussed and endorsed the policy of Andrew Johnson, and instructed them to find bills of indictment against those gentlemen who should respond to the call of the president of the convention and the Governor of the State.[27]

In a letter to the mayor, according to the report, the Union general informed the mayor that the meeting had not sought and did not need permission to meet: "If these persons assemble, as you say is intended, it will be, I presume, in virtue of the universally-conceded right of all loyal citizens of the United States to meet peaceably, and discuss freely questions concerning their civil governments."[28] According to the report, when the convention met, its members were massacred with the knowledge and connivance of local authorities.[29]

After their convention, southern unionists campaigned for Republicans throughout the North. In Trenton, New Jersey, Governor Hamilton of Texas spoke on what he saw as the central issue of the campaign.

> The claims of Andrew Johnson to their confidence were predicated on the declaration that he wants the Union restored. They all wanted that, he said; but as for his part, althoug [sic] much was said about the Union as it was and the Constitution as it is. He wanted the Union as it wasn't and the Constitution as it isn't. He wanted a Union of loyal men in which all, even the humblest, can exercise the rights of American freemen every where—not the least of which are the rights to speak, to write and to impress their thoughts on the minds of others. . . . Any other [Union] than one which guaranteed these fundamental rights was worthless to him.[30]

Southern loyalists were not the only Republican activists to read the rights of citizens to include the rights in the Bill of Rights. A speech by Governor Joseph Roswell Hawley of Connecticut to a "Loyal Meeting" at National Hall in Philadelphia also shows a broad reading of the rights of American citizens. As reported by the *Philadelphia Inquirer*:

He claimed liberty, not only for men of Connecticut or Pennsylvania, not simply for men of the Anglo-Saxon race, but for men of every race and color. . . . It was said that the whole country was now free, and yet men now assembled in the Loyal Convention in Philadelphia were denied the right of meeting to petition for a redress of grievances.

There were men who had been honorably discharged from our armies who had been ruthlessly stripped of the very weapons given them by the Government for their fidelity to it. He claimed that the war was not over until every man should have free and uninterrupted possession of every right guaranteed him by the Constitution.[31]

Senator Yates suggested that the former rebellious states should be barred from the Union until "every American citizen can travel to every village and hamlet in these States, and speak his sentiments freely, and be protected in his property, and enjoy his Constitutional rights." "Do you suppose," Yates asked in his speech, "any of you can go down South and express your sentiments freely in safety? No; and yet the Constitution of the United States guarantees to the citizens of each State all privileges and immunities in the several States."[32]

On another occasion Yates also referred to freedom of speech. Speaking to a Republican rally in Illinois, Yates contrasted the position of Republicans to Johnson supporters who had met in a convention in Philadelphia: "We are now on the proud basis of Union, for the full freedom of speech and freedom of discussion on every foot of American soil." "We will rally around the flag," Yates concluded, "shouting the battle cry of freedom." According to the *Illinois State Journal*, Yates's brief remarks were met with "tremendous applause." After Yates spoke the Decatur Glee Club led the crowd in singing "Rally Around the Flag."[33]

Denial of First Amendment rights was a recurring theme. Congressman William D. Kelley spoke to a "grand meeting" at the Illinois statehouse. Northerners could go South, Kelley said, but once there "they could not express their thoughts as freemen and receive the protection they were entitled to as citizens of the Republic."[34]

Congressman Columbus Delano of Ohio, a centrist Republican in 1866, struck the same note in a speech at Coshocton, Ohio. The first section of the amendment was a definition of citizenship. "It provides that the privileges and immunities of these citizens shall not be destroyed or impaired by state legislation, and it provides that no man shall be deprived of life, liberty, or property without due process of law." The need for the amendment was proved by history. "I know very well that the citizens of the South and of the North going South have not hitherto been safe in the South, for want of constitutional power in Congress to protect them. I know that white men have for a series of years been driven out of the South, when their opinions did not concur with the chivalry of Southern slaveholders." Delano concluded, "We are determined that these privileges and immunities of citizenship by this amendment of the Constitution ought to be protected."[35]

In Pennsylvania one "Col. Forney" spoke to a mass meeting in Clinton County, discussing the Fourteenth Amendment at length. He read it to create a body of national rights. "The first [section of the amendment] declares that citizens of the United States shall be clothed with the same rights, and entitled to the same protection in all the States of the Republic," he asserted. "History demanded" and "experience justified" this "glorious Republican enunciation."

> For more than fifty years the Southern country was almost as hermetically sealed against Northern progressive enterprise as China. No Northern man could either travel through or reside in the South unless he consented to become the slave of slavery. Under the baneful influence of this infernal institution all intelligence was crushed or discouraged.
>
> That section is intended to secure to the colored man and the white man of the southern section the same immunities, the same privileges, the same protection as are secured to the colored man and the white man in Pennsylvania. . . . It is simply to declare the citizenship of all the people of the country, at the same time asserting that the majesty of the laws shall be exercised in the courts in their behalf. Is it not an extraordinary thing that, in a republican Government like this, we had to wait nearly a century before the rights of person and property in one of the most populous and flourishing sections of our country could be secured?[36]

The idea that the Thirteenth Amendment clothed blacks with all the rights of citizens was expressed by Republicans out of Congress, just as it had been expressed by those in Congress. Judge Noah Davis spoke to the Republican Union State Convention, held in Syracuse on September 5, 1866. A lawyer who had been appointed a trial judge by New York's governor, Preston King, Davis was elected to Congress in 1868 and later still became United States Attorney for the Southern District of New York and, once again, a trial judge.[37]

Congress, Davis noted, had been given the power to enforce the Thirteenth Amendment by appropriate legislation. That amendment, Davis insisted, was intended to do more than merely "change the name of a great evil."

By force of the amendment the former slaves were at once made
freemen, possessed of the rights that belong under the federal Constitution to persons who are free. The right freely to buy and sell; to
do lawful labor and have its fruits; peaceably to assemble and petition against grievances; to keep and bear arms; to be free from
unreasonable searches and seizures; to have liberty of conscience; to
migrate from one State to another, carrying with them these constitutional rights; to "due process of law," in the protection of life,
liberty and property; to the care and custody of their own children
and families—all these with their necessary incidents became theirs
as absolutely as they ever were the rights of the proudest of their
masters. . . . It is a badge of slavery when a freeman, without conviction of a crime, is made subject, without his consent, to laws depriving him of these rights, or unjustly restricting their exercise, and
especially to such laws as do not equally affect all other citizens of
the state.[38]

"Who will say," Davis asked, "that Congress has not power to protect all
citizens everywhere, when necessary, in the enjoyment of rights
expressly secured to them by the Constitution itself?"[39]

Judge Davis's discussion of section 1 was brief. It was, in his judgment,
"simply declaratory of existing law."[40] But, he conceded, many
disagreed. The amendment was needed to clarify the law, to secure
the rights of all inhabitants of the rebel states. "The first and most
important of these is the right of citizenship both of the United States
and of the State, and to prevent the deprivation by States of the rights
to life, liberty and property, and the denial of the equal protection of
the laws."[41]

The New York Soldiers and Sailors State Convention also supported
the proposed amendment and the Republicans who advocated it.[42]
The address adopted by the convention demonstrates, once again,
that for many the Fourteenth Amendment was declaratory of existing
rights of citizens already enforceable in the states. As read by a General Martindale, the address insisted that if freedom "has not been
secured, if it is not entrenched and fortified in the Constitution and
the laws by the most complete and undeniable guarantees, we demand
that it shall be entrenched and guaranteed beyond all doubt and
misconstruction."[43]

The address complained of denial of rights basic to freedom. As an
example, it cited a South Carolina law that restricted the rights of
blacks to sell, keep arms, travel, and work without a license as mechanics or shopkeepers. The address found "this infamous code" violative
of "freedom and of the United States Constitution," which "provided

that 'the right of the people to keep and bear arms shall not be infringed,' also that the 'citizens of each State shall be entitled to the privileges and immunities of citizens in the several States,' [and] that no person 'shall be deprived of life, liberty or property without due process of law.'"[44] If the Thirteenth Amendment was not adequate to secure freedom to blacks, the address concluded, loyalists were duty bound to support "still further amendments and appropriate legislation."[45]

Several congressmen who spoke about the amendment after Congress adjourned equated section 1 of the Fourteenth Amendment with the Civil Rights bill.[46] The equation is understandable. Both defined citizenship and, in the view of Republicans, thereby secured to all persons made citizens the rights, privileges, and immunities of American citizenship.[47] Senator Trumbull spoke in Illinois about the amendment.

> The next step taken by Congress in the work of reconstruction was the submission to the States, for their ratification, of an amendment to the Constitution. The first clause of this amendment secures civil liberty to all citizens of the United States whether native born or naturalized, and declares that no State shall deprive any person of life, liberty, or property without due process of law, nor deny to any person within its jurisdiction the equal protection of the laws. An unnecessary provision, perhaps since the abolition of slavery and the passage of the Civil Rights Bill; still the declaration of the great principles of individual freedom and civil liberty cannot be too often repeated, and may well find a place in the fundamental law of the land.[48]

It is possible, of course, that Trumbull believed that the great principles of individual freedom and civil liberty did not include the rights to free speech, freedom of religion, to be free from unreasonable searches and seizures, to bear arms, or to be free from cruel and unusual punishments. He may have believed that the great principles of civil liberty that he described were limited to the right to make and enforce contracts, to sue, to give evidence, and to inherit, lease, purchase, and sell real and personal property. But this is unlikely. From his remarks in Congress, we know that Trumbull believed the Thirteenth Amendment gave Congress power to secure practical freedom. Trumbull thought that state laws depriving blacks of the right to teach, preach, or own property violated the rights of a free person.[49] Some of Trumbull's colleagues in Congress suggested that the freedom guaranteed by the Thirteenth Amendment included liberties in the Bill of Rights.[50] By making blacks citizens, the Civil

Rights bill secured to them all rights, privileges, and immunities of citizens of the United States.[51]

Today the term *civil rights* is often used to describe the rights in the Bill of Rights. In 1866 Republican use of the term often was equally broad. Senator Waitman Willey, speaking in Congress, said that blacks must be guarantied "every civil right of man." They must "be fully protected in the enjoyment of 'life, liberty, and the pursuit of happiness.'"[52] All agreed, Willey said, to "yield to the negro equality of civil rights" that included "all that enters into the security and enjoyment of 'life, liberty and the pursuit of happiness.'"[53]

A speech by Senator Nye in Nevada after Congress adjourned shows that Republicans believed that the Civil Rights bill had a broad and libertarian effect. "The gist of the whole bill," Nye said, "was that it clothed these heretofore downtrodden slaves with the vesture of American citizenship. . . . If the cry 'I am a Roman citizen' protected the Roman in his mongrel republic, with what redoubled forces does the cry that I am an American citizen protect me."[54] From Nye's remarks in Congress, we know that he believed the guaranties of the Bill of Rights were rights of citizens that limited the state as well as the federal government.[55] Nye concluded his speech by hailing the spirit of determination "that the fruits of this great victory shall not be lost; that it shall result in securing in its perfection and fullness the sweets of political and personal freedom to every citizen on this continent."[56]

On October 4 the *Philadelphia Inquirer* reported a speech by Hannibal Hamlin, Lincoln's first vice-president. Hamlin, the paper reported, went into "a long and able discussion of the principles involved in the constitutional amendment." The paper's brief account included the following discussion of section 1. "The first section embodies the civil rights bill, which says that every child born under our flag shall be an American citizen. The President vetoed the law; unwilling to give every man in the country complete protection of his person and property."[57]

The passage gives some insight into the identity many Republicans saw between the Civil Rights bill and the amendment. The bill had made all persons born in the country and subject to its jurisdiction citizens. Citizenship, by Republican thought, protected the citizen from state violation of basic liberties, including those in the Bill of Rights. Hamlin simply assumed that citizenship provides complete protection and went into no further discussion. He did not mention the due process clause. It seems to be subsumed under the "complete protection of [the citizen's] person and property."

Judge Phillip B. Swing spoke for the Republicans in Ohio. According to the *Cincinnati Commercial*, Swing and others spoke to a huge crowd in Court Street Marketplace in a meeting marked by a "torch-light procession of the boys in blue" and by "patriotic pyrotechnics." The meeting had its share of men destined for high political success. Rutherford B. Hayes, who became president in 1876, also spoke to the crowd. Stanley Matthews, who would later become a Justice of the Supreme Court, was on the political committee.[58]

Judge Swing discussed the Fourteenth Amendment section by section. The first section, he noted, declared who should be citizens of the United States. "To Congress the right of citizenship is a national right, character, or condition, and does not pertain to the individual states separately considered."[59] Negro citizenship had not been seriously questioned until the *Dred Scott* decision, which made it necessary that a definition of citizenship become part of the Constitution.

The privileges or immunities clause followed from the national character of citizenship. "For if the General Government alone can declare who shall be citizens, no state, as a matter of course, can pass any law abridging or enlarging their rights as citizens of the United States." The third clause of the amendment provided "that no State shall deprive a person of property, life or liberty, without due process of law, nor deny equal protection of its laws. This is rather more than the Bill of Rights; and it is the boast of our country that in this free land of ours every man, woman, and child is entitled to equal and exact justice."[60]

Congressman Woodbridge spoke to the Vermont legislature about the amendment. He "read the proposed Constitutional amendment, and dwelt at length upon each section."[61] Unfortunately, the newspaper account of his speech did not, giving only the following "synopsis":

> The question to be considered by the people was, are these amendments republican in form? Are they general in their application? Are they just to the whole country? And will they answer the desired ends? They wish to cement the Union, that any of us can go into any State in the Union with the declaration "I am an American citizen" with the same consciousness of protection as of old it was sufficient for any citizen of the Roman empire to say "I am a Roman citizen."[62]

Representative Lawrence spoke about the Fourteenth Amendment in August. Lawrence asked, "but what are the 'privileges and immunities' which no state shall abridge?" Lawrence answered by harking back to the language used by Justice Washington.

> This is confined to those privileges and immunities which are in their nature fundamental, which belong of right to citizens of all free Governments. . . . They may be comprehended under the fol-

lowing general heads: protection by the Government, the enjoyment of life and liberty, with the right to acquire and possess property of every kind, and to pursue and obtain happiness and safety.

Lawrence mentioned the right to pass through and reside in a state, to claim the benefit of the writ of habeas corpus, to maintain court actions, and to be exempt from higher taxes than other citizens of the state as a few of the privileges or immunities of citizens.[63]

When Lawrence spoke later in Congress about the amendment, he gave more specific content to "liberty." He insisted that the amendment secured the right to civil jury trial against state abridgment.[64] In another speech Lawrence cited Bingham's statement that the amendment was designed to require the states to respect the Bill of Rights.[65]

One Republican paper discussed the privileges or immunities clause at some length. As the writer noted,

> The privileges and immunities, respecting which the hireling writer makes inquiry, are those of not having your private letters opened and read by emissaries of the oligarchy to ascertain your sentiments and correspondents; of not having your political sentiments regulated by the same absolute authority; of not being beaten, maimed, murdered or driven away for exercising the freedom of speech or of the press; of holding meetings or conventions for lawful purposes; the privilege of looking after your own property in your own way; of collecting your debts by lawful means, without being bound as an incendiary; of organizing your political party and voting your own ticket without intimidation or molestation.[66]

Congressman James Wilson of Iowa defended the amendment as necessary to secure First Amendment rights:

> We must still guarantee to those boys the liberty of going into any part of the United States and causing their type to speak as freely as when our army was there to back them. They must have the same liberty of speech in any part of the South as they always have had in the North. He would have no more cross road committees to wait upon liberty loving men. . . . The validity of the national debt shall never be questioned. The rebels never should be remunerated for the loss of their slaves.[67]

Congressman William Boyd Allison of Iowa explained why a change in the Constitution was needed: "If any man asks me if I want the Constitution as it was and the Union as it was, I tell him, No. I want a Constitution and Union where free speech is possible, and where a man is a man and not three fifths of a man."[68]

Congressman Bingham also discussed the amendment during the campaign. The proposal, he said, imposed a limitation on the states to correct their abuses of power. It secured equal protection of the laws. It was essential to the peace and safety of the Republic. "Hereafter the American people cannot have peace, if, as in the past, States are permitted to take away freedom of speech, and to condemn men, as felons, to the penitentiary for teaching their fellow men that there is a hereafter, and a reward for those who learn to do well."[69]

Their discussions of section 1 show that Republicans read it to cover a broad range of fundamental rights, including liberties set out in the Bill of Rights. A reading of Republican speeches during the campaign reveals that discussion of section 1 was often cursory. Some speakers did not mention particular rights in the Bill of Rights.[70] Many, however, insisted on the need for protection of rights in the Bill of Rights, and many demanded full protection of the constitutional rights of loyalists in the South.[71]

Debate on Ratification of the Amendment

Most of the state legislatures that considered the Fourteenth Amendment either kept no record of their debates, or their discussion was so perfunctory that it shed little light on their understanding of its meaning. Messages by governors are available, but most are quite general,[72] as the following selection suggests.

The message of the governor of Maine treated the amendment as the basis for readmission of the southern states. The terms proposed reflected "magnanimity without parallel." The "sorrows and burdens" of the rebellion were to be forgotten in return for a few simple conditions. One was that "the providential and inevitable results of the war as affecting the rights of American citizenship should be recognized in good faith, and practically embodied in enactment and institution." As a result of the war, the people had become the great expounders of the Constitution. They had shown what "they mean by the declaration that all men are created equal. They have decided that this shall be a Republic of People, not a Republic of Municipalities." The states and the rights of states would be preserved, but the people had insisted "on the duties of states as well."[73]

The governor of New Jersey summarized section 1 as a provision "defining citizenship." He did not mention the due process, privileges or immunities, or equal protection clauses.[74]

In Nebraska the governor devoted a single sentence to section 1:

In extending the right of citizenship to "all persons born or naturalized in the United States and subject to the jurisdiction thereof,"
and prohibiting the denial of equal protection of the laws to any
such person, it accepts fully and forever vindicates . . . the idea that
was the corner stone of American Independence, but has been for a
time rejected by the builders of the national superstructure.[75]

Governor Thomas C. Fletcher of Missouri also explained section 1 as
protecting the rights of citizens:

The first section of the proposed amendment secures to every
person, born or naturalized in the United States, the rights of a
citizen thereof in any of the States. It prevents a State from depriving any citizen of the United States any of the rights conferred on
him by the laws of Congress, and secures to all persons equality of
protection in life, liberty, and property, under the laws of the State.[76]

Governor Paul Dillingham of Vermont, like other Republican
governors, supported Congress against President Johnson. Political
power in the rebellious states had reverted to the hands of those who
actively supported the rebellion or who gave it aid and comfort. Without the imposition of further conditions than Johnson imposed, those
in political control of those states would "use that control to oppress
and put under ban" those who had supported the Union. Complete
evidence of the inherent error of Johnson's scheme was furnished by
the riots at New Orleans and Memphis. Congress had been willing to
go along with the presidential plan "so far as it could do so . . . with a
proper regard to the security and protection of the property, liberty
and lives of all the people of the United States."[77]

In Connecticut, Governor Hawley read the amendment as confirm-
ing the results of the war—the destruction of slavery in fact as well as
in name, security "against taxation to pay the debts contracted in aid
of treason," and "full protection, safety and honor everywhere for the
rights of all loyal citizens everywhere, without distinction of race or
color."[78]

The governor of Nevada explained section 1 of the amendment in a
few words. It extended the protection of life, liberty, and property to
the weak. The amendment would "surround liberty with new barriers
alike impregnable to anarchy and despotism."[79]

A common theme in messages by the governors was that the amendment would protect the "rights" or "liberty" of citizens of the United
States. Several governors seem to have treated the word *rights* as equivalent to the words *privileges or immunities*. "Are not all persons born or
naturalized in the United States subject to its jurisdiction rightly

citizens," asked the governor of Illinois, "and justly entitled to all the civil and political rights citizenship confers?" The governor insisted that ours is a government carefully guarding the rights of all.[80]

The messages are silent on exactly what rights the governors thought were encompassed by the phrase "rights of the citizens of the United States." Except for their insistence that the amendment would protect liberty, governors failed to discuss its legal effect. Still, the messages are fully consistent with an intent to apply the Bill of Rights to the states. To read the messages as inconsistent with that goal, one has to assume that references to "rights of citizens of the United States" or to "liberty" exclude the liberties in the Bill of Rights.

There are a few cases where Republicans during the ratification debates spelled out in more detail rights to be protected by the Fourteenth Amendment. The exceptions are significant because of the silence of most of the ratification record.

In his message Governor Cox of Ohio described the amendment as necessary to protect "immunities" such as freedom of speech.

> The [provisions] consist, first, of the grant of power to the National government to protect the citizens of the whole country in their legal privileges and immunities, should any State attempt to oppress classes or individuals, or deprive them of equal protection of the laws. . . .
>
> A simple statement of these propositions is their complete justification. The first was proven necessary long before the war, when it was notorious that any attempt to exercise freedom of discussion in regard to the system which was then hurrying on the rebellion, was not tolerated in the Southern States; and the State laws gave no real protection to immunities of their kind, which are the very essence of free government.[81]

Debates on the amendment in Pennsylvania were both lengthy and recorded. Much of the debate involved partisan wrangling between Republicans and Democrats. The dispute covered such topics as John Brown and responsibility for the Civil War. Judging by the number and frequency of their appeals to racism, Democrats considered it one of their most potent political weapons. Still, there was some, often quite general, discussion of section 1. Some speakers noted a correspondence between section 1 and the Civil Rights bill.[82]

Representative Browne of Lawrence saw the issue as a battle between Republicans on one side "engaged in defending a constitutional amendment to secure civil rights to every individual born in the land, and upon the other side a party opposed to giving this security to civil liberty and to civil right."[83] The amendment, Browne noted, defined citizenship for the first time.[84]

Without it, a man born on "the soil of Massachusetts, and a [presidential] elector might be incarcerated in South Carolina, and sold for jail fees into interminable slavery."[85] Browne wanted the government to have the power to protect its citizens. He noted that "it is for the rights of States these gentlemen are concerned. Are, then, States of more importance than men? For what are States created but to conserve the rights of men?"[86]

Representative Mann, another Republican supporter of the amendment, answered those who claimed that the amendment was useless by recounting the suppression of free speech in the South before the war. Those who ruled the South

> denounced the *Tribune* as an abolition paper, and they only had to say that any paper was an abolition paper to justify the rifling and burning of mails. And from 1838 down to the surrender of Lee, there was an entire suppression of the freedom of speech in those States. Not a syllable was uttered publicly or privately against slavery, unless surrounded by walls so thick that no one outside could hear for fear [o]f vigilance committees and star chamber courts.[87]

According to Mann, there had been rifling of the mails and "a denial of the constitutional right of free speech." Whoever "went down South was obliged to put a padlock on his mouth."[88] Mann hailed the amendment because it would secure equality before the law.[89] The provision would also

> enable the Government to accomplish the object for which its founders declared that Governments were established. . . . What is the worth of a Government that wilfully neglects to protect all its citizens in their rights of life, liberty and property? And what reasons did the signers of the Declaration of Independence give to the nations of the earth as a sufficient excuse for throwing off their allegiance to the mother government . . . ? Their reason was that the old Government had failed to maintain those rights of citizenship, of liberty and property, that it had failed to secure to the inhabitants of these territories those rights to secure which was the chief object of government.[90]

Representative M'Camant of Blair County insisted that the amendment was "necessary to secure to us the blessings of peace and the freedom of every man, woman and child in the country—that freedom of speech and action which before the war was denied and even now is denied to every man who has not been a rebel or rebel sympathizer, a secessionist, or a traitor."[91] He concluded by asking Democrats to be

> as true to the Constitution as has been the Republican organization. Stand by us in demanding from the South that our citizens and loyal men everywhere be protected by their laws in the enjoyment of all their constitutional rights. . . . We demand the freedom of speech and of the press; we demand, sir, a Union reconstructed upon the principles of universal justice to all men, whether they be white or black.[92]

Representative Allen of Warren County compared the first section of the amendment to the Pennsylvania Constitution and found no contradiction.[93] Allen equated the citizenship clause, and indeed the entire first section, with the first section of the Pennsylvania "Declaration of Rights" that provided: "All men are born equally free and independent, and have certain inherent and indefeasible rights, among which are those of enjoying and defending life and liberty, of acquiring, possessing and protecting property and reputation, and of pursuing their own happiness."[94] Section 1 would not require black suffrage, but would secure to blacks all the rights provided for in the Constitution. "I want to do to those colored men what I want to do to any honest, deserving men. I want to give them the right of the protection of the law, the right to hold property, and all the rights which the Constitution provides for men—all the rights which this amendment indicates—in full."[95] Allen apparently read the amendment's privileges or immunities clause to mean literally what it said—all rights guarantied by the Constitution would be protected.

Democrats claimed that the amendment provided for "consolidation" and revolutionized the federal system.[96] Their reading of the privileges or immunities clause was exceptionally broad. A privilege, Representative Wallace insisted, meant "everything it is desirable to have."[97] Representative Kurtz believed the privileges or immunities clause permitted Congress to confer suffrage on blacks.[98]

The report of the Committee on Federal Relations of the Massachusetts House of Representatives also provides a detailed statement of how Republicans read section 1. In Massachusetts the amendment faced strong opposition from Radical Republicans because it did not directly provide suffrage to blacks. The majority report of the Committee of the State House recommended rejection because of this shortcoming and because the amendment provided no new securities to liberty.[99] The report repeated old Republican refrains: it implicitly rejected the *Dred Scott* decision by insisting that free blacks were citizens of the United States, and it implicitly rejected *Barron v. Baltimore* by insisting that the Bill of Rights limited the states.

In response to the question whether the amendment gave any additional guaranties to human rights, the majority compared section 1 to the original Constitution, which it read much as Joel Tiffany had. Two questions emerged at the outset: "First. Does it give any additional guarantees to human rights? Second. Does the proposed amendment impair or endanger any rights now recognized by the Constitution?"[100] The committee responded:

> It is difficult to see how these provisions differ from those now existing in the Constitution. The preamble to the Constitution grandly and solemnly declares: "WE, the people of the United States, in order to form a more perfect union, establish justice, insure domestic tranquillity, provide for the common defense, promote the general welfare, and secure the blessings of liberty to ourselves and our posterity, do ordain and establish this Constitution for the United States of America."
>
> Many of our ablest jurists agree with the opinion of the late Attorney-General Bates, that all native-born inhabitants and naturalized aliens, without distinction of color or sex, are citizens of the United States. The Constitution (Article IV, section 2) declares, —"The citizens of each state shall be entitled to all privileges and immunities of citizens in the several states."
>
> "Sect. 4. The United States shall guarantee to every state in this Union a republican form of government."

The committee then cited the First, Second, Sixth, and Seventh amendments and the due process clause. It asserted:

> Nearly every one of the amendments to the Constitution grew out of a jealousy for the rights of the people, and is in the direction, more or less direct, of a guarantee of human rights.
>
> It seems difficult to conceive how the provisions above quoted, taken in connection with the whole tenor of the instrument, could have been put into clearer language; and, upon any fair rule of interpretation, these provisions cover the whole ground of section one of the proposed amendment.
>
> .   .   .   .
>
> We are brought to the conclusion, therefore, that this first section is, at best, mere surplusage; and that it is mischievous, inasmuch as it is an admission, either that the same guarantees do not exist in the present Constitution, or that if they are there, they have been disregarded, and by long usage or acquiescence, this disregard has

hardened into constitutional right; and no security can be given that similar guarantees will not be disregarded hereafter.[101]

The minority report did not dispute the merits of the amendment. Nor did it dispute the interpretation given it by the majority report. It simply found the amendment "a declaration of the true intent and meaning of American citizenship."[102]

By January and February 1867 many southern states had rejected the proposed Fourteenth Amendment. Some southerners joined with President Johnson to prepare an alternative. Section 1 of the congressional amendment was modified only with reference to the privileges or immunities clause. The congressional version had provided, "no state shall make or enforce any law which shall abridge the privileges or immunities of citizens of the United States." Johnson's substitute provided, "citizens of each state shall be entitled to all privileges and immunities of citizens in the several states."[103]

Joseph James suggests that the change proposed by President Johnson was "highly significant" and that the purpose of the change was to limit the role of the federal courts in determining the federal rights of citizens.[104] At any rate, the Johnson proposal tracked exactly the language of Article IV, section 2, a provision that could be read as merely providing temporary visitors from other states an equality of certain basic rights under state law with citizens of the state.[105] On the other hand, the Fourteenth Amendment, which protected the privileges or immunities of citizens of the United States, seems designed to protect fundamental rights of American citizens from state action. It was designed, that is, to write the way leading Republicans read article IV, section 2 explicitly into the Constitution.

Although Republicans in the state legislatures often said nothing about the meaning of the Fourteenth Amendment, Democratic opponents and southerners were more vocal.

In New Hampshire opponents of the amendment listed their reasons for opposition. These included a claim that the amendment would pave the way for the destruction of the entire constitutional system as it had been; a claim that the amendment was "a dangerous infringement upon the rights and independence of the States"; and that several different subjects should not be contained in an omnibus proposal.[106]

A similar theme was reiterated in the Texas legislature. There, a legislative committee insisted that the amendment was a virtual repeal of the Tenth Amendment.[107]

In the closing weeks of the campaign of 1866 Orville H. Browning, secretary of the interior in Johnson's cabinet, had written a long political letter in opposition to the amendment. The letter was treated as an official statement of the administration's views. According to Joseph James, "it was discussed with great animation in the Democratic press both North and South." The amendment, Browning insisted, would provide power "substantially to annihilate the state judiciary." Browning focused on the due process clause.

> It is to subordinate the State judiciaries to Federal supervision and control; to totally annihilate the independence and sovereignty of State judiciaries in the administration of State laws, and the authority and control of the States over matters of purely domestic and local concern. If the State judiciaries are subordinate, all the departments of State Governments will be equally subordinated, for all State laws, let them relate to whatever department of Government they may or to what domestic and local interests, will be equally open to criticism, interpretation and adjudication by the Federal tribunals, whose judgments and decrees will be supreme and will override the decisions of the State Courts and leave them utterly powerless.[108]

Browning's claims were reasserted by opponents in southern state legislatures. The North Carolina legislative committee objected that the amendment would "break down and bring into contempt the judicial tribunals of the States, and ultimately transfer the administration of justice, both in criminal and civil cases, to Courts of federal jurisdiction."[109] Other southern legislatures made similar objections.[110] The objection that the amendment would centralize power and allow federal courts to decide if citizens were being denied their rights were common refrains of opponents, North as well as South.[111]

By December 1866 seven southern states had rejected the proposed Fourteenth Amendment. By February 1867 the number was up to ten.[112] The effect of these rejections was to undercut the moderate Republican position on Reconstruction.

John Bingham was a leading moderate on Reconstruction. He had been determined to get a guaranty of the rights of all individuals against the power of the state government.[113] With this guaranty plus a reduction in southern representation in Congress if blacks were denied the vote, Bingham had been ready to admit the southern states. He had opposed disfranchisement of southern whites[114] and had sought cooperation with the leaders of the South on the basis of equal rights and constitutional guaranties.[115]

Faced with mounting violence and refusal to ratify by the southern states, Bingham and other moderate Republicans were eventually willing to accept military Reconstruction as a temporary device to maintain order until the southern states were readmitted.[116] For the moderates, military rule in the South, like the Civil War itself, was a distasteful constitutional anomaly. They accepted it with substantial misgiving, hoping to end it at the earliest possible date.

Chapter 6

Congressional Interpretation

After the Fourteenth Amendment was adopted, Congress tried to interpret it and to enforce it. Later statements by congressmen about the amendment should be scrutinized carefully as an indication of congressional intent in 1866. People change their minds and are apt to read the amendment to suit later and different purposes. Where remarks made later corroborate what was said during the enactment of the amendment, however, they shed further light on the purposes of its framers.

The first legislative action arguably bearing on the meaning of the amendment took place before it was ratified. Southern states were readmitted under reconstructed state constitutions, after they ratified the Fourteenth Amendment. Charles Fairman has argued that the way Congress handled the admission of the rebellious southern states shows that it did not read the amendment to apply the Bill of Rights to the states.[1]

The Reconstruction act under which the southern states were admitted required that they have a government in conformity with the Constitution of the United States. Congress did examine the constitutions of the southern states prior to their readmission. None were rejected because of conflict with the Bill of Rights. Fairman found several state constitutions which, he believed, might possibly have been inconsistent with the Fourteenth Amendment (construed to require the states to obey the Bill of Rights) and one that he thinks actually was. Since Congress admitted the states, Fairman believed, it must have believed that the amendment did not require the states to adhere to the Bill of Rights.[2] There is less to this argument than meets the eye.

By 1868 President Johnson and Republicans in Congress had reversed positions. Congressional Republicans were now pushing hard for the readmission of reconstructed southern states. Their reasons related to the Fourteenth Amendment and to the upcoming election of 1868.[3] After Democrats won control of some northern legislatures, they had passed ordinances repealing their previous ratification of the Fourteenth Amendment.

To avoid any question as to the validity of the amendment, Republicans needed additional states to ratify it. For these ratifications they looked to the reconstructed southern states. Senators Henry Wilson and Jacob Howard implored their colleagues to admit the seven states in question and, as Wilson put it, "thus secure the twenty eight States necessary to make the amendment part of the Constitution."[4] The southern states in question ratified the amendment and were admitted. As a result, the secretary of state on July 20, 1868, certified that the requisite number of states had adopted the amendment. A concurrent resolution to the same effect was passed by Congress on July 21, 1868.[5]

Several of the provisions of southern state constitutions on which Fairman relies to refute application of the Bill of Rights could possibly have allowed presentment instead of grand jury indictment in some cases where indictment would be required under the Fifth Amendment. By Fairman's own analysis, these provisions were "not necessarily inconsistent with the terms of the fifth amendment." Still, if Congress had checked further, it would have found that some of the statutes of these states violated the Fifth Amendment.[6] Fairman's complaint is that such further investigation was not made.

Second, Fairman seems to have found one state where he believes there was a clear conflict with the provisions of the Bill of Rights. Two provisions of the Georgia constitution, he believes, conflicted with the Bill of Rights. First, there was one that provided for jury trial before the district judge when demanded by the accused. But the jury would consist only of seven persons.

The district judge had jurisdiction of all cases not punishable with death or imprisonment in the penitentiary, including misdemeanors. Since the federal right to jury trial has been limited to cases where the possible imprisonment exceeds six months,[7] in cases involving less than six months' imprisonment, the Georgia provision was more liberal than the Bill of Rights, as currently interpreted. The conflict Fairman found with the federal Bill of Rights rests on the assumption that there were a class of cases in which the Sixth Amendment would require a jury of twelve while Georgia allowed one of seven. Whether the Georgia provision could meet the requirement of the Sixth Amendment was, Fairman thought, "obscure." The answer would require "minute examination," an examination Fairman does not make. His complaint is that congressional Republicans also failed to make such a minute examination to see if the Georgia constitution violated the amendment, whose ratification as part of the Constitution was then in doubt.[8]

Fairman's whole argument on this point turns on the number of jurors. The Bill of Rights does not specifically say twelve jurors are required. A majority of the modern Supreme Court has read the Fourteenth Amendment and the Seventh Amendment to allow juries of less than twelve.[9] The Court may well be wrong. But its decision helps to show that Fairman's example of possible violation of the Sixth Amendment simply could have been overlooked.

A second inconsistency was in a Georgia constitutional provision that allowed the superior court to "render judgment without the verdict of a jury in all civil cases, founded on contract, where an issuable defense is not filed on oath." Fairman thinks that this provision should have been discussed as a violation of the Seventh Amendment.[10] It is hard to see why. On its face it seems only to require an answer under oath that raises a defense to the complaint before a jury is required. A number of modern procedures allow judges to decide cases without a jury—default judgment where a party fails to answer, judgment on the pleadings where a party's pleadings fail to create an issue for trial, and so forth. Such provisions are not thought to violate the right to trial by jury. Nothing Fairman has presented suggests that the approach was different in 1866.

In dramatic contrast to Fairman's argument from silence in the debates on the readmission of the southern states is what congressmen actually said and did about the amendment in the years after 1868. Congressmen had much to say because by the 1870s the meaning of the amendment was a critical issue.

Under congressional Reconstruction acts, southern states had given blacks the vote in the South as part of Reconstruction. Then the Fifteenth Amendment prohibiting abridgment of the right to vote based on race, color, or previous condition of servitude had been adopted. Meanwhile, the Ku Klux Klan had been organized and by 1871 it was using terrorism in an attempt to drive blacks and their Republican allies from power in the South. Its tactics consisted of political murders, whippings, and other outrages.[11] For example, in 1871 in Meridian, Mississippi, blacks who had made "inflammatory speeches" were placed on trial in an atmosphere dominated by the Klan. Blacks who gathered to show support for their leaders were shot, and those accused of inflammatory speeches were taken from jail and hanged. According to Philip Paludan, the incident was typical of others throughout the South.[12]

Senator Adelbert Ames of Mississippi described conditions in his state this way:

> The condition of Republicans there previous to the campaign was much the same as was that of Republicans in other States of the South. They had been . . . subjected to every kind of outrage from murder and whippings to the meanest insults man can offer to his fellow-man . . . .
>
> In some counties it was impossible to advocate Republican principles, those attempting it being hunted like wild beasts; in others speakers had to be armed and supported by not a few friends.[13]

In March 1871 Congress considered an act to enforce the Fourteenth Amendment. In its original form the bill provided a civil action against any person who under color of law, statute, ordinance, regulation, or custom subjected or caused to be subjected any person to deprivation of any rights, privileges, or immunities under the Constitution of the United States. Another section sought to punish conspiracies to deprive persons of their rights, privileges, and immunities under the Constitution and laws of the United States.[14] Congress enacted provisions similar to these.[15] The section reaching denial of constitutional rights under color of law was enacted without substantial change. But the criminal conspiracy section was changed to outlaw conspiracies to interfere with equal constitutional rights or with state protection when the conspiracies were for the purpose of violating constitutional rights.

The attempt to reach private conduct in the proposed 1871 statute was challenged by Democrats and some Republicans as a violation of states' rights. State governments with wide powers had had great appeal for Republicans. Federalism in this sense served important functions. It reinforced democracy by leaving regulation of local problems to the people closest to the problems.[16] For the federal government to take over the vast domain of state law was unacceptable. For states to violate or leave unprotected the basic rights of citizens was equally unacceptable to Republicans. The Fourteenth Amendment had sought to reconcile these two competing interests. It provided that no state should deprive citizens of privileges or immunities, or deprive any person of due process or equal protection. The right to protection would play a key role in the 1871 debate.

The concept of equal protection was rooted in Republican ideas about natural law. Under the Declaration of Independence, a document revered by Lincoln and the rest of his party, the government existed to protect people and their rights to life, liberty, and property. Protection from violence was a central purpose of government. Republicans had had plenty of experience with state and local governments that failed to protect opponents of slavery from mob action. The Republican view of protection was summed up by Congressman Lawrence in the Thirty-ninth Congress. States could violate their duty of equal protection by affirmatively violating the citizens' rights or by failing to supply that protection without which the rights were meaningless.[17]

What was unclear in 1866 is exactly how the rights in the Fourteenth Amendment would be enforced. Action could be taken against government officials who violated constitutional rights, by their action or inaction. But could the government indict private perpetrators of mob violence, when the purpose of the mob was to deprive blacks or Republicans of constitutional rights? That issue was raised starkly in 1871. On this issue Republicans split. Still, in 1871 most Republicans thought that when states failed to provide adequate protection, Congress could supply it by laws operating directly on private individuals.

The Republican split over state action is reminiscent of the division over direct federal protection to life, liberty, and property in the debate over Bingham's prototype of the Fourteenth Amendment. Indeed, several Republicans cited rejection of the prototype to prove that Congress did not intend to allow legislation under the Fourteenth Amendment to reach purely private conduct.[18] Other Republicans insisted that if state governments would not or could not provide the necessary protection for citizens' constitutional rights, then the federal government could and should see that the citizen was protected.[19] Others insisted that private persons could be prosecuted only if they conspired to influence local officials to deny equal protection.

The denial of equal protection by local officials was a major problem that concerned the Republicans. As Representative Aaron F. Perry of Ohio noted, states "shall neither abridge or permit to be abridged these rights, deny nor fail to afford equal protection of the laws to any persons." Still, "where these gangs of [Klan] assassins show themselves the rest of the people look on, if not with sympathy, at least with forbearance. . . . sheriffs, having eyes to see, see not; judges, having ears to hear, hear not."[20] Local failures to protect individual rights influenced Congress to provide direct federal protection.

Still, for many Democrats and some Republicans in Congress the deceptively simple answer to the plight of blacks and Republicans in the South came in the form of a state action syllogism. The Fourteenth Amendment provided that no state could deprive persons of its protections. Private individuals are not the state. Therefore, they argued, the amendment did not reach private action. In spite of its surface appeal, this argument was less conclusive than it appeared. It ignored the repeated insistence, in the debates on ratification of the amendment, that the amendment would provide protection to blacks and loyalists in the South. Indeed, Republicans cited events such as the New Orleans massacre and a race riot in Memphis to show the need for the amendment.[21] Admittedly, however, the question of how the protection was to be supplied was left unclear.

To further understand the problems of the state action syllogism, one needs to look back at the fugitive slave clause of the Constitution. The history of the clause highlights the legal assumptions on which a number of Republicans operated.

The fugitive slave clause had provided that no slave escaping into another state shall "in consequence of any law or regulation therein, be discharged, but shall be delivered up." Obviously, the clause could be read to incorporate a state action syllogism. The clause protected against emancipation by state law or regulation. Private parties are not states. So, one could argue, the federal law could not reach the action of abolitionists who aided or harbored the fugitive. In fact, of course, the Congress had enforced the clause so as to secure the right of the slaveholder and to permit the prosecution of private individuals who helped the escaping slave.[22] In 1859 in sweeping dicta the Supreme Court pronounced the law constitutional in all respects.[23] This was so, even though the fugitive slave clause contained no explicit grant of legislative power to enforce it, as the Fourteenth Amendment did. Earlier, in *Prigg v. Pennsylvania*, the Supreme Court had insisted that the right to have the slave returned implied a remedy.[24] The decision in *Prigg* upholding the fugitive slave law had been relied on by Republicans in 1866 as a precedent for enforcement provisions of the Civil Rights bill, and some relied on it again to justify reaching private conduct under the Fourteenth Amendment.[25]

To support legislation reaching private conduct, some supporters of the 1871 bill pointed to the decision of the Supreme Court in *Prigg v. Pennsylvania*.[26] Just as the Court in *Prigg* had read the fugitive slave clause to allow Congress to pass laws operating directly on private individuals within the state, the Fourteenth Amendment, these congressmen insisted, should be read to reach private conduct.[27] If, as the Court thought, a federal constitutional right to get a slave back implied a remedy, the right to have the privileges secured by the Fourteenth Amendment should provide a remedy. Still, some Republicans seemed to have stopped short of providing for prosecution of private individuals for violations of constitutional rights.[28]

The state action argument could have been resolved in favor of individual liberty. The rights of the individual to free speech, to vote, and to other basic rights are rights of the individual that government is designed to secure. The rights are recognized by the Constitution and, after passage of the Fourteenth Amendment, were protected against state or federal infringement. Bill of Rights liberties could be seen not just as rights against government, but as positive preexisting rights of individuals that were recognized by the Bill of Rights and the Fourteenth Amendment. The constitutional recognition of the right to have a fugitive slave returned had been enough to allow Congress to secure the right by federal statutes reaching private conduct. So it seemed the federal government could enforce (against all who would violate them) the rights recognized by the federal Constitution.

Before he wrote the majority opinion in the *Civil Rights Cases*[29] (a decision that used the state action syllogism to hold unconstitutional the Civil Rights Act of 1875 granting equal accommodations to blacks), Justice Joseph Bradley had found that the federal government could reach the actions of private persons under the Fourteenth Amendment. Answering a question from Judge Woods about the case of *United States v. Hall*, Bradley had written a letter to Woods suggesting that the federal government could reach private conduct that violates constitutional rights. Bradley's letter was largely appropriated by Judge Woods and became his opinion in *United States v. Hall*.[30]

As finally drafted, the conspiracy section of the 1871 act provided punishment

> if two or more persons within a State or territory of the United States shall conspire together . . . or go in disguise upon the public highway or upon the premises of another for the purpose, either directly or indirectly, of depriving any person or a class of persons of the equal protection of the laws, or equal privileges or immunities under the laws, or for the purpose of preventing or hindering constituted authorities of any State from giving or securing to all persons within said State equal protection of the laws.[31]

Republicans had debated the state action question, and some had argued that the federal government could not reach purely private conduct designed to violate constitutional rights. But at least in the face of private conduct aimed at depriving political and racial groups of equal constitutional rights and equal protection of the law, Congress, as the language of the act shows, seems to have come down against the state action limitation.

Whether the 1871 decision was consistent with the purposes of the Fourteenth Amendment has been the subject of much scholarly debate. The evidence on the question is puzzling and runs in different directions. I do not seek to resolve it here. But the argument against a pure state action limitation is far stronger than it first appears.[32]

Some scholars have suggested that rigid adherence to federalism was a fatal flaw in the Fourteenth Amendment and Reconstruction generally.[33] For blacks and Republicans in the South facing political terrorism, a Constitution that denied all federal power to reach private conspiracies to deprive people of constitutional rights was flawed.[34]

In addition to arguing about state action, congressmen also described the type of rights to be protected by the Enforcement Act. One section of the 1871 act was directed against those who violated the rights, privileges, or immunities of citizens under color of law. Republicans generally agreed that Congress had constitutional power to pass that portion of the act. The rights Congress intended to secure under the Enforcement Act included those in the Bill of Rights. Congressman Horace Maynard, a lawyer and former attorney general of Tennessee, understood the reference to "rights, privileges, or immunities" in the act to include personal rights that the Constitution guaranteed to the citizen, including those in the Bill of Rights.[35]

In a speech on the Enforcement Act, Bingham discussed the meaning of the privileges or immunities clause of the Fourteenth Amendment. Now, after the 1868 case of *Paul v. Virginia*, he read the cases as limiting article IV, section 2 to protection under state law. He explained why he had changed the form of his amendment from his first version.

In reexamining that case of Barron, Mr. Speaker, after my struggle in the House in February, 1866, to which the gentleman has alluded, I noted and apprehended as I never did before, certain words in that opinion of Marshall. Referring to the first eight articles of amendments to the Constitution of the United States, the Chief Justice said: "Had the framers of these amendments intended them to be limitations on the powers of the State governments, they would have imitated the framers of the original Constitution, and have expressed that intention." *Barron v. The Mayor, &c.,* 7 Peters, 250.

Acting upon this suggestion I did imitate the framers of the original Constitution. As they had said "no State shall emit bills of credit, pass any bill of attainder, ex post facto law, or law impairing the obligations of contracts;" imitating their example and imitating it to the letter, I prepared the provision of the first section of the fourteenth amendment as it stands in the Constitution, as follows:

"No State shall make or enforce any law which shall abridge the privileges or immunities of the citizens of the United States, nor shall any State deprive any person of life, liberty, or property without due process of law, nor deny to any person within its jurisdiction the equal protection of the laws." I hope the gentleman now knows why I changed the form of the amendment of February, 1866.

Mr. Speaker, that the scope and meaning of the limitations imposed by the first section, fourteenth amendment of the Constitution may be more fully understood, permit me to say that the privileges and immunities of citizens of the United States, as contra distinguished from citizens of a State, are chiefly defined in the first eight amendments to the Constitution of the United States. Those eight amendments are as follows.[36]

Bingham then read word for word each of the first eight amendments.[37] Because Bingham's reading of the privileges or immunities clause of the Fourteenth Amendment is consistent with his prior statement of purpose to make the Bill of Rights enforceable against the states and consistent with Senator Howard's interpretation of the clause, it is entitled to weight in considering the purpose of the framers of the Fourteenth Amendment.

Some scholars have argued that Bingham's 1871 explanation of the privileges or immunities clause as including the rights in the Bill of Rights "was plainly not shared by his fellows."[38] The 1871 debate was addressed mainly to the question of state action. Controversy about the Bill of Rights was, as several congressmen pointed out, a side issue.[39] But the argument that Bingham's analysis was rejected by his colleagues in the House is not supported by the record. A number of Bingham's colleagues supported his reading of the privileges or immunities clause of the Fourteenth Amendment to include rights in the Bill of Rights.[40] A few Republicans did take positions that seem inconsistent with application of the Bill of Rights to the states.[41] Most, like Garfield, who have been read as disagreeing with Bingham, never said that they believed the amendment did not make the Bill of Rights a limitation on the states.[42] Although they did make remarks that can be read as inconsistent with Bingham's position, these remarks are, on balance, not conclusive.

Representative George F. Hoar, like Bingham speaking in 1871, believed that the "privileges and immunities"[43] in the Fourteenth Amendment referred to "all the privileges and immunities declared to belong to the citizen by the Constitution itself" together with "those privileges and immunities which all Republican writers of authority agree in declaring fundamental and essential to citizenship."[44]

Representative James Monroe, another Republican who spoke in 1871, accepted Hoar's analysis of the "meaning of the words 'privileges and immunities'" in the Fourteenth Amendment.[45] And Representative Benjamin Butler seems also to have embraced both Bingham's and Hoar's views.[46] Another Republican who seems to have read the amendment as protecting all the basic liberties of the citizen was John B. Hawley from Illinois. Hawley accepted the view that the Bill of Rights limited the states even prior to the passage of the Fourteenth Amendment and that the Fourteenth Amendment was designed to effectuate the true meaning of the Constitution.

> Sir, before the late war it is a matter well known to you and to every man born and reared in this land that throughout the southern States of the Union there was no freedom of speech, no freedom of person, no freedom to express the opinions which were entertained by freemen unless those opinions were in consonance and in conformity with the opinions of the dominant class of the southern States.
>
> Sir, we have in the Constitution of the United States and have always had, sufficient guarantees, in my judgment, to protect the citizens of the United States in all parts of the great Republic. It was not necessary that we should amend the Constitution of the United States in order to give to the citizens of the United States the right to be protected throughout the length and breadth of the land. But, sir, the Constitution of the United States was perverted, and those rights which were guarantied by it were not executed in behalf of the citizens of the United States. But if these rights inhered in the Constitution before the war and before the adoption of the constitutional amendments, how much more do they now attach to every American citizen.[47]

Several Republicans said that the rights of American citizens protected by the Fourteenth Amendment included rights to freedom of speech.[48] In addition to these men, Senator Joseph Fowler and Representative Horace Maynard, both of Tennessee, apparently adhered to Bingham's views.[49]

Representative Henry L. Dawes had been a conservative Republican member of the Thirty-ninth Congress. In 1871 he described rights in the Bill of Rights as "privileges and immunities"[50] and, in a reference to the Fourteenth Amendment, said that "every person born on the soil was made a citizen and clothed with them all."[51] Dawes spoke in support of the 1871 enforcement bill, a bill he saw as protecting all liberties set out in the Constitution.

> The rights, privileges, and immunities of the American citizen, secured to him under the Constitution of the United States, are the subject matter of this bill. They are not defined in it, and there is no attempt in it to put limitations upon any of them; but whatever they are, however broad or important, however minute or small, however

estimated by the American citizen himself, or by his Legislature, they are in this law. The purpose of this bill is, if possible, and if necessary, to render the American citizen more safe in the enjoyment of those rights, privileges, and immunities. No subject for legislation was ever brought before the American Congress so broad and comprehensive, embracing as it does all other considerations hitherto affecting the life, liberty and pursuit of happiness of every citizen of this Republic.

Dawes then characterized rights secured by the Bill of Rights —freedom of speech and religion, to bear arms, and against unreasonable search and seizures—as privileges and immunities, and he summarized parts of amendments one through four.

> Then, again, as if that were not enough, by another amendment he was secured against trial for any alleged offense except it be on the presentation of a grand jury, and he was protected against ever giving testimony against himself. Then, sir, he was guarantied a speedy trial, and the right to confront every witness against him. Then in every controversy which should arise he had the right to have it decided by a jury of his peers. Then, sir, by another amendment, he was never to be required to give excessive bail, or be punished by cruel and unusual punishment. And still later, sir, after the bloody sacrifice of our four years' war, we gave the most grand of all these rights, privileges, and immunities, by one single amendment to the Constitution, to four millions of American citizens who sprang into being, as it were, by the wave of a magic wand. *Still further, every person born on the soil was made a citizen and clothed with them all.* Lastly, sir, every one of them was given the ballot.
>
> It is all these, Mr. Speaker, which are comprehended in the words "American citizen," and it is to protect and to secure him in these rights, privileges, and immunities this bill is before the House. [Emphasis supplied.][52]

Other congressmen speaking in other contexts agreed. Senator Fredrick Frelinghuysen believed that "the right that private property shall not be taken without compensation is among those privileges" and was protected by the privileges or immunities clause of the Fourteenth Amendment.[53] And in 1872 Senator John Sherman, who had been a member of the Thirty-ninth Congress, said that the "right to be tried by an impartial jury is one of the privileges included in the fourteenth amendment; and no State can deprive any one by a State law of this impartial trial by jury."[54]

Sherman spoke in 1872, in support of a bill by Charles Sumner to guaranty blacks and other citizens equal access to public accommodations. Like a number of other Republicans, Sherman thought that the privileges or immunities clause of the Fourteenth Amendment included rights not explicitly listed in the Constitution. He noted that the antifederalists "insisted upon the old amendments to the Constitution which bristle all over with the word 'rights.'" "But," Sherman insisted, "these amendments to the Constitution do not define all of the rights of American citizens. They define some of them." He cited the Ninth Amendment to the effect that the enumeration of some rights did not deny or disparage others retained by the people.

Sherman clearly recognized that the Fourteenth Amendment included rights in the Bill of Rights. "What are those privileges and immunities?" he asked. "Are they only those defined in the Constitution, the rights secured by the amendments? Not at all."[55] To define the "privileges or immunities" secured by the Fourteenth Amendment, Senator Sherman suggested that the courts should look "first at the Constitution of the United States as the primary foundation of authority. If that does not define the right they will look for the unenumerated powers to the Declaration of American Independence, to every scrap of American history, to the history of England, to the common law of England . . . and so on back to the earliest recorded decisions of the common law."[56] Sherman said that he did not distinguish between the words *privileges, immunities,* and *rights.*

In a speech in 1871 Representative Lawrence complained about a proposed act of Congress about education that failed to provide for a jury trial in certain eminent domain proceedings. Lawrence had been a leading member of the Thirty-ninth Congress and a centrist Republican. He insisted that the Seventh Amendment guaranty to a jury trial was included within due process (as to the federal government) and was also encompassed in the due process clause of the Fourteenth Amendment as well as in the privileges or immunities clause.[57] Lawrence noted:

Now let us see what *security for property* our own great Constitution has provided. The 5th article of Amendments provides that—

"No person" . . . "shall be" . . . "deprived of life, liberty, or property without due process of law, nor shall private property be taken for public use without just compensation."

In article seven it is provided that—

"In suits of common law where the value in controversy shall exceed $20.00 the right of jury trial shall be preserved."

The fourteenth article of amendments contains a provision as follows:

"Nor shall any state deprive any person of life, liberty or property without due process of law."

> And by this same article "the privileges and immunities of citizens"
> are protected so that they cannot be abridged by State authority.
> And now what mean all these sacred guarantees?[58]

Lawrence concluded that: "Where the power of eminent domain is to
be exercised under State authority . . . a trial at law by a common law
jury is now a matter of constitutional right. I know doubts have been
entertained on this subject prior to the adoption of the fourteenth
article of amendments to the Constitution. . . . But since the adoption
of the fourteenth article it may well be maintained that a common law
jury trial is secured."[59] Lawrence seems not to have agreed with the
original interpretation that the Seventh Amendment did not limit the
states: "The true original interpretation of the Constitution ought to
have been that the right of trial by jury was preserved by it."[60]

Many of the guaranties contained in the Bill of Rights are "process"
guaranties. Prior to the framing of the Fourteenth Amendment, in *Murray's Lessee v. Hoboken Land and Improvement Co.*,[61] the Court suggested
that the procedural guaranties set out in the Constitution were part of
the process required by the due process clause. Lawrence cited the same
case as authority for the proposition that "Congress cannot arbitrarily by
law declare that to be due process of law which is not so at common law."[62]

Even a number of Democrats in the early years after the adoption of
the amendment accepted and advocated the idea that the privileges or
immunities secured by the Fourteenth Amendment included rights in
the Bill of Rights and other rights explicitly provided for by the Constitution. In 1871 several Democrats accepted the argument that the privileges or immunities clause included the privileges and immunities in
the Bill of Rights[63] or assumed, for the sake of argument, that Bingham's
position was correct.[64] All denied that the privileges or immunities
clause provided the constitutional power necessary to pass the Ku Klux
Act,[65] which was under consideration. Democrats generally accomplished this feat by insisting that the amendment reached only state
action. Although Democrats consistently rejected broad readings of the
privileges or immunities clause such as that suggested by Senator
Sherman, a number believed that the privileges or immunities referred
to in the Fourteenth Amendment included Bill of Rights liberties.

In 1874 Representative Roger Mills spoke in opposition to the Civil
Rights bill guarantying blacks equality of access to public accommodations. In opposing the idea that the Fourteenth Amendment provided
congressional power over such subjects, Mills explained what he thought
the amendment did mean. He noted that the demand for a Bill of
Rights followed the federal convention that drafted the Constitution.
And he said, "These first amendments and some provisions of the

Constitution of like import embrace the 'privileges and immunities' of citizenship as set forth in Article 4, section 2 of the Constitution and in the fourteenth amendment."[66] Mills asked what the rights, privileges, and immunities of citizens of the United States were.

> It is clear that the privileges and immunities mentioned in the fourteenth amendment are only such as are conferred by the Constitution itself as the supreme law over all; that they are fundamental, such as lie beneath the very foundation of the Government; that they are fixed and absolute. . . . These privileges are among others, the right to enjoyment of life, liberty, property, and the pursuit of happiness; the right of peaceable assemblage for all purposes not criminal, freedom of speech, of the press, and of religion; immunity of one's person, house, and papers against unlawful seizure and search; trial by jury when held to answer for crime. . . [etc.].[67]

These privileges were the same in every state, Mills noted, and states were "impotent" to abridge them.[68]

Senator Thomas Norwood, Democrat of Georgia, spoke to the same effect about the public accommodations bill. He also believed that the privileges or immunities of citizens of the United States protected by the Fourteenth Amendment included all rights in the Bill of Rights, together with other rights provided by the Constitution. These, Norwood observed, included the privilege of the writ of habeas corpus; immunity from bill of attainder, from ex post facto laws, and from slavery or involuntary servitude except for punishment of crime; and the right not to be deprived of the right to vote on account of race, color, or previous condition of servitude.[69]

Norwood said that the argument that the amendment conferred no new rights was true in one sense, but not in another. "No new rights are enumerated; the amendment simply refers to existing rights, and in this sense no new privileges were conferred."[70] But "while not technically conferring new rights," Norwood explained, the Fourteenth Amendment had "given additional protection to existing rights."[71] This was so, he said, because before the adoption of the Fourteenth Amendment a state "could have deprived its citizens of any of the privileges and immunities contained in the first eight [amendments]."[72] Before its adoption "any State might have established a particular religion, or restricted freedom of speech and of the press, or the right to bear arms . . . [or] inflicted unusual and cruel punishment, and so on."[73] But, he said, "the instant the fourteenth amendment became a part of the Constitution, every State was from that moment disabled from making or enforcing any law which would deprive any citizen of a State of the benefits enjoyed by citizens of the United States under the first eight amendments to the Federal Constitution."[74] Other Democrats also seem to have accepted the idea that the privileges or immunities secured by the Fourteenth Amendment included the rights in the Bill of Rights.[75] Mills's and Norwood's remarks show that finding the Bill of Rights and other explicit constitutional rights *and nothing else* in the Fourteenth Amendment's privileges or immunities clause was one way of limiting the reach of the amendment. Many leading Republicans, while finding the amendment applied the Bill of Rights to the states, did not believe it was limited only to Bill of Rights liberties.[76]

Victoria Woodhull submitted a memorial to Congress asking the Congress to enact womens' suffrage under the privileges or immunities clause of the Fourteenth Amendment. On January 30, 1871, Bingham presented a report from the Committee of the Judiciary of the House recommending that the relief requested be denied. The majority of the committee noted:

> The clause of the fourteenth amendment, "no state shall make or enforce any law which shall abridge the privileges or immunities of citizens of the United States," does not, in the opinion of the committee, refer to privileges and immunities of citizens of the United States other than those privileges and immunities embraced in the original text of the Constitution, article IV, section 2. The fourteenth amendment, it is believed, did not add to the privileges or immunities before mentioned, but was deemed necessary for their enforcement as an express limitation upon the powers of the States. It had been judicially determined that the first eight articles of amendment of the Constitution were not limitations on the power of the States, and it was apprehended that the same might be held of the provisions of the second section, fourth article.[77]

The majority report went on to define the privileges protected by article IV, section 2 in accordance with Judge Washington's decision in *Corfield v. Coryell*. They were those privileges and immunities that were fundamental and could be classified under general headings, including protection by the government and "enjoyment of life and liberty."[78] In addition to describing rights like those set out in *Corfield*, the committee also quoted from Justice Story to the effect that article IV conferred a general citizenship and "communicated all the privileges and immunities which a citizen of the same state would be entitled under the same circumstances."[79] In short, the committee seemed to treat article IV as protecting both fundamental rights and as protecting against discrimination in certain rights under state law.[80] If, however, the report gives article IV a reading that limited it to equality under state law, it is inconsistent with Bingham's prior and subsequent statements and with the contemporaneous view of the framers of the Fourteenth Amendment.

Some scholars treat remarks by congressmen made in 1876 on the Blaine amendment as the "clincher" in their effort to prove that the framers of the Fourteenth Amendment did not understand it to apply the Bill of Rights to the states.[81] The Blaine amendment had been proposed as a result of concern with the use of public funds for sectarian schools. Among other things, it prohibited states from establishing religion or interfering with free exercise of religion.[82] As one writer noted, "Not one of the several Representatives and Senators who spoke on the proposal even suggested that its provisions were implicit in the amendment ratified just seven years earlier. . . . Remarks of Randolph, Christiancy, Kernan, Whyte, Bogy, Eaton, and Morton give confirmation to the belief that none of the legislators in 1875 thought the Fourteenth Amendment incorporated the religious provisions of the First."[83] Theodore F. Randolph, Isaac P. Christiancy, Francis Kernan, William P. Whyte, Lewis V. Bogy, and William Eaton were Democrats who spoke ten years after the Fourteenth Amendment debates.[84] Four of the six voted against the Senate version of the Blaine amendment,[85] and several of them suggested that it would violate states' rights to require the states to obey the religious guaranties of the First Amendment.[86]

The question scholars relying on the Blaine amendment seek to answer is what senators and representatives understood the Fourteenth Amendment to mean in 1866. The claim that the Fourteenth Amendment was not intended to require the states to obey the guaranties of religious liberty contained in the First Amendment is inconsistent with the view that Congressman Bingham and Senator Howard expressed at the time the Fourteenth Amendment was presented to Congress.[87] As a means of discovering congressional purposes in 1866, remarks by senators and representatives on the Blaine amendment debates are significant only if they shed light on this subject—if they prove that Bingham's and Howard's views were not shared by their colleagues.[88] But as we have seen, the Bingham-Howard interpretation of the amendment was explicitly accepted by a number of Republicans,[89] and explicitly rejected by few, if any.

By 1876, when most of the debate on the Blaine amendment took place, the earlier broad support for the Bingham-Howard reading of the Fourteenth Amendment had evaporated. Democrats insisted that the rights in the First Amendment did not limit the states and further insisted that application of the Bill of Rights to the states would violate states' rights.[90] Some Republicans also said that the religious guaranties of the First Amendment did not limit the states.[91] At least during the Blaine amendment debates themselves, no one seems to have said that the privileges or immunities clause of the Fourteenth Amendment protected the rights set out in the Bill of Rights.

How can this remarkable transformation be explained? The answer, I believe, lies in two Supreme Court decisions handed down very shortly before most of the debate on the Blaine amendment took place. In March 1876 in *United States v. Cruikshank*[92] the Court held that the right of peaceable assembly and the right to bear arms were not privileges secured by the Fourteenth Amendment. These and other rights in the Bill of Rights were said to be merely limitations on the powers of the national government.[93] All the Justices except one concurred in the Court's opinion.[94] In April of that year in *Walker v. Sauvinet*[95] the Court held that the Seventh Amendment right to trial by jury was not a privilege or immunity of national citizenship protected by the Fourteenth Amendment and that the right was also not protected by the due process clause. Justices Nathan Clifford and Stephen J. Field dissented.[96]

Congressmen had been reluctant to accept the idea that the Fourteenth Amendment privileges or immunities clause had no significant meaning. Even after the constricted reading given to the privileges or immunities clause in the *Slaughter-House Cases*, many believed and continued to assert that the clause protected fundamental liberties of American citizens set out in the Bill of Rights.[97] But the decisions in *Cruikshank* and *Walker* were unequivocal.

On the issue of rights of American citizens, the Supreme Court was more royalist than the king, more devoted to a restricted states' rights interpretation of the Constitution than even some southern Democrats. In the context of the Court's then recent decisions in *Cruikshank* and *Walker*, it is not surprising that congressmen did not repeat the earlier broad belief that the privileges or immunities clause of the Fourteenth Amendment protected at least the Bill of Rights. Nor is it surprising that some congressmen said that the religious guaranties of the First Amendment did not limit the states. After rulings by the high Court, that was clearly the law. The true and intended meaning of the Fourteenth Amendment was, by this time, of only academic interest.

Senator Oliver Morton, speaking on the Blaine amendment, noted the sad fate that had befallen the Fourteenth Amendment at the hands of the Court.

> The fourteenth and fifteenth amendments which we supposed broad, ample, and specific, have, I fear, been very much impaired by construction, and one of them in some respects, almost destroyed by construction. Therefore I would leave as little as possible to construction. I would make [the proposed provisions of the Blaine amendment] so specific and so strong that they cannot be construed away and destroyed by the courts.[98]

Chapter 7

The Amendment Before the Courts

(Part One)

After the ratification of the Fourteenth Amendment in 1868, the battle over its meaning shifted to the courts. By 1873 the Supreme Court began dismantling the amendment. In that year it nullified the privileges or immunities clause.[1] In a companion piece to Charles Fairman's article, Stanley Morrison read the record of the Court's decisions as a further vindication for the claim that the amendment was never intended to encompass all Bill of Rights liberties.[2] However, as Leonard Levy notes, Morrison proved "that the Supreme Court had never accepted the incorporation theory . . . but he did not prove that the several rejections of that theory had a scintilla of historical support."[3] According to Levy, the record of the Court's decisions cited by Morrison is "a melancholy litany of judicial errors."[4]

It is too easy to assume that the Court followed the only available road in rejecting application of the Bill of Rights to the states. In the years between 1868 and 1873, in fact, there was significant support for a libertarian reading of the amendment. In one early case, *United States v. Hall*, decided in 1871, a lower federal court held that the Fourteenth Amendment did apply the Bill of Rights to the states.[5] In *Hall* the defendants were charged with conspiring to deny other citizens their rights of freedom of speech and assembly. The defendants claimed that even if the charge were true it did not constitute a federal crime—because rights to freedom of speech and assembly were not privileges or immunities of citizens of the United States. Judge (later Justice) William B. Woods rejected the defense. He also held that the statute under which the defendants were charged could constitutionally reach the acts of private individuals within the states intended to deprive citizens of First Amendment freedoms.

Woods had been born in Ohio. He was admitted to the bar in 1847.

In 1857, as a Democrat, he was elected speaker of the Ohio House. In the Civil War he sided with the Union, enlisted, and was a brigadier general by the end of the war. He settled in Alabama and was appointed to the Fifth Circuit by President Ulysses S. Grant in 1869. Woods would later join with Bradley on that court in holding that a New Orleans monopoly on slaughtering animals violated the Fourteenth Amendment.[6] In later years Woods would uphold the separate but equal doctrine. In 1880 he was appointed to the Supreme Court.[7]

In deciding *Hall*, Judge Woods considered the privileges or immunities clause of the Fourteenth Amendment, a clause he understood exactly as Bingham and Howard had intended.

> By the original constitution citizenship in the United States was a consequence of citizenship in a state. By this clause this order of things is reversed. Citizenship in the United States is defined; it is made independent of citizenship in a state, and citizenship in a state is a result of citizenship in the United States. So that a person born or naturalized in the United States, and subject to its jurisdiction, is, without reference to state constitutions or laws, entitled to all the privileges and immunities secured by the constitution of the United States to citizens thereof. The amendment proceeds: "No state shall make or enforce any law which shall abridge the privileges and immunities of citizens of the United States." What are the privileges and immunities of citizens of the United States here referred to? They are undoubtedly those which may be denominated fundamental; which belong of right to the citizens of all free states and which have at all times been enjoyed by citizens of the several states which compose this Union from the time of their becoming free, independent, and sovereign. Corfield v. Coryell [Case No. 3,230]. Among these we are safe in including those which in the constitution are expressly secured to the people, either as against the action of federal or state governments. Included in these are the right of freedom of speech, and the right peaceably to assemble. . . . We think, therefore, that the right of freedom of speech, and the other rights enumerated in the first eight articles of amendment to the constitution of the United States, are the privileges and immunities of citizens of the United States.[8]

As Robert Kaczorowski has shown, in the years before 1873 a number of federal prosecutors and federal judges read the amendment as Judge Woods did. A letter in the Bradley papers shows that Justice Joseph P. Bradley agreed with the views Woods expressed in *Hall*.[9]

One early academic writer interpreted the Fourteenth Amendment to apply the limits of the Bill of Rights to the states. John N. Pomeroy was a professor of law first at New York University, then at Hastings. He was a prolific and highly respected author. In his 1868 *Introduction to Constitutional Law* Pomeroy insisted that section 1 of the Fourteenth Amendment would bring civil rights under the protection of the nation. Both *Dred Scott* (holding blacks not entitled to federal constitutional protection) and *Barron v. Baltimore* (holding that the Bill of Rights did not limit the states) would be corrected.[10]

In the United States Supreme Court, Bill of Rights liberties did not fare so well. In its early cases considering the amendment, the Court read it narrowly, so narrowly that the privileges or immunities clause was virtually read out of the Constitution. These early decisions share several common characteristics. The history of abuses that led to the amendment received superficial and cursory attention at best.[11] The legislative history of the amendment— including Senator Howard's full statement as to the purpose of the privileges or immunities clause —received no attention at all. By the time the Court finally discussed Howard's remarks in 1900,[12] it had repeatedly held that the guaranties of the Bill of Rights did not limit the states and was clearly reluctant to overrule a long line of its cases on the subject. In its early misconstructions of the Fourteenth Amendment, the Court also ignored the implication of some of its own prior decisions, particularly *Dred Scott v. Sandford*,[13] *Barron v. Baltimore*,[14] and *Murray's Lessee v. Hoboken Land & Improvement Co.*[15]

Dred Scott v. Sandford had been decided in 1857. There, in accordance with Chief Justice Taney's view of the "original intentions" of the framers, the Court had held that blacks, even free blacks, had belonged to a degraded class at the time the Constitution was written and, short of a constitutional amendment making them citizens, could never be citizens of the United States or entitled to any of the "rights and privileges and immunities guaranteed by [the Constitution] to the citizen," including those in the Bill of Rights.[16]

One object of the Fourteenth Amendment (which made all persons born or naturalized in the United States citizens of the United States and of the state where they resided) was to overrule *Dred Scott* and make blacks citizens. As Crosskey has noted, *Dred Scott* had treated rights in the Bill of Rights and other privileges in the Constitution as belonging only to the class composed of citizens of the United States, a class that excluded all blacks, even those who might be citizens of a particular state.[17] The Court in *Barron v. Baltimore*, of course, held that rights in the Bill of Rights did not limit the states. So, when the Fourteenth Amendment provided that "all persons born or naturalized in the United States . . . and subject to the jurisdiction thereof are citizens of the United States and of the state wherein they reside" and that "no state shall make or enforce any law which shall abridge the privileges or immunities of citizens of the United States," it had a twofold object: first, to extend citizenship of the United States and of the states to blacks, and second, to provide that the privileges of citizens of the United States (previously defined in *Dred Scott* to include Bill of Rights liberties) should no longer be abridged by the states.[18]

Another antebellum case had similar implications for all of the procedural guaranties of the Bill of Rights. In 1856, about ten years prior to the framing of the Fourteenth Amendment, the Court had suggested that the procedural guaranties set out in the Constitution were part of the process required by the due process clause.[19] Most of the guaranties in the Bill of Rights—the right against self-incrimination, the right to counsel, the right to confront witnesses, and the like—are procedural. So it could have been a simple matter, under prior law, for the Court to have found that the Fourteenth Amendment applied these rights in the Bill of Rights to the states.

Neither the Court nor counsel made any reference to the Fourteenth Amendment in the first case in which the Bill of Rights question was raised in the Supreme Court after the amendment's ratification.[20] Pennsylvania had passed a statute changing the requirements for an indictment for murder or manslaughter. It was no longer necessary to specify in the indictment the means by which the death was caused. George S. Twitchell, who was convicted under such an indictment, claimed that it violated the guaranties of the Fifth and Sixth Amendments, particularly the Sixth Amendment guaranty to the accused "to be informed of the nature and cause of the accusation against him."

The Court disposed of the case by noting that the Fifth and Sixth Amendments had been held, in a long line of cases, not to apply to the states. If that "were an open question" it might be the Court's duty to hear argument on the case. However, the Court considered the question closed.[21] The opinion was written by Chief Justice Chase, an antislavery Republican activist, and joined by other Republican appointees. The Supreme Court said nothing about the Fourteenth Amendment. Apparently, counsel for the defendant had not thought to raise it.

The first time the Supreme Court considered the meaning of the Fourteenth Amendment privileges or immunities clause was in the *Slaughter-House Cases*.[22] A state statute had given one corporation a monopoly on slaughtering animals in New Orleans. Other butchers in the city went to court to attack the ordinance. Among other claims, they asserted that the monopoly violated the privileges or immunities clause of the Fourteenth Amendment. Counsel for the butchers in one of their briefs to the court cited the congressional legislative history of the amendment, including statements by Bingham and Senator Howard indicating an intent to apply the Bill of Rights to the states.[23] The Bill of Rights question was not directly presented by the *Slaughter-House Cases*, but by its construction of the Fourteenth Amendment the Court effectively nullified the intent to apply the Bill of Rights to the states. The Supreme Court upheld the monopoly statute by a vote of 5 to 4. Justice Samuel F. Miller wrote for the majority.

Miller had been trained as a doctor and left medicine for law, practicing in Kentucky as a doctor and a lawyer. There he had advocated gradual emancipation. In politics Miller had been a Whig, a follower of Henry Clay. He was propelled into the Republican party by the passage of the Kansas-Nebraska Act. Moving to Iowa in 1850, he ran for and lost elections for state senator and governor. In 1860 he was a strong Lincoln supporter. He was on the Court by 1862.[24] Like most of his fellow Justices, he would take a narrow view of the rights of blacks in the years after the Civil War.[25]

Miller thought that the "most cursory glance" at the Thirteenth, Fourteenth, and Fifteenth Amendments discloses a "unity of purpose, when taken in connection with the history of the times." The purpose was to prevent discrimination against blacks and to protect them from those who had "formerly exercised unlimited domination over" them. Miller found it unlikely that the clause was intended to protect fundamental rights of a citizen of a state against the legislative power of his own state.[26]

Miller distinguished between the privileges and immunities of citizens of a state and the privileges and immunities of citizens of the United States. The privileges of a citizen of a state embraced "nearly every civil right for the establishment and protection of which organized government is instituted. They are, in the language of Justice Washington, those rights which are fundamental."[27] The privileges and immunities of a citizen of the United States were a narrow class of privileges, enjoyed by virtue of United States citizenship and including things such as protection on the high seas. According to Justice Miller the Fourteenth Amendment was not designed to transfer the protection of civil rights from the states to the federal government.[28] So by Justice Miller's construction of the Fourteenth Amendment the fundamental rights of American citizens were left to the protection of the states, a strange reading of the language of the Fourteenth Amendment.

Miller's reading also flew in the face of legislative history. Leading Republicans in the Thirty-ninth Congress had believed that the fundamental rights referred to by Justice Washington and embraced within article IV, section 2 were absolute privileges of citizens of the United

States that states could not abridge.[29] These absolute rights had other incidental rights connected with them, and Congress had power to enforce protection of such civil rights.[30] Justice Miller turned the plan for the Fourteenth Amendment on its head.

Miller did identify (lest it should be said that none existed) privileges and immunities of citizens of the United States that were protected by the amendment. These included such things as the right to go to and from the seat of government, free access to the seaports, protection on the high seas or when under the jurisdiction of foreign governments, and the right to use navigable waters.[31] Why an amendment, which Miller incorrectly thought was designed only to protect blacks, would focus on things such as traveling back and forth to Washington, D.C., and to the seaports and protection on high seas and in foreign countries, Justice Miller did not explain. He also mentioned the right to petition and assemble for redress of grievances as privileges of citizens of the United States, though later it became apparent that the Court intended to limit such rights to assembling to petition the federal government.[32]

In dissent, Justice Bradley, joined by Justice Noah H. Swayne, wrote that the privileges or immunities of citizens of the United States would include those guarantied by the Bill of Rights. The fact that the majority opinion did not follow this obvious explanation, but resorted to privileges such as protection on the high seas, indicates that it was unsympathetic with Bradley's interpretation.[33]

Bradley insisted that citizenship was not "an empty name, but had connected with it certain incidental rights, privileges and immunities of the greatest importance." "And to say that these rights and immunities attach only to state citizenship, and not to citizenship of the United States, appears to me to evince a very narrow and insufficient interpretation of the constitutional history and the rights of men, not to say the rights of American people."[34] Because of the similarity of the original privileges and immunities clause and that of the Fourteenth Amendment, Bradley looked at article IV, section 2, which he gave a broad reading. The section, Bradley insisted, "seems fairly susceptible of a broader interpretation than that which makes it a guarantee of mere equality of privileges with other citizens."[35] Bradley went on explicitly to interpret the privileges or immunities clause of the Fourteenth Amendment to protect all rights of citizens of the United States specified in the Constitution.

> The Constitution, it is true, as it stood prior to the recent amendments, specifies, in terms, only a few of the personal privileges and immunities of citizens, but they are very comprehensive in their

character. The States were merely prohibited from passing bills of attainder, *ex post facto* laws, laws impairing the obligation of contracts, and perhaps one or two more. But others of the greatest consequence were enumerated although they were secured, in express terms, from invasion by the federal government; such as the right of habeas corpus, the right of trial by jury, the free exercise of religious worship, the right of free speech and of free press, the right peaceably to assemble for the discussion of public measures, the right to be secure against unreasonable searches and seizures, and above all and including almost all the rest, the right of not being deprived of life, liberty, or property without due process of law. These, as well as still others, are specified in the original Constitution or in the early amendments of it, as among the privileges and immunities of citizens of the United States, or, what is still stronger for the force of the argument, the rights of all persons whether citizens or not.[36]

Justices Chase and Field also dissented, but they did not reach the Bill of Rights question.

By the Court's opinion in the *Slaughter-House Cases* the most basic civil liberties were to be protected only by state laws and state constitutions. In this respect the situation was much as it had been before the Civil War.[37] The Court had reversed one of the main nationalizing results of the Civil War. Justice Swayne, one of the *Slaughter-House* dissenters, protested: the Court had turned "what was meant to be bread into a stone."[38] Protests came from Congress as well. Senator George Franklin Edmunds, one of the framers of the amendment, said the Court had "radically differed" from the intent of the framers.[39]

In 1890 political scientist John W. Burgess wrote a premature epitaph for the *Slaughter-House* decision. According to Burgess the Court had attempted to restore "that particularism in the domain of civil liberty, from which we suffered so severely before 1861." It threw away the "great gain in the domain of civil liberty won by the terrible exertion of the nation by appeal to arms. I have perfect confidence that the day will come when it will be seen to be intensely reactionary and will be overruled."[40]

For years to come, the decision was extremely influential. In the years that followed the *Slaughter-House* decision—a decision that suggested that the amendment was designed almost exclusively to protect blacks—it was cited to justify decisions denying them a wide range of rights.[41]

When the *Slaughter-House Cases* were decided in 1873, the influence of antislavery ideology in the Republican party had seriously declined. As antislavery stalwarts grew old, died off, or were defeated at the polls, more and "more Republicans began to emphasize the issue of states' rights."[42] President Grant, a defender of the rights of blacks, found himself increasingly isolated.[43] Blacks could be protected only by federal "force," and each new application of force brought defections. With the Force Act of 1870, the once radical Carl Schurz, the United States senator from Missouri, declared himself for states' rights.[44]

The Klan was omnipresent in the 1870s. Assassination of black leaders and Republicans was becoming frequent. At first, Congress and the Grant administration acted forcefully to protect citizens. Grant suspended the writ of habeas corpus in nine South Carolina counties. A number of Klansmen were tried under federal anti-Klan statutes, and fifty-five were found guilty of violating civil rights. According to historian Page Smith more than five thousand Klansmen were arrested under the federal acts, and for a time the Klan was suppressed. Federal prosecutors and judges often had acted on the theory that Klan violence deprived citizens of their Bill of Rights privileges, privileges secured by the Fourteenth Amendment and the Reconstruction acts.[45]

The question of the constitutionality of congressional Reconstruction acts designed to protect blacks and Republicans in the states would soon reach the Supreme Court. The *Slaughter-House* decision was not encouraging. In March of 1876 the Supreme Court decided the case of *United States v. Cruikshank*.[46] A group of armed whites had killed over sixty blacks. The defendants were indicted for conspiring to oppress, threaten, injure, and intimidate blacks to prevent them from exercising their right to assemble and their right to bear arms.

By the time *Cruikshank* was decided the Court considered the meaning of the Fourteenth Amendment settled. The Court noted that "no rights can be acquired under the Constitution or laws of the United States, except such as the government of the United States has the authority to grant or secure. All that cannot be so granted or secured are left under the protection of the States."[47] The Court found that the right to assemble was not a right granted to the people by the Constitution. The First Amendment was merely a limitation on the national government. It only guarantied the right to assemble against congressional interference. "For their protection in its enjoyment, the people must look to the States."[48] Still, had the indictment alleged that the assembly was for the purpose of petitioning Congress, the Court said that the case would have been within the statutory conspiracy and the defendants could have been punished. The Court also found that the right to bear arms was not granted by the Constitution. The Second Amendment merely restricted the power of Congress.[49]

The *Cruikshank* case raised two related questions: What was the scope of the guaranties of the Bill of Rights? and Could the government directly protect rights of its citizens when their First Amendment right to assemble and Second Amendment right to bear arms were violated? In the latter respect the Court held that the Fourteenth Amendment added nothing to the rights of one citizen as against another.[50]

The view of the federal system espoused in the *Slaughter-House Cases* was reaffirmed and extended in *Cruikshank*.[51] It was becoming judicial orthodoxy. Historian Philip Paludan and others suggest that *Cruikshank's* limitation of the reach of the Fourteenth Amendment to "state action" represented Republican commitment to federalism coming home to roost. As Paludan seems to recognize, the federalism of 1866 was at the least a federalism where states stayed within their orbits, orbits carefully marked by the guidelines of the federal Bill of Rights.[52] *Cruikshank* went beyond the state action question to free states from the constitutional constraints of the Bill of Rights.

For reasons not entirely clear, Republican judges were abandoning a commitment to enforcement of Bill of Rights liberties and the rights of blacks. Part of the reason may have been concern for federalism. Another may have been the conclusion that the protection of blacks was not worth the enormous effort it required and the conflict it produced. At any rate, views were changing—almost as fast as they changed during the Civil War, but in the opposite direction. In 1871 Justice Bradley had believed that the federal government could prohibit private conspiracies in states aimed at abridging Bill of Rights liberties. By 1874, after the *Slaughter-House Cases*, he held the government could do nothing about a politically motivated armed attack by whites that killed sixty blacks.[53] He had completely changed positions.

On one occasion, failure to require the states to obey the Bill of Rights actually enhanced the situation of blacks. In *Walker v. Sauvinet*,[54] decided in 1876, the Court considered the right to trial by jury in civil cases. In that case a black had been denied equal accommodations in violation of the state law. When the jury failed to agree, the judge—in accordance with state law—decided the case in favor of Sauvinet and against the defendant Walker, who had refused him refreshments. Walker claimed that he was entitled to trial by jury under the Seventh Amendment. The amendment, the Court held, related only to trials in courts of the United States. "A trial by jury in suits at common law pending in State Courts is not, therefore, a privilege or immunity of national citizenship which the States are forbidden by the Fourteenth Amendment to abridge."[55] Nor did the provision violate due process. Only Justices Clifford and Field dissented.[56]

While the Court was reading Bill of Rights liberties out of the Fourteenth Amendment it was also seriously restricting the power of Congress to protect blacks under the Fourteenth and Fifteenth Amendments. For example, in 1876 in *United States v. Reese*,[57] Reese was prosecuted for refusing to receive and count the vote of black citizens. The Court read the statute under which Reese was prosecuted to prevent other types of interference with the right to vote in addition to those based on race. As a result the Court held the statute unconstitutional.[58]

Developments in the Court paralleled those in the nation at large. In 1876 the Democratic presidential candidate won a majority of the popular vote. The electoral vote was close and hung on the outcome in disputed southern states. By the compromise of 1877 the election was given to the Republicans. In return, federal troops were to be withdrawn from the South, leaving blacks and southern Republicans to their own devices.[59]

For a brief shining moment during and after the Civil War, protection of blacks had been associated with the cause of the Union. By the mid-1870s protection of blacks seemed to disrupt national unity, and the commitment to protection of their rights faded away as quickly as it had come. The state action limitation was a primary judicial rationalization for the retreat.

In 1883, in an opinion by Justice Woods, the Court held a section of the Enforcement Act of 1871 unconstitutional because it attempted to protect the constitutional right to equal protection against invasion by private individuals, as opposed to state officials.[60] Also in 1883 the Court in an opinion by Justice Bradley voided the Civil Rights Act of 1875, which guarantied blacks equal accommodations.[61] In 1903 in *James v. Bowman*[62] the Court indicated that the Fifteenth Amendment, like the Fourteenth, could not reach private action.

After *Walker v. Sauvinet* the Supreme Court delivered several major decisions bearing on the Fourteenth Amendment. In 1884 in *Hurtado v. California*[63] the Court considered the meaning of the due process clause of the Fourteenth Amendment, a clause the Court had earlier said would have to be defined by a gradual judicial process of exclusion and inclusion.[64] As *Hurtado* shows, in the judicial process of exclusion and inclusion, exclusion was winning out.

Hurtado had discovered that his wife was having an affair with another man. According to witnesses he wept frequently and raved and tore his hair when he discussed his problem. Hurtado confronted both his wife and her lover, and the man promised to leave the city. Instead, he continued to pursue Hurtado's wife. Finally, Hurtado shot and killed him.[65]

At the time federal courts and most state courts required indictment by grand jury for serious crimes. In California, however, state law permitted charge by information—essentially a procedure by which the prosecutor prepared the charge of crime without the intervention of a grand jury.[66] Charged by information, Hurtado was tried and convicted of first degree murder and sentenced to death. After losing his appeal in state court, he took his case to the United States Supreme Court.

Hurtado argued that the due process clause protected ancient "common law rights" that Americans had inherited from England. There was some precedent to support Hurtado's contention, particularly an 1856 case[67] in which the Supreme Court had suggested that due process should be defined by the procedures set out in the Constitution. For procedures that did not violate an explicit constitutional guaranty, the Court said it would look to English usage that had been accepted here after settlement of the colonies.[68]

There was also historical support for Hurtado's position. The revolutionary generation of Americans, fighting for their liberty against England, looked to history to justify their resistance. The history uppermost in the minds of the colonists was the fight by Parliament for the liberties of Englishmen against the tyranny of the king. A leading prophet of the seventeenth-century resisters was Sir Edward Coke, prosecutor, judge, and member of Parliament. Coke had written a legal treatise on the Magna Carta. For Coke, the Magna Carta was a fundamental law protecting the citizen against oppression by government. Passages in Coke seemed to support the contention that Magna Carta required grand jury indictment.[69] William Penn, founder of Pennsylvania, cited and relied on Coke and the Magna Carta in his book *The Excellent Privilege of Liberty & Property Being the Birth-Right of Free Born Subjects of England.*[70] A part of the privilege of liberty which, according to Penn, was protected by the Magna Carta was grand and trial juries.[71]

John Adams reached similar conclusions. On Christmas Day, 1765, Adams was thinking about "taxation without consent." Adams wrote in his diary for that day a paraphrase of Coke's commentaries on the Magna Carta—to the effect that an act of Parliament that allowed proceedings based on information instead of presentment by a grand jury affronted the Magna Carta.[72] Chief Justice Lemuel Shaw had also construed the law of the land clause of the Massachusetts constitution to require grand jury indictment in serious felonies, relying on a statement by Coke that the "law of the land" required indictment or a presentment by a grand jury.[73] Since the law of the land clause of the Magna Carta is generally recognized as the origin of the due process clause, that, one might suppose, would be that.

The Supreme Court took a different approach. In a thoughtful study of the use of history by the Supreme Court, Charles Miller has noted that, faced with "obstinate historical facts," the Court follows several strategies: "The first of these responses is to devise a different interpretation of history that would permit a different outcome for the case. The second is to dispute the clarity of the historical record and to hold, on that basis, that history is of no real aid in settling the issue. A third response is to ignore history altogether."[74] A fourth rather unusual approach is to admit that history is not on the Court's side and to decide the case on other principles.[75] A fifth hybrid method is to escape from history by insisting on constitutional "flexibility." In *Hurtado*, Justice Stanley Matthews followed a combination of methods one, two, and five.

Matthews had graduated from Kenyon College in Ohio. There he met and formed a lasting friendship with Rutherford B. Hayes. In politics Matthews became a Stephen Douglas Democrat. He was appointed United States attorney for the Southern District of Ohio by President Buchanan. In that office he prosecuted a newspaper reporter who had helped a fugitive slave escape. The reporter was sentenced to jail but received much public support. Matthews fought for the Union in the Civil War and had served as a judge. In 1872 he flirted with Liberal Republicanism (an anti-Grant, more states' rights approach). He was a close associate of Hayes in 1876 and soon was placed on the Court.[76]

In *Hurtado* Matthews first argued that indictment by grand jury was treated by Coke as one form of due process but not as essential to due process.[77] Matthews argued that in England grand jury indictment was not required in all capital cases — only those instituted by the king. It was not required, as even Coke recognized, in all criminal cases instituted by the king. Misdemeanors, for example, were an exception.

Second, Matthews insisted that the Constitution must be kept up to date. Limiting due process to traditional procedure "would be to deny every quality of the law but its age, and to render it incapable of progress or improvement. It would be to stamp on our jurisprudence the unchangeableness attributed to the laws of the Medes and the Persians."[78]

There is an unquestionable tension between the common law tradition, in which judges create law based on precedent and social policy, and the interpretation of the Constitution, in which judges expound a particular historical text, limited to some degree at least by its language, history, and traditions.[79]

Recently, applying provisions of the Bill of Rights to the states has been treated as the child of broad construction, unrooted in the intent of the framers, unsupported by historical tradition.[80] Ironically, the Court in *Hurtado* took the opposite tack, suggesting that the English heritage of American liberty was too parochial and constricting a guide to be followed in construing the Constitution.[81]

According to the Court in *Hurtado*, the due process clause would be read to protect liberty—"not particular forms of procedure, but the very substance of individual rights to life, liberty and property."[82] What was acceptable would be determined not by what Coke thought, or by what the framers thought about acceptable procedure, or by procedure specified in the Bill of Rights but by what the Justices thought: "Any legal proceeding enforced by public authority whether sanctioned by age and custom or newly devised in the discretion of the legislative power, in furtherance of the general public good which regards and preserves those principles of liberty and justice [i.e., those the Justices found fundamental], must be held to be due process of law."[83] So due process did not require indictment by grand jury in capital cases. The Court upheld Hurtado's conviction.

The Court in *Hurtado* had supported its conclusion by a second line of analysis. The due process clause in the Fourteenth Amendment was identical in language to the same clause of the Fifth Amendment. But the Fifth Amendment contained a separate clause that guarantied indictment by grand jury in cases of infamous crimes. On this fact the Court constructed its argument. According to what the Court insisted was a "recognized canon of construction" (applicable in the absence of clear reason to the contrary), the Court must conclude that no part of the Fifth Amendment was superfluous. To hold that the due process clause included the right to indictment by grand jury would make the grand jury clause superfluous. Therefore, the due process clause did not include grand jury indictment.[84]

The Court's conclusion was only as true as its premises. Lawyers say everything at least twice. But the Court's canon of construction assumed that the framers of the Constitution, a group that included a large number of lawyers, was incapable of redundancy. Taken literally, the doctrine of nonsuperfluousness would mean that the due process clause excluded all rights in the Bill of Rights including, as Justice Harlan pointed out, such things as the right of an accused to be informed of the nature of the accusation against him, to be confronted with witnesses against him, to have the assistance of counsel, and so forth. Furthermore, as Justice Harlan noted, a contrary inference could be drawn from the double protection of certain procedural guaranties—that the framers intended to make the rights in question doubly secure.[85]

John Marshall Harlan was the lone dissenter in *Hurtado*. He was an extraordinary Justice. He had been born in Kentucky in 1833. His father was a Whig and supporter of Henry Clay. Harlan was raised to defend both slavery and Union.[86] He had become a lawyer and later for one term a county judge.

In 1860 he opposed Lincoln. When the Civil War broke out, however, Harlan supported the Union, formed a company of volunteers, and fought with distinction. But he continued to support the right to hold slaves. He opposed the Emancipation Proclamation, opposed Lincoln's election in 1864, and came out against the Thirteenth Amendment. About this time he was elected attorney general of Kentucky.

After the war Harlan faced a choice between Democrats, far more racist than he was, and the Radicals, whose commitment to the rights of blacks had gone far beyond his own.[87] He chose the Radicals and supported Grant in 1868. Faced with violence against blacks and violent criticisms of himself, Harlan began to change his views. He accepted the post–Civil War amendments. In 1871 Harlan was defeated for governor of Kentucky. In the 1876 Republican convention he led the Kentucky delegation to Hayes. In 1877 Hayes appointed him to the Court.[88]

As a Justice, Harlan stood almost alone for constitutional protection for blacks. He dissented from the *Civil Rights Cases*,[89] which held an act of Congress granting blacks equal accommodations unconstitutional, and he would later dissent from the separate-but-equal doctrine of *Plessy v. Ferguson*.[90] On the income tax and antitrust laws and government regulation of business, Harlan tended to be populist or at least to support government regulation in these areas.

Harlan's commitment to liberty surfaced again and again—including a long line of cases on application of the Bill of Rights to the states. He spoke with eloquence and force. In his dissent in *Hurtado* Justice Harlan insisted on the heritage of English liberty. "Those who had been driven from the mother country brought with them as their inheritance, which no government could rightfully impair or destroy, certain guarantees of the rights of life, liberty and property, which had long been deemed to be fundamental in Anglo-Saxon institutions."[91]

The purpose of the due process clause, Harlan insisted, was to impose on the states in proceedings involving life, liberty, or property the same restrictions that had been imposed on the federal government. While the Court looked to general principles of justice to define due process, Harlan would look to the Bill of Rights to determine what rights were fundamental to liberty. "Does not the fact that the people of the original states required an amendment to the national Constitution, securing exemption from prosecution, for a capital offense, except upon indictment or presentment by a grand jury prove that, in their judgment such an exemption . . . was a fundamental principle of liberty and justice?"[92] As to the argument that the law must be allowed to grow and improve, Harlan did not find the change an improvement.

Finally, Harlan summed up his opposition to the method chosen by the Court to determine what rights were fundamental to liberty and so protected by the due process clause.

> The court, in this case, while conceding that the due process of law protects the fundamental principles of liberty and justice, adjudges, in effect, that an immunity or right, recognized at common law to be essential to personal security, jealously guarded by our national constitution against violation by any tribunal or body exercising authority under the General Government, and expressly or impliedly recognized when the Fourteenth Amendment was adopted, in the Bill of Rights or constitution of every state of the Union is not yet a fundamental principle.[93]

Justice Harlan's position was twofold. First, that at least in capital cases grand jury indictment was required. Second, that grand jury indictment was required in all cases covered by the provisions of the Fifth Amendment—in all cases of infamous crimes.

Against Harlan's powerful argument, Charles Fairman has marshaled significant evidence that points to a contrary inference. Several states that ratified the Fourteenth Amendment, according to Fairman, did not require grand juries in all cases of infamous crimes: Connecticut,[94] Kansas,[95] Indiana, and Michigan.[96] The argument is that these states would not have ratified an amendment inconsistent with their legal systems. Furthermore, as Fairman notes, these states did not institute grand juries after the passage of the Fourteenth Amendment.[97]

The Fourteenth Amendment, however, was a compromise that contained a number of independent provisions. No legislative compromise is entirely satisfactory to all its supporters. Voting on the amendment involved weighing pros and cons. It does not seem likely that Republican politicians in the state legislatures, if they thought about the grand jury system at all, would reject the amendment because of that feature. The alternative, at that point, was to swell the political power of the recently rebellious states by allowing them to count for purposes of representation all of their disfranchised black population.

In 1887 the Supreme Court considered the case of *Spies v. Illinois*.[98] The petitioners in that case were anarchists in Chicago sentenced to death in connection with the Haymarket affair. Counsel for the petitioners, J. Randolph Tucker, mounted a powerful attack on the Court's position on application of the Bill of Rights to the states.

Tucker was a lawyer, teacher, and congressman from Virginia. Before the Civil War he had been a states' rights politician and a Democratic elector in 1852 and 1856. After the war he taught law at Washington and Lee, served in Congress, and practiced law. In Congress he was an "old fashioned strict constructionist, states rights logician."[99] In 1893 he became dean of the Washington and Lee Law School.

In 1887, when he appeared in *Spies,* Tucker was nearing his final term in Congress. When friends expressed surprise at his defense of the Chicago anarchists, Tucker replied, "I do not defend anarchy. I defend the Constitution."[100] After the decisions in the *Slaughter-House Cases,*[101] *Hurtado,*[102] and the rest, Tucker faced an uphill battle in *Spies.* Still, he argued that the privileges or immunities clause required the states to respect the guaranties of the Bill of Rights.

> One other provision of the Fourteenth Amendment will now be considered which is more comprehensive in its protection of personal rights than the one just considered. It is that:
> "No State shall make or enforce any law which shall abridge the privileges or immunities of citizens of the United States." The meaning of this clause turns chiefly on what shall be deemed "privileges and immunities of citizens of the United States." A privilege is a special and peculiar right. An immunity is an exemption or relief from burden or charge. These words are used once in the Original Constitution, Art. 4, § 2; and in respect to those privileges and immunities which are enjoyed by citizens of a State. What they are has been judicially defined partially in the judgment of Mr. Justice Washington in the case of *Corfield v. Coryell,* 4 Wash. C.C. 371. He says: "We have no hesitation in confining these expressions to those privileges and immunities which are *fundamental,* which belong of right to the citizens of all free governments, and which have at all times been enjoyed by citizens of the several States which compose the Union from the time of their becoming free, sovereign, and independent." . . .
> When the Constitution was proposed by the Federal Convention September 17, 1787, to the several States for ratification, many of them in their conventions expressed an apprehension that by enlarged construction of the powers delegated to the General Government, and by enforced implication, the rights of the States and of the people would be endangered. The preamble of the Congress proposing them to the States shows this. It is stated that "the conventions of a number of the States having at the time of their adopting the Constitution declared a desire, in order to prevent misconstruction or abuse of its powers, that further declaratory and restrictive clauses should be added," etc. Those amendments have been held, chiefly upon the basis of this historic fact, to be confined

to their operation as limitations on the Federal power over States and citizens.

But when the late war closed and all slaves were made free by the Thirteenth Amendment, the non-slave-holding States apprehended (whether justly or not is not here in question) that the late slave-holding States would make, or enforce already existing laws abridging the rights of the African race; and, jealous of state power, as our fathers had been jealous of Federal power, they gave American citizenship to the former slaves, and prohibited the States from abridging the privileges and immunities of persons holding such citizenship. Congress made a ratification of this amendment a precondition to the admission of the Southern States to representation in the union.[103]

Tucker insisted that restraining the power of the states as to personal rights was consistent "even with the genius of the original Constitution." He proceeded to consider the purposes of the Fourteenth Amendment.

Looking, then, to the purpose in view in adopting this Fourteenth Amendment, and to the historic condition of things which suggested it, and to the general consistency of its purpose with that which led to the original Constitution, I cannot think that we can go wrong in holding, as a canon for its true construction, that it shall have a liberal interpretation in favor of personal rights and liberty. If the views of the minority of the court in the *Slaughter-House Cases*, 16 Wall. 36, be adopted, the argument I shall present would only be the stronger, but I shall rest upon that of the majority, as above cited.

I hold the privileges and immunities of a citizen of the United States to be such as have their recognition in or guaranty from the Constitution of the United states. Take then the declared object of the Preamble, "to secure the blessings of liberty to ourselves and our posterity," we ordain this Constitution—that is, we grant powers, declare rights, and create a Union of States. See the provisions as to personal liberty in the States guarded by provision as to *ex post facto* laws, etc.; as to contract rights—against States' power to impair them, and as to legal tender; the security for *habeas corpus*; the limits imposed on Federal power in the Amendments and in the original Constitution as to trial by jury, etc.; the Declaration of Rights—the privilege of freedom of speech and press—of peaceable assemblages of the people—of keeping and bearing arms—of *immunity* from search and seizure—*immunity from self-accusation*, from second trial—and privilege of trial by due process of law. In these last we find the privileges and immunities secured to the citizen by the Constitution. It may have been that the States did not secure them to all men. It is true that they did not. Being secured by the Constitution of the United States to all, when they were not, and were not required to be, secured by every State, they are, as said in the *Slaughter-House Cases*, privileges and immunities of citizens of the United States.

The position I take is this: Though originally the first ten Amendments were adopted as limitations on Federal power, yet in so far as they secure and recognize fundamental rights — common law rights — of the man, they make them privileges and immunities of the man as citizen of the United States, and cannot now be abridged by a State under the Fourteenth Amendment. In other words, while the ten Amendments, as limitations on power, only apply to the federal government, and not to the States, yet in so far as they declare or recognize rights of persons, these rights are theirs, as citizens of the United States, and the Fourteenth Amendment as to such rights limits state power, as the ten Amendments had limited Federal power.

. . . .

[T]he propounders of the Fourteenth Amendment were looking to the protection of the freedmen from the peril of legislation in the South against those fundamental rights of free speech; of freedom from unreasonable searches; of double jeopardy; of self-accusation; of not being confronted with witnesses and having benefit of counsel and the like: and if these are construed as the privileges and immunities of citizens of the United States, the Fourteenth Amendment secures them; otherwise not. The fundamental nature of these rights, as common law rights, which were recognized at the time of the Revolution as the inherited rights of all the States may be seen by reference to Tucker's Blackstone App., p. 305, Story, Constitution, § 1779, 1781–2–3. As to searches, self-accusation, etc., see Story, § 1895; May's Const. History of England, Vol. 3, Ch. 11; and especially *Boyd v. United States*, 116 U.S. 616.[104]

Some of Tucker's clients were aliens. In addition to insisting that their procedural rights, such as the right to an impartial jury, were secured by the due process clause, Tucker also found protection for them under the privileges or immunities clause.

One word more on this point. If the State cannot abridge the privilege of a citizen of the United States, the same limitation applies to an alien, for *no person* shall be denied the equal protection of the laws. So that all of these defendants are, whether citizens or aliens, alike protected from the abridgment of these privileges and immunities of citizens.[105]

In refusing to hear the *Spies* case, the Supreme Court recited the litany of cases refusing to hold the Bill of Rights applicable to the states.[106] *Hurtado* had only been the most recent in a long line.

Probably no "canon" of constitutional construction is more regularly and correctly ignored than the doctrine of nonsuperfluousness that had been announced in *Hurtado*. It was not long before the Supreme Court itself ignored the rule. The 1897 *Chicago Burlington and Quincy Railroad Case*[107] was the first of many departures from the doctrine of nonsuperfluousness. Chicago had extended a street across the property owned by the railroad. The railroad insisted on compensation. The city claimed that the railroad was entitled to only minimal compensation because the street across the tracks did not significantly impair the ability of the railroad to use the track.

When the railroad failed to win what it considered adequate compensation in state court, it appealed to the United States Supreme Court. The attorney for the railroad argued that just compensation was required by the due process clause and that the Fourteenth Amendment was designed to apply the Bill of Rights to the states.[108] The railroad won the battle but lost the war. The Court concluded that the due process clause required just compensation but that the railroad had received adequate compensation.

Since the Fifth Amendment contains the due process, grand jury, and just compensation clauses, the *Hurtado* rule of nonsuperfluousness seemed to preclude application of the just compensation clause to the states.[109] The Supreme Court treated the problem with an elegantly simple method courts sometimes use when precedent seems to preclude the desired result. The Court ignored the precedent. Perhaps it was unaware of the conflict. Since the *Burlington* decision was written by Justice Harlan who had dissented in *Hurtado* and vigorously criticized the nonsuperfluousness doctrine, this explanation seems unlikely. The more likely reason is that the members of the Court decided to let sleeping doctrines lie, at least for the moment.

Some Supreme Court Justices gave detailed consideration to the Bill of Rights issue in the case of *O'Neil v. Vermont*.[110] O'Neil was a New York liquor merchant. Selling liquor in New York was legal; selling liquor in Vermont was not. A number of ingenious Vermonters hit on the simple expedient of ordering their liquor by mail from O'Neil in New York. All went well until the State of Vermont charged O'Neil with violating its liquor laws. He was tried in Vermont and convicted of 307 offenses, fined $6,140, and sentenced to imprisonment for thirty days at hard labor. Furthermore, if he failed to pay his fine (a

large sum in those days), he was to be imprisoned at hard labor for
19,194 days.[111]

O'Neil claimed that his conviction violated the exclusive power of
Congress over interstate commerce and also subjected him to cruel
and unusual punishment. The majority of the Supreme Court held
that O'Neil had not raised the cruel and unusual punishment claim
properly and upheld his conviction.

Justice Field, joined by Justices Harlan and Brewer,[112] dissented.
Field thought the convictions violated the exclusive power of Congress over interstate commerce but also imposed a cruel or unusual
punishment. He noted:

> In *Slaughter-House Cases*, 83 U.S. 16 WALL 36, it was held that the
> inhibition of [the Fourteenth Amendment] was against abridging
> the privileges or immunities of citizens of the United States as
> distinguished from privileges and immunities of citizens of the
> States. Assuming such to be the case, the question arises: What
> are the privileges and immunities of citizens of the United States
> which are thus protected? These terms are not idle words to be
> treated as meaningless, and the inhibition of their abridgement
> as ineffectual for any purpose, as some would seem to think. They
> are of momentous import, and the inhibition is a great guaranty
> to the citizens of the United States of those privileges and immu-
> nities against any possible state invasion. It may be difficult to
> define the terms so as to cover all of the privileges and immunities
> of citizens of the United States but . . . the privileges and
> immunities of citizens of the United States are such as have their
> recognition in a guaranty from the Constitution of the United
> States. . . . This definition is supported by reference to the history
> of the first ten amendments to the Constitution and of the amend-
> ments which followed the late Civil War.[113]

After summarizing rights in the federal Bill of Rights and noting
that the federal government had been prohibited from violating them,
Field pointed out that when the Civil War ended there was legislation
in slaveholding states inconsistent with rights in the Bill of Rights,
"and a general apprehension arose in a portion of the country
—whether justified or not is immaterial—that this legislation would
still be enforced and the rights of freed men would not be respected."[114]

Field concluded that the privileges or immunities clause meant
what it said: "Insofar as the first ten amendments declare or recognize
the rights of persons, their rights belong to them as citizens of the
United States under the Constitution; and the 14th Amendment as to
all such rights, places a limit upon state power by ordaining that no

State shall make or enforce any law which shall abridge them."[115]

By 1892 six people who sat as Justices on the Supreme Court had concluded that the privileges or immunities clause of the Fourteenth Amendment applied the Bill of Rights to the states: Justice Woods,[116] before his elevation to the Court; Justices Bradley and Swayne in the *Slaughter-House Cases*;[117] and Justices Field, Brewer, and Harlan in the case of *O'Neil v. Vermont*.[118] Unfortunately, they did not sit and reach their conclusions at the same time.

Justice Harlan's career has already been noted. Field was a Democrat appointed to the Court by Abraham Lincoln. On issues of Reconstruction he tended to take a negative view of military reconstruction and to oppose it as a violation of basic civil liberties.[119] Many of his opinions were civil libertarian, though far less consistently than those of Justice Harlan. Guaranties of liberty, Field once wrote, "should be broadly and liberally interpreted so as to meet and protect against every form of oppression . . . in whatever shape presented."[120] He had objected to opening sealed letters and post office interference with freedom of the press; he took a broad view of the privilege against self-incrimination; and he had objected to discriminations against the Chinese. In *O'Neil* he wrote in favor of full incorporation of the Bill of Rights. Still, he had concurred in *Hurtado*.[121]

Field's great passion after the 1870s was "protection of the property" against government regulation. He joined opinions striking down regulation of railroad rates as unreasonable, narrowing the antitrust act, and striking down the income tax. He also joined in opinions restricting the power of the federal government to protect blacks.[122]

Brewer was Field's nephew. He had joined the Court in 1889. On economic matters he was also an extreme supporter of "liberty of contract" and an opponent of economic regulation of business.[123]

In 1898 William D. Guthrie published his *Lectures on the Fourteenth Article of Amendment to the Constitution of the United States*. Guthrie was a prominent New York lawyer, one of the attorneys who had earlier persuaded the Court to invalidate the income tax. His book insisted that the privileges or immunities clause of the Fourteenth Amendment prohibited the states from impairing "the fundamental rights of the individual which are mentioned in the first eight amendments to the Constitution."[124] Guthrie argued that *Hurtado* would have been decided differently if the clear intention of the framers, including Senator Howard's speech, had been called to the attention of the Court.[125]

The idea that the Court could be persuaded to apply the Bill of Rights to the states by the legislative history of the Fourteenth Amendment was explicitly refuted in *Maxwell v. Dow*.[126] Charles Maxwell was convicted of bank robbery in the state of Utah, a state that had had a long and vigorous history of experimenting with jury trial. The territorial legislature had provided for less than unanimous verdicts in civil cases, and the practice was upheld by the Utah Territorial Supreme Court.[127] Subsequently, it was held invalid by the Supreme Court of the United States.[128] After Utah became a state, it reduced the number of criminal trial jurors to eight and attempted to try a defendant whose crime had been committed prior to the new law by a new eight-person jury. The Supreme Court in the case of *Thompson v. Utah*[129] held the practice an unconstitutional ex post facto law. The jury referred to in the Sixth Amendment, the Court said, required twelve persons. To change the rules after the crime had been committed was impermissible.

Maxwell's crime was committed after Utah had become a state and after the state had provided for an eight-person criminal jury in such cases. The state had also eliminated the need for grand jury indictment. Maxwell challenged both of these innovations as violations of his basic constitutional rights. In *Maxwell v. Dow*,[130] decided in 1900, the Court held that a jury of eight (instead of twelve as required by the Court's reading of the Sixth Amendment) and a prosecution based on information instead of indictment (as required by the Fifth Amendment) did not violate either the privileges or immunities clause or the due process clause of the Fourteenth Amendment.[131]

The *Maxwell* decision was written by Justice Rufus W. Peckham. On economic matters Peckham was an arch-conservative Democratic New York lawyer and judge. He was appointed to the Court by President Grover Cleveland. For Peckham the liberty of the Fourteenth Amendment was primarily liberty of contract. The liberty protected the right of bakers to work more than ten hours a day and sixty hours a week and the right of miners to work more than eight hours a day. Government regulations designed to protect workers violated Peckham's view of the Fourteenth Amendment. So did many other attempts to regulate business.[132] If such statutes were passed, he felt, people would soon be "at the mercy of legislative majorities."[133] If "a little unhealthfulness" could justify limiting hours, Peckham warned, there would be "no end of meddlesome interference with the rights of the individual."[134]

In *Maxwell* Peckham relied on and repeated the rule laid down in the *Slaughter-House Cases*: "The protection of the citizen and his rights as a citizen of the state still remains with the state."[135] Indeed, the Court noted that the principle had been reiterated by it again and again. "The protection of rights of life and personal liberty within the respective states, rests alone with the states."[136] Any other rule, it said, would "entirely" destroy states' sovereignty over Bill of Rights liberties. Justice Peckham recited an impressive litany of cases in which liberty after liberty in the Bill of Rights had been held not to apply to the states.[137] Here a claim was based on Fifth and Sixth Amendment rights. The Court had previously denied such a claim based on Seventh Amendment rights. Justice Peckham insisted that there was no logical basis for distinguishing between the various amendments in the Bill of Rights. "Is any one of the rights secured to the individual by the fifth or by the sixth amendment any more privilege or immunity of a citizen of the United States than those secured by the seventh?"[138]

For the first time the Court made reference to legislative history. Maxwell's lawyer cited Howard's speech to the Court. Peckham was unimpressed.[139] He treated the speech as that of a single senator, neglecting to note that Howard spoke on behalf of the Joint Committee that had charge of the Fourteenth Amendment. Statements of individual representatives and senators, the Court held, were to be given little weight: "What individual Senators or Representatives may have urged in debate, in regard to the meaning to be given to a proposed constitutional amendment, or bill, or resolution, does not furnish a firm ground for its proper construction, nor is it important as explanatory of the grounds on which the members voted in adopting it."[140] The way to interpret the amendment was "to read its language in connection with the known condition of affairs out of which the occasion for its adoption may have arisen, then to construe it, if there be therein any doubtful expressions, in a way, so far as reasonably possible, to forward the known purpose or object for which the amendment was adopted."[141] The "known condition of affairs" apparently required little historical investigation by the Court. Had the Court been familiar with the history leading up to the amendment, its method would have been fully adequate to apply the Bill of Rights to the states.[142]

Peckham and the Court also rejected Maxwell's argument based on due process. It cited *Hurtado* for the proposition that abolishing the grand jury did not violate due process and concluded that the "same course of reasoning established the right to reduce the number of trial jurors."[143]

For Peckham, historically established liberties had less appeal than "liberty of contract." In the area of civil liberties, diversity and experimentation were acceptable, even desirable. "It is emphatically a case of the people by their organic laws providing for their own affairs and we are of the opinion that they are much better judges of what they ought to have in these respects than anyone else can be," Peckham wrote. "It is a case of self protection and the people can be trusted to look out and care for themselves."[144]

Justice Harlan dissented. It did not solve the question to say that the first ten amendments had only been intended to limit the states.

> For, if, prior to the adoption of the Fourteenth Amendment, it was one of the privileges or immunities of citizens of the United States that they should not be tried for a crime in any court organized or existing under national authority except by a jury composed of 12 persons, how can it be that a citizen of the United States may now be tried by a state court for crime, particularly for an infamous crime, by eight jurors, when the amendment expressly declares that "no state shall make or enforce any law which shall abridge the privileges or immunities of citizens of the United States?"[145]

Harlan noted that the Court's decision left the states free to violate all the liberties in the Bill of Rights.

He rejected the idea that the Court's decision did little harm because the states could be relied upon to protect Bill of Rights liberties under their local constitutions.

> If it be said that there need be no apprehension that any state will strike down the guaranties of life and liberty which are found in the national Bill of Rights, the answer is that the plaintiff in error is now in the penitentiary of Utah as a result of the mode of trial that would not have been tolerated in England at the time American Independence was achieved, nor even now, and would have caused rejection of the Constitution in every one of the original states if it had been sanctioned by any provision in that instrument when it was laid before the people for acceptance or rejection. Liberty, it has often been said, depends not so much upon the absence of actual oppression, as upon the existence of constitutional checks upon the power to oppress. These checks should not be destroyed or impaired by judicial decision. . . .
> If some of the guaranties of life, liberty, and property which at the time of the adoption of the national Constitution were regarded as fundamental and as absolutely essential to the enjoyment of freedom, have in the judgment of some ceased to be of practical value, it is for the people of the United States to so declare by an amendment to that instrument. But, if I do not wholly misapprehend the scope and legal effect of the present decision, the Constitution of the United States does not stand in the way of any state striking down guaranties of life and liberty that English speaking people have for centuries regarded as vital to personal security, and which men of the revolutionary period universally claimed as the birthright of free men.[146]

Finally, Harlan noted the *Burlington* case. Under the Fourteenth Amendment, he wrote, "It would seem that the protection of private property is of more consequence than the protection of the life or liberty of the citizen."[147]

In fact, Harlan was prophetic. As the amendment shrank as a protection of liberties explicitly written into the Bill of Rights, it grew as a protection of liberty of contract. In the years that followed *Maxwell* the Court often found that legislation designed to protect workers interfered with the liberty protected by the Fourteenth Amendment. For example, in *Lochner v. New York*[148] the Court struck down a New York law providing a ten-hour day and sixty-hour week for bakery workers. Only in the 1930s after Court appointments by Franklin Roosevelt did the process begin to go into reverse. The Roosevelt Court left the regulation of economic matters almost exclusively to the states or Congress but required ever stricter adherence to at least some basic liberties of citizens set out in the Bill of Rights.[149]

After *Maxwell* the Bill of Rights question was raised again in 1908 in the case of *Twining v. New Jersey*.[150] That case involved an instruction that the jury could draw an adverse influence from the failure of the defendant to take the stand. The defendant argued that the instruction violated the Fifth Amendment because the first eight amendments were among the privileges and immunities of citizens of the United States which the Fourteenth Amendment protected against state action.

The Court rejected the defendant's privileges or immunities argument because it considered the matter closed: "It is, however, not profitable to examine the weighty arguments in its favor for the question is no longer open in this court."[151] The *Twining* opinion was written by Justice William H. Moody, who had been appointed by Theodore Roosevelt. As far as the Fifth Amendment went, Moody referred the rights of the individual to the democratic process. "If the people of New Jersey are not content with the law as declared in repeated decisions of their courts, the remedy is their own hands."[152]

In *Twining* Justice Moody indicated that the Court might be inclined to read the due process clause to protect some basic rights in the Bill of Rights. "It is possible," he noted, "that some of the personal rights safeguarded by the first eight Amendments against national action may also be safeguarded against state action, because a denial of them would be a denial of due process of law." The crucial thing was that the right was implicit in the due process clause, not that it was explicit in the Bill of Rights. The meaning of the clause would be "ascertained from time to time by judicial action." Due process would include fundamental principles of liberty and justice inherent in the very idea of a free government.[153] It would include, in other words, those principles held in high regard by the Justices.

Justice Moody's formulation had potential for growth. It was remarkably similar to that of Justice Washington in *Corfield v. Coryell*[154] and to the way that at least some framers of the Fourteenth Amendment described what it would accomplish. The major difference was that Republicans tended to view all or almost all the rights in the Bill of Rights as fundamental to a free society and as essential to liberty. The Supreme Court, on the other hand, held many of the guaranties in lower regard.

Chapter 8

The Amendment Before the Courts

(Part Two)

In the twenty-seven years prior to the twentieth century, the Supreme Court had liquidated the privileges or immunities clause. After doing so, however, it gradually began to read certain guaranties of the Bill of Rights into the due process clause of the Fourteenth Amendment. The result was that rights that were viewed solicitously by the Justices began to have federal protection against state abridgment.

As we have seen, the expansion of the due process clause had begun in 1897 when the Court read the due process clause to prohibit taking private property for public use without just compensation.[1] In 1925 in *Gitlow v. New York*[2] the Supreme Court suggested that freedoms of speech and the press were fundamental rights that were protected under the due process clause.

Benjamin Gitlow was a twenty-eight-year-old man who had advocated revolution in the United States. He was arrested under a state law that prohibited advocacy of overthrow of the government by violent means. Gitlow claimed that the statute, as applied to his conduct, violated the Fourteenth Amendment. In rejecting this claim, the Supreme Court had suggested in *dictum* that freedom of speech was protected by the due process clause. But the *dictum* in *Gitlow* was just that. The Court had assumed that the due process clause protected freedom of speech because it was convinced that what Gitlow had been doing was not protected by the First Amendment in any case.

Although *Gitlow* suggested that the First Amendment applied to the states, the Court had not yet found any state statute in violation of its terms. In 1931 the Court decided two significant free speech cases, *Near v. Minnesota*[3] and *Stromberg v. California*.[4] Both held that free speech and freedom of the press applied to the states under the Fourteenth Amendment. By 1931 the personnel of the Court was changing. Since the *Gitlow* opinion, President Herbert Hoover had appointed Charles Evans Hughes to replace Chief Justice William H. Taft and Owen Roberts to replace Justice Edward T. Sanford, author of the *Gitlow* opinion. Both of the new Justices had a strong commitment to civil liberties.[5] The change in personnel may have produced a change in result.

In *Near* the Court considered the fate of *The Saturday Press*, an anti-Semitic scandal sheet that claimed to be exposing links of political officials to organized crime. After a series of attacks on public officials, Jews, the chief of police, major newspapers in Minneapolis, and the county attorney, the county attorney got an injunction silencing the paper. Under the Minnesota law the truth of the charges was irrelevant. In a landmark decision Chief Justice Hughes held that the injunction against further publication of the newspaper was a prior restraint that violated the freedom of press protected by the Fourteenth Amendment.[6]

In 1932 in *Powell v. Alabama*[7] the court considered the right to counsel in capital cases. *Powell* involved some young black men accused of raping white women in Alabama. Public feeling ran high against the accused, and troops were required to protect them. No counsel had been appointed to represent the defendants until the day of trial. On that day, unprepared counsel began a pro forma appearance for the defendants, who were on trial for their lives. The defendants were convicted and sentenced to death.

The Supreme Court reversed. The Court held that the Fourteenth Amendment due process clause required appointment and effective assistance of counsel in capital cases. The Justices confronted and disposed of the *Hurtado* doctrine of nonsuperfluousness. Justice George Sutherland, writing for the Court, candidly admitted that *Hurtado* "if it stood alone" would have made it difficult to find a right to counsel under the due process clause of the Fourteenth Amendment. (The original Bill of Rights contained a guaranty of right to counsel *and* of due process of law.)[8] Justice Sutherland cited the *Burlington* case,[9] the *Gitlow* case,[10] and the *Near* case[11] to show that the doctrine of nonsuperfluousness set out in *Hurtado* was "not without exceptions."[12]

In *DeJonge v. Oregon*,[13] decided in 1937, the Court considered the case of a Communist who participated in a meeting called to denounce police raids on the Communist party and to denounce the shooting of a longshoreman by police during a strike. Oregon's Criminal Syndicalism Act had made it a crime to assist in the assemblage of any group that advocated force or violence as a means of political change. At trial the state proved that the party advocated violent overthrow and that DeJonge had assisted in a meeting arranged by the party. It did not, however, prove that any advocacy of unlawful action had occurred at the meeting. In Oregon juries could convict by a vote of 10 to 2. DeJonge was convicted by just such a vote.[14]

The United States Supreme Court reversed DeJonge's conviction. Freedom of assembly was fundamental and was protected by the Fourteenth Amendment.[15] Communists enjoyed the rights of free speech and were entitled to take part in peaceable assemblies called for lawful purposes. This was so, even when the assemblies were called by the party itself. Speaking for the Court, Justice Hughes held that discussing public issues and seeking a redress of grievances—when done without inciting violence—were "of the essence" of the liberty protected by the Fourteenth Amendment.[16]

By the time the Court decided *Palko v. Connecticut*[17] in 1937, the rights protected by the due process clause had expanded, and the privileges or immunities clause was a dead letter.

Palko had been convicted of second degree murder in the state of Connecticut. The state appealed and, because of an error in his trial, was allowed a new trial. At the second trial the jury found him guilty of first degree murder, and he was sentenced to death.[18] In a federal prosecution the second conviction for a higher offense would have violated the double jeopardy clause as construed by the Supreme Court of the United States. Palko's counsel argued that the right against double jeopardy was protected under the privileges or immunities clause and also the due process clause.

Speaking through Justice Benjamin N. Cardozo, the Court rejected the argument that all the guaranties of the Bill of Rights applied to the states. Cardozo noted that states could prosecute people by information rather than by indictment, that persons could be compelled to be witnesses against themselves in state court, that people were not entitled to jury trials in state criminal or civil cases, and he noted that certain other guaranties of the Bill of Rights did not limit the states.[19] On the other hand, he pointed out that the due process clause of the Fourteenth Amendment may make it unlawful for a state to abridge freedom of speech or of the press or free exercise of religion or the right of peaceable assembly or the right of the accused to the benefit of counsel.[20]

In all of this Cardozo saw a rationalizing principle, one that justified failing to protect people against state infringement of some of the rights in the Bill of Rights.

The exclusions of these immunities and privileges from the privileges and immunities protected against the action of the States has not been arbitrary or casual. It has been dictated by a study and ap-

preciation of the meaning, the essential implications, of liberty itself.

We reach a different plane of social and moral values when we pass to the *privileges and immunities* that have been taken over from the earlier articles of the federal bill of rights and brought within the Fourteenth Amendment by a process of absorption.[21]

So in his opinion Cardozo, speaking for eight of the nine Justices, describes rights in the Bill of Rights as "privileges and immunities." Some of these privileges and immunities of citizens of the United States were so important that they were protected from state violation by the due process clause. Other of these immunities and privileges were less significant and the states would be permitted to violate them.[22] Why the states should be permitted to disregard some privileges and immunities of citizens of the United States set out in the Bill of Rights when the Fourteenth Amendment said that "no state shall abridge the privileges or immunities of citizens of the United States" Cardozo did not explain. The issue was so well settled by its previous decisions that the Court was apparently unaware of the irony implicit in its opinion.

When it needs to come up with a short collective phrase to describe rights in the Bill of Rights, the Supreme Court has often referred to them as privileges or immunities.[23] Use of the same language for the same purpose by John Bingham and his colleagues has, oddly enough, never been considered adequate.

Professor Crosskey has underlined the difference between expositions of the constitutional text and expositions of the Justices' decisions about the text. The decision in *Palko* is a clear example of that duality. As Crosskey notes,

> The justices, it ought not to be forgotten, rarely read, study or discuss the Constitution; they read, and study, and discuss instead, their pronouncements about it and those of their predecessors on the Court. One Chief Justice, with somewhat surprising candor, once declared that "the Constitution is what the Judges say it is." . . . As a consequence, the Court's product incorrectly called Constitutional law has come to have almost no connection with the rather sensible straight forward document on which it is supposed to be based. . . . [The Justices] simply drift along with the current without paying much attention to the ancient document they are sworn to uphold.[24]

One need not accept Crosskey's criticism at face value to see how well it describes the process in *Palko v. Connecticut.*

After *Palko* the Court continued to expand the protections of the Fourteenth Amendment. In *Cantwell v. Connecticut* and *Everson v. Board of Education*[25] the clauses protecting free exercise of religion and prohibiting establishment of religion were applied to the states.

A major assault on the judicial status quo represented by *Palko* occurred in the case of *Adamson v. California*.[26] Adamson was tried and convicted of first degree murder. During his trial the prosecution was permitted to comment adversely on his failure to take the stand. Adamson insisted that the prosecutor's comment violated his rights under the Fifth Amendment privilege against self-incrimination as well as his rights under the Fourteenth Amendment. Five Justices voted to uphold the death sentence. They held that the right against self-incrimination did not limit the states. Justice Hugo Black and three colleagues dissented.

Black was born in Alabama in 1886. He studied law, became a police court judge, district attorney, and later a successful personal injury lawyer. Black had grown up with and come to share most of the Populist outlook on business and government. In 1925 he ran successfully for the United States Senate. "I am not now," he announced proudly, "and never have been, a railroad, power company, or corporation lawyer."[27] In the Senate, Black's record was one of advanced liberalism. Throughout his career Black had taken stands that showed a strong personal philosophy. As a prosecutor, he had investigated police brutality. As a senator, he opposed custom controls over subversive and obscene publications, insisting on freedom of speech.[28]

In 1937 President Franklin D. Roosevelt appointed Black to the Supreme Court. For Roosevelt, one crucial issue was the question of economic substantive due process—the power the Court had assumed under the Fourteenth Amendment to strike down economic and social legislation. On this issue Black stood squarely against the power that had been exercised by the Court. As a result of Roosevelt appointments, the Court soon buried economic substantive due process.

On questions of civil liberties Black became one of the leading libertarian justices. He was a textualist, and he took his text from the Constitution, particularly the Bill of Rights. He often read the provisions with a literalism that was disarming or infuriating, depending on one's views. For Black, precedent occupied a secondary position. His approach to application of the Bill of Rights to the states is an example. The fact that case after case had rejected total application of the Bill of Rights to the states did not deter Justice Black.[29]

In *Adamson* Black argued that the Fourteenth Amendment was intended to overrule earlier Supreme Court decisions and to make the first eight amendments to the Constitution a limitation on the states. Justice Black examined the congressional history of the Fourteenth Amendment and found an intent to require the states to obey the Bill of Rights.[30] He argued that the privileges or immunities clause was the primary device used to accomplish this end and that reference to privileges and immunities was a reasonable way to apply the Bill of Rights to the states.[31] In addition Black also relied on the due process clause.

Justices Frank Murphy and Wiley B. Rutledge agreed with Black that the Bill of Rights should be applied to the states under the first section of the Fourteenth Amendment. They were not prepared to say that section 1 was necessarily limited by the Bill of Rights.[32] Although Justice Black's argument for total incorporation was rejected by the Court, the Supreme Court began to find more and more guaranties in the Bill of Rights fundamental and so protected under the due process clause of the Fourteenth Amendment.

The "incorporation" movement made great strides in the 1960s. In the Warren Court "federalism" was less of a virtue than it had been in the past.[33] Conversely, the protection of individual rights against the states, particularly the rights of blacks, occupied a higher scale in the Court's scheme of values. In *Brown v. Board of Education*[34] the Court struck down segregated public school education. Federalism would be subordinated to protecting the rights of blacks. In case after case the Court of the 1960s applied guaranties of the Bill of Rights to the states. The Court had applied guaranties of the First Amendment securing free speech and press and freedom of religion and the Sixth Amendment right to counsel in capital cases to the states in the 1930s and 1940s.[35] In 1961 the Court treated the Fourth Amendment protection against unreasonable searches and seizures as fully incorporated by the Fourteenth. Evidence from such illegal searches would have to be excluded from the jury's consideration in state courts, the Justices declared, as it had been for some time in federal court cases.[36] In 1963 the right to counsel in all felony cases was held to be required by the due process clause of the Fourteenth Amendment. The Court required appointed counsel for indigents in such cases.[37] In 1964 the Court held the privilege against self-incrimination limited the states, overruling its prior decisions to the contrary.[38] In 1968 in *Duncan v. Louisiana*[39] the Court held that the Sixth Amendment right to trial by jury was applied to the states by the Fourteenth Amendment.

In *Duncan* Justice Black reiterated his view that the words "'no state shall make or enforce any law which shall abridge the privileges or immunities of citizens of the United States' seem to me an eminently reasonable way of expressing the idea that henceforth the Bill of Rights shall apply to the States."[40] In looking at congressional history, Black insisted, one should look at what was said, not at what was not.[41]

Justices Harlan and Stewart dissented in *Duncan*. They rejected the argument for total incorporation of rights in the Bill of Rights. They believed that the "overwhelming historical evidence marshalled by Professor Fairman demonstrates . . . conclusively" that the framers of the Fourteenth Amendment did not apply the Bill of Rights to the states. The test was fundamental fairness. The "principal original virtue of the jury trial—the limitations a jury imposes on a tyrannous judiciary" had, Harlan and Stewart thought, largely disappeared.[42]

In *Benton v. Maryland*[43] the Court finally overruled *Palko* and found that "the double jeopardy provision of the Fifth Amendment represents a fundamental ideal in our constitutional heritage, and that it should apply to the States through the Fourteenth Amendment." The Court discarded the fundamental fairness test. Once it was decided that a particular Bill of Rights guaranty was "fundamental to the American scheme of justice the same standards apply against the state and federal governments."[44]

By the end of the 1960s most of the guaranties had been applied to the states. Those that had not included the right to bear arms, against quartering troops in private homes (an issue that has not often arisen), the Fifth Amendment right to a grand jury, and the Seventh Amendment right to a civil jury trial. Of these, the Second Amendment right to bear arms and the Seventh Amendment right to a jury trial were regarded by framers of the Fourteenth Amendment as particularly precious rights, a view less in vogue today.

At the same time the Warren Court was reading the Bill of Rights back into the Fourteenth Amendment, it was also reading the amendment to afford substantial protection to blacks. Most members of the Court concluded that Congress could outlaw racially motivated private conspiracies to interfere with Fourteenth Amendment rights, whether or not state action was present.[45] For a whole range of issues from desegregation[46] to voting rights,[47] the Court gave the post–Civil War amendments a broad interpretation. And the First Amendment rights of those protesting segregation (as well as those opposing integration) also received protection of federal law.[48]

Warren Court decisions applying criminal procedure guaranties of the Bill of Rights to the states were often unpopular. Those accused of crimes are always the beneficiaries of such guaranties. It was an easy step to see the rights merely as protection for criminals. The guaranties are necessarily general and neutral: they protect the savory and unsavory alike.

Other Warren Court decisions also produced hostile public reactions, notably those finding that school prayers violated the prohibition against establishment of religion;[49] those protecting civil liberties of

Communists;[50] and also (in certain sections of the country at least) those protecting blacks.[51]

In addition to applying the Bill of Rights to the states, the Court interpreted a Reconstruction statute designed to give citizens a right of action against state officials who violated their constitutional rights to mean what it said.[52] As a result, public officials found themselves repeatedly called to answer damage actions alleging that they had violated constitutional rights.[53] (State legislators, judges, and ultimately others were held immune from suit.)[54] Still, litigants ranged from those claiming that they had been illegally arrested or searched to government employees claiming that they had been fired for the exercise of First Amendment rights.[55]

Throughout the Warren Court's march toward application of the Bill of Rights to the states, Justice John Marshall Harlan, grandson of the first Justice Harlan, protested that the effect of the Court's action would be to dilute the strength of the guaranties as applied to the federal government.[56] To make it easier for states to comply, Harlan argued, the Court would tend to water down the protections. At least in the area of trial by jury, there is reason to believe that he was correct.

By the 1960s Supreme Court precedent had made it fairly clear that the jury referred to in the Constitution contained twelve members and had to be unanimous. From its decision in *Barron v. Baltimore* in 1833 until the 1960s, the Supreme Court had indicated that the jury trial provisions of the Sixth and Seventh Amendments did not apply to the states. (As far as the Seventh Amendment is concerned, the rule remains undisturbed.) As a result, some states had experimented with different types of juries—less-than-unanimous juries and juries of fewer than twelve.

Once the Sixth Amendment right to jury trial was applied to the states, the Warren Court faced the prospect of overturning a number of otherwise lawful convictions or at least of voiding procedures established by several states. When the Court had held that the right to jury trial applied to the states in the case of *Duncan v. Louisiana*, it had sidestepped the question of whether or not the jury trial was to be defined, in accordance with the Court's precedents, as requiring twelve unanimous jurors.[57]

The first assault on the conventional idea of a jury was the 1970 Supreme Court decision in *Williams v. Florida*[58] holding that juries of twelve were not constitutionally required. Justice Marshall was the lone dissenter. It seemed possible that the Court might require the states to provide jury trial but strip the institution of all of its historic characteristics.

Next, by a margin of 5 to 4, the Court, now under Chief Justice

Burger, held in 1972 that state criminal juries need not be unanimous.[59] The effect of these two decisions—allowing nonunanimous jury verdicts and juries of less than twelve—was to change the nature of constitutionally required juries. Juries of less than twelve were less apt to include minority members of the community or those sympathetic to minority rights. The result was that the institution provided less protection to the politically or religiously unorthodox or to racial or other minorities. Nonunanimous jury verdicts had the same effect, to an even greater degree. If a couple of jurors insisted on protecting the rights of members of an unpopular political, religious, or racial minority, their views could simply be ignored.[60]

With a Court strongly devoted to civil liberties, the effect of these rules would be mitigated. DeJonge's Oregon conviction by a vote of 10 to 2 for addressing a rally sponsored by Communists, for instance, had been overturned by the Supreme Court.

The jury system in seventeenth-century England and eighteenth-century America was seen as a protection against a government determined to crush its political enemies. For this function, imperfectly realized as it is, size and unanimity were crucial. Courts, on the other hand, were viewed with suspicion—more likely than jurors to do the bidding of the government against claims of individual liberty. The years of the Warren Court tended to obscure the extent to which this assessment of the role of the courts has been true throughout much of American history.[61]

Whether the Fourteenth Amendment applies a single standard to the states and national government also arises in the context of guaranties of freedom of expression. The second Justice Harlan and others argued for a dual standard. As William W. Van Alstyne noted, a dual standard could actually provide greater protection for speech and press at the federal level.[62] States, necessarily, must have broader police powers than the federal government.

To these intriguing questions, the debates surrounding the Fourteenth Amendment provide no clear answers. Still, the restrictions of freedom of speech and other basic liberties in the South before the Civil War were justified under the police powers of the states. The framers of the Fourteenth Amendment believed that the courts had done an inadequate job of protecting citizens from such abuses of state power. And Republicans had little patience with the argument that protection of individual rights would interfere with the legitimate rights of states.[63]

Partly as a result of the civil rights revolution and support given to it by Democratic administrations, the once solidly Democratic South was becoming more and more Republican. In the long run, this political shift would have significant impact on the personnel of the Court.

With the election of Richard Nixon, the personnel and philosophy of the Court gradually began to change. Nixon, like Barry Goldwater before him, had campaigned against the Supreme Court. The Court, he said in his 1968 Republican nomination acceptance speech, had gone too far in strengthening the criminal forces against the "peace forces."[64] The answer to the problem was a "strict construction" of the guaranties of individual liberty, particularly those connected with criminal justice. Ironically, the Nixon years would show that the line between the "peace forces" of the government and the criminal forces was less distinct than one might wish.[65]

Nixon appointed four justices to the Court. In contrast to the Warren Court, the Nixon Court began to follow a strict or narrow interpretation of the rights in the Bill of Rights and a broad interpretation of the power of the government. The issue of application of the Bill of Rights to the states presents two separate questions: whether the guaranty should be applied, and the scope or meaning of the guaranty. In the Supreme Court so far, most of the controversy has centered on the second question. The typical restrictive method of the Justices has been to read the guaranties narrowly. The trend has continued under President Ronald Reagan.[66]

The Burger Court has (with some notable exceptions)[67] refused to expand the protection afforded by Bill of Rights liberties and has instead contracted the protection afforded by them.[68] A brief look at a number of cases reveals the trend. The overall effect of the cases is expansion of government power and contraction of individual rights.

In a wide range of cases the Court has restricted Fourth Amendment rights. For years, to justify the search, a search warrant was required to be supported by an affidavit containing a statement of probable cause. If the cause was not set out in the affidavit, the product of the search could not be used in evidence. In *United States v. Leon*[69] the Court abrogated that rule. Fruits of searches based on an officer's "reasonable" reliance on a warrant that was not based on probable cause would not necessarily be suppressed.[70]

Three Justices dissented from the new rule. Justice John Paul Stevens relied on history.

The notion that a police officer's reliance on a magistrate's warrant is automatically appropriate is one the Framers of the Fourth Amendment would have vehemently rejected. The precise problem that the Amendment was intended to address was the *unreasonable issuance of warrants*. As we have often observed, the Amendment was actually motivated by the practice of issuing general warrants

—warrants which did not satisfy the particularity and probable cause requirements. The resentments which led to the Amendment were directed at the issuance of *warrants* unjustified by particularized evidence of wrongdoing. Those who sought to amend the Constitution to include a Bill of Rights repeatedly voiced the view that the evil which had to be addressed was the issuance of warrants on insufficient evidence.

. . . .

In short, the Framers of the Fourth Amendment were deeply suspicious of warrants; in their minds the paradigm of an abusive search was the execution of a warrant not based on probable cause. The fact that colonial officers had magisterial authorization for their conduct when they engaged in general searches surely did not make their conduct "reasonable." The Court's view that it is consistent with our Constitution to adopt a rule that it is presumptively reasonable to rely on a defective warrant is the product of constitutional amnesia.[71]

Stevens suggested that the Court was converting the Bill of Rights "into an unenforced honor code that the police may follow at their discretion." "If the Court's new rule is to be followed," he concluded, "the Bill of Rights should be renamed."[72]

In other cases the Court has suggested that private diaries may be seized and used to convict the writer of a crime,[73] overruling *Boyd v. United States*;[74] that a person mistakenly labeled and advertised by the government as an active shoplifter has no federal protection against such conduct, although some remedy may be available at state law;[75] that private shopping centers may ban free speech on their premises, overruling prior cases to the contrary;[76] that the death penalty may be imposed in spite of a jury recommendation of mercy even when the law at the time of the crime made the recommendation of mercy conclusive;[77] that states may convict persons of crimes by nonunanimous juries;[78] and that it is not a cruel or unusual punishment to sentence a repeated writer of bad checks to life in prison.[79] The Court is changing the face of American liberty and law.

Ironically, two Nixon Justices participated in expanding the reach by the Fourteenth Amendment to liberty not explicitly covered by guaranties in the Bill of Rights. The expansion had begun in *Griswold v. Connecticut*,[80] where the Court found that a Connecticut statute banning birth control devices violated the right of privacy secured by the Fourteenth Amendment. The decision produced a dissent by Justice Black,[81] who had never accepted the idea that liberties beyond those spelled out in the Bill of Rights were encompassed by the Fourteenth

Amendment. The *Griswold* doctrine soon produced a storm center of constitutional controversy, the decision in *Roe v. Wade*[82] prohibiting general state laws outlawing all abortions. The decision was written by Justice Harry A. Blackmun, a Nixon appointee, and was joined in by Chief Justice Burger.

Some constitutional guaranties such as the Fourth Amendment and the privilege against self-incrimination have their origin in English law. Others, such as the First Amendment, may have been designed to change English law.[83] Much of the progress in the history of liberty resulted from a very libertarian reading (or, more accurately, misreading) of the intent of the framers of the Magna Carta. Any attempt to freeze understanding of liberty at a certain period in history confronts the historical fact of evolution. Judicial evolution has never been a one-way street.

Although government power is greater than ever, today there are serious calls to restrict individual rights. Perhaps the historical purposes of the guaranties should at least set a floor, a minimal level below which Bill of Rights liberties should not be permitted to fall.

If history were treated as a minimum standard of liberty, constitutional law would have a very different shape. Many would not find the change an improvement. The right to bear arms, for example, would have to be taken seriously. In some respects, prosecution of those accused of crimes would be more difficult.[84]

Justice Stevens's dissenting opinion in *Zurcher v. Stanford Daily*[85] is an example of an interpretation focused on history. A student newspaper had published photographs of a clash between demonstrators and police at a hospital. Armed with a search warrant, the police had searched the newspaper office for evidence bearing on the crime. The question presented was whether the police could search the newspaper's files or had to proceed by way of a subpoena. The majority of the Supreme Court upheld the search.

Justice Stevens, in dissent, noted that the police power of search had been vastly expanded by the decision in *Warden v. Hayden*,[86] a Warren Court decision. That case had abolished the "mere evidence" rule. The result was that warrants authorizing the search for and seizure of private papers became possible. Stevens noted that the framers would have thought the private papers were protected from seizure[87] and so, in Stevens's view, had not specifically directed the Fourth Amendment to protect against such abuses.

Because of the privacy interest in an innocent party's private papers, Stevens suggested that a subpoena (which presumably would minimize intrusions into privacy) instead of a search warrant was ordinarily required by the Fourth Amendment. The reasonableness requirement of the Fourth Amendment was to be read in light of the amendment's history and in light of the protection historically provided to private papers. Stevens's opinion in the *Stanford Daily* case may not have gone far enough. But his dissent there, like his dissent in *Leon*, clearly tried to read and interpret the Fourth Amendment in light of its history.

As the Court has taken a narrower and narrower view of individual rights, state courts have been increasingly reluctant to follow its lead. The result has been to reawaken interest in state constitutions and bills of rights. In a number of cases, state courts have construed their state constitutions to provide liberties the Supreme Court has not found in the federal Bill of Rights.[88] Just as some opponents of slavery were supporters of states' rights when the "slave power" had control of the federal government and the courts, then changed position when opponents of slavery got control of the federal government, libertarians are now developing a new appreciation for states' bills of rights.[89]

Two writers have noted the changing positions of Justice William J. Brennan, Jr., and Chief Justice Burger on the federalism issue.[90] In 1964 Justice Brennan wrote that "the Bill of Rights is the primary source of expressed information as to what is meant by constitutional liberty."[91] In 1977 he emphasized that the legal revolution "which has brought federal law to the fore must not be allowed to inhibit the independent protective force of state law—for without it the full realization of our liberties cannot be guaranteed."[92] Meanwhile, Chief Justice Burger has switched from urging state experimentation with criminal procedure to scolding state courts that find more protection for liberty under state constitutions than the Chief Justice and his colleagues find in the federal Constitution. "When state courts interpret state law to require more than the Federal Constitution requires, the citizens of the state must be aware that they have the power to amend state law to ensure rational law enforcement."[93]

Under present law the federal protection of individual liberty is a minimum that states can exceed, at least so long as there is no conflict with federal law. State courts that clearly rely on state court constitutional provisions (as opposed to federal provisions) are supposed to be free from Supreme Court reversal. In fact, the federal Supreme Court has been increasingly reluctant to find state court decisions supported by an independent state constitutional ground.[94] Where the reliance on state law is crystal clear, the Court has typically not disturbed the state decision.[95]

The case of *Pruneyard Shopping Center v. Robins*[96] decided in 1980 underlines some of the potential complexity of the issue of incorporation for libertarians. In the 1930s the Court developed a rule that public streets were a public forum for free speech. By the 1970s the crowds the speaker might wish to reach had moved from downtown streets to private shopping malls. In 1968 the Court balanced the right of the property owners and the importance of freedom of expression and found a right to free speech in common areas of shopping centers.[97] As the personnel of the Court changed, however, the rule changed.[98] The First Amendment no longer created a public forum in shopping centers.

Then the California Supreme Court interpreted its state constitution to provide a right to speak in shopping centers. The California court concluded that its state constitution "broadly proclaims speech and petition rights. Shopping centers to which the public is invited can provide an essential and invaluable forum for exercising those rights."[99] The shopping center appealed, claiming denial of *its* Bill of Rights liberties under the First and Fifth Amendments.

In an opinion by Justice Rehnquist, the Supreme Court affirmed the California decision. Justice Marshall, concurring, "applauded" the California decision. It was part of "a very healthy trend of affording state constitutional provisions a more expansive interpretation than this court has given to the Federal Constitution."[100]

Justices Byron R. White and Powell concurred specially. They thought the California rule raised serious questions under the First and Fifth Amendments and indicated that in a proper case they would find that the rule creating a public forum in common areas of shopping centers violated the federal Bill of Rights.

The Burger Court has read the federal Bill of Rights increasingly narrowly. Usually, however, the Court has *not* held that the guaranties do not apply fully to the states. On occasion, though, the question is crucial. In *Apodaca v. Oregon*,[101] Justice Powell found that the Fourteenth Amendment did not require full or literal application of the Sixth Amendment to the states. The upshot was that states could convict people in criminal cases by nonunanimous juries. Later, in *Ballew v. Georgia*,[102] two Justices, Burger and Rehnquist, joined Justice Powell's position that the Fourteenth Amendment did not fully incorporate the Sixth Amendment right to jury trial as a limit on the states.[103] But in *Ballew* the difference in philosophy did not produce a difference in result. All the Justices agreed that states could not convict people by five-person juries. The majority reached this result under the Sixth Amendment, which it found incorporated by the Fourteenth. Justices Powell, Burger, and Rehnquist reached the same result under a "fundamental fairness" reading of the due process clause.[104]

So far, at least, the broad call to free the states from the commands of the federal Bill of Rights has received very little encouragement from decisions of the Supreme Court. The call to restrict the content of the guaranties has already had considerable judicial success. That demand entered the political system earlier and has had fairly broad public support.

In the long run, decisions of the Court are affected by the philosophy of the Justices. The fact that a growing body of political opinion is clamoring to free the states from federal protection of the guaranties of individual liberty contained in the Bill of Rights is a disturbing development.

The Court can change direction—if it chooses—and allow states to violate the Bill of Rights. It cannot, however, justify this result by a fair reading of history.

Conclusion

Opponents of slavery never had much success in the courts. In the early years of the Republic a few state decisions held that slavery violated libertarian guaranties of state constitutions. As time went on, however, the judiciary paid less and less attention to the claims of liberty and more and more attention to the needs of slaveholders.[1]

Robert Cover, in his original and thoughtful study of the antislavery cause and the judicial process, argued that even antislavery judges followed a positivist approach to constitutional law. According to Cover, they rendered decisions against fugitive slaves because of their conception of the proper role of a judge. The judge followed positive law (whether it was morally right or wrong). He was bound by the intention of the framers, in the case of a constitution, or of the legislature, in the case of a statute. He operated on neutral principles —the values he pursued were those of others, not his own. Cover found that the judicial response to antislavery was formal and mechanical. He concluded that "given a particular juristic competence, there will be very specific consequences to and limits on the performance of judges caught in the moral-formal dilemma. If a man makes a good priest, we may be quite sure he will not be a great prophet."[2]

Judges who conscientiously follow the law do find their discretion limited by the legal process. Judges operate within a tradition that requires them to honor rules set by others, to follow the text of constitution and statutes, and to make decisions within an historical tradition. But the area of discretion is far wider than is typically recognized.

In some cases the text, history, and the intent of the framers provide fairly clear answers. By the prevailing jurisprudence of the nineteenth century, at least, in such cases the judge was required to follow the law, even if it produced morally unacceptable results. The question of the legality of slavery in the original southern states was one where text (if read in light of the records of the federal convention), history, and intent pointed in the same direction. By prevailing nineteenth-century legal thought, a federal judge in Mississippi was simply without power to free one of Mississippi's slaves. The law did not give the judge the power to prevent a crime against humanity.

Even this case, however, is not perfectly clear. As the radical constitutional abolitionists showed, a strong antislavery argument could be made on behalf of the slave in Mississippi—based only on the constitutional text.[3] If one goes beyond the text to look at history, intent, or past interpretations, the argument loses much of its force.

To view the radical abolitionist argument solely in terms of legal methodology (and to give it a failing grade on that score) is to miss much of its point. The argument highlighted the contradiction of a union established to promote liberty but that protected slavery. It confronted slavery with the words of the Bill of Rights. Although the argument never persuaded most opponents of slavery, it probably had a significant role in producing a second, more moderate antislavery constitutional theory.

Under this moderate antislavery theory, the federal government lacked power to abolish slavery in the original southern states. But the Constitution, under the due process clause, made slavery illegal in all federal territories. The Constitution also protected the right of American citizens to go to southern states and speak against slavery and protected the other rights of citizens in the Bill of Rights. Furthermore, the Constitution protected the rights of free blacks and guarantied them procedural protections before they were kidnapped or seized by federal officers and shipped off to a state where they were presumed slaves because of their color.

The mainstream of antislavery legal thought operated at the margins. At first, at least, it did not go to the heart of the evil by finding slavery illegal in the southern states. But it contained the institution within its boundaries, protected the rights of its opponents to attack the evil at its point of origin, and insisted on constitutional protections for free blacks. It called upon a grand tradition of American history, the tradition of liberty.

Although radical antislavery legal thought was impossible to reconcile with the history of slavery and was difficult to reconcile with parts of the constitutional text, mainstream antislavery thought was a different matter. It was a more reasonable, if creative, application of the traditional legal method. That some of its conclusions were doubtful as a matter of history does not distinguish it from other legal ideas that have achieved, for a time at least, the force of law.

Robert Cover noted that judges who decided in favor of slavery insisted that the law required the result they reached.[4] In fact, of course, even within a formal and mechanistic system that followed a positivist approach to the law, the judges had far more latitude than they admitted—and used that leeway to protect slavery. This fact is underlined by the decision in *Prigg v. Pennsylvania*.[5]

In the 1830s blacks in northern states faced capture and transportation south as alleged slaves. Northern states, concerned with the plight of blacks in their states, responded by passing personal liberty laws. The laws guarantied procedural rights to blacks before they were shipped south. Pennsylvania passed an antikidnapping law as well, punishing those who removed blacks from Pennsylvania without proper legal process. Prigg had been convicted of kidnapping for capturing a fugitive slave in Pennsylvania and taking him to Maryland without legal process. In the Supreme Court, Justice Story reversed Prigg's conviction. According to Story, the fugitive slave clause of the Constitution was self-executing. The slaveholders had a "positive unqualified right" to recapture a slave by private effort anywhere in the country.[6]

As Don Fehrenbacher noted, *Prigg* held that the slaveholder in effect carried the law of his slaveholding state with him into the free states: "One half of the nation must sacrifice its presumption of freedom to the other half's presumption of slavery, and the historic English principle of *in favorem libertas* was reversed where fugitive slaves were involved." Furthermore, Fehrenbacher noted, "Story coolly ignored . . . the argument of counsel for Pennsylvania that the law of 1793, in certain of its provisions, violated the personal rights guarantied by the privileges and immunities clause, by the Fourth Amendment, and by the due process clause of the Fifth Amendment." Blacks wrongfully claimed as slaves were deprived of basic constitutional rights.[7]

Whatever else one may say for the decision, it was not the inevitable result of the commands of the law, whatever the system of jurisprudence used. The decision was one based on policy. It sought to promote the stability of the Union at the expense of the constitutional rights of individual blacks. In the final analysis the policy may have been misguided. Like the later *Dred Scott* decision, *Prigg* may have contributed as much to disunion as to union.

Fehrenbacher suggested that racism was fundamental to the decision. The Court refused to pay any attention to the problem of kidnapping of free people—"a refusal that would have been inconceivable if the victims had been white."[8]

One segment of the antislavery movement essentially accepted the Court's view of the Constitution as a proslavery compact and "focused on the nature of moral obligation to such laws." The other part of the movement, according to Cover, "was forced to the anomalous position that the Constitution could not mean what the Justices were saying it meant."[9] But unless one surrenders entirely to positivism, the Constitution is not simply what the judges say it is. The law in a particular case is what the judges say it is. The Constitution is a different matter. The document has a text, history, and tradition of its own. There is nothing anomalous about the argument that the judges were misreading it.

The argument that the Supreme Court had misread and perverted the Constitution was made by leading Republicans. Probably the most notable case was Abraham Lincoln's response to the *Dred Scott* decision. Lincoln thought the decision was wrong and refused to accept it as a rule of political action. "We propose," he said, "so resisting it as to have it reversed if we can, and a new judicial rule established in its place."[10]

Republican legal thought departed, on a number of points, from judicial orthodoxy established by the Supreme Court and perhaps also from historic purposes of the Constitution. To dismiss it for that reason ignores the high function it served. For such legal thought was not simply or even primarily directed at convincing courts that their precedents required an antislavery or libertarian result in specific cases. It served a prophetic function, the function of recalling Americans to their commitment to liberty. It mustered the Bill of Rights into the political battle against slavery.

By 1866 leading Republicans in Congress and in the country at large shared a libertarian reading of the Constitution. The Constitution meant what its preamble said. It established liberty. Liberty was understood in terms of the fundamental guaranties of liberty set out in the Constitution itself. For many Republicans that did not exhaust the meaning of the word, but that was its core. With the abolition of slavery, liberty extended to all citizens, white and black.

The idea that the Constitution protected fundamental liberties of citizens against state action was accepted by Republicans of all political persuasions. Its most ardent exponent was John Bingham, a conservative to centrist Republican. Bingham's greatest problem in getting the final draft of his proposal for a Fourteenth Amendment accepted was not that it departed from what Republicans thought appropriate. It was that many Republicans had so convinced themselves of the correctness of their constitutional views that they considered the Fourteenth Amendment superfluous. They thought blacks were already citizens; that states were already prohibited from depriving free persons of due process; that all the privileges or immunities or rights of American citizens protected them throughout the nation, even in the South. A major part of Bingham's argument in favor of his amendment was to point to the decision in *Barron* where the Court had held the guaranties of the Bill of Rights did not limit the states. What, Bingham asked, have gentlemen to say to that?

At least one thing the gentlemen had to say was to point out that Bingham had not gone far enough. For Bingham also believed that the Bill of Rights limited the states and that the Supreme Court decisions on the subject were wrong. His first draft merely gave Congress power to enforce the Bill of Rights, failing to protect the rights if the old proslavery coalition returned to political power.

The power to enforce the Bill of Rights was a central concern for Republicans. The chairman of the House Judiciary Committee had justified the Civil Rights bill on that basis.[11] But the power to enforce alone was not sufficient to make the rights secure. A second complaint by Radical Republicans was that the amendment left out a basic liberty —the right of blacks to vote. A third complaint with the prototype of Bingham's amendment was that it would allow Congress to pass laws on all subjects traditionally covered by state law.

Another problem was that the first draft of the amendment used the words in article IV, section 2 in defining privileges and immunities. The use of the very language of article IV tied Bingham's proposal to words whose meaning was disputed. Did the article mean only, as Democrats insisted, that the citizens of each state should be entitled when visiting other states on a temporary basis to the same basic rights enjoyed by the citizens of the state visited under its state law? Were the privileges merely and solely created by state law? Did Republicans in Virginia enjoy exactly the same freedom of speech to attack slavery as citizens of Virginia enjoyed—that is to say none? Obviously, such a cramped reading of article IV had little appeal to Republicans.

In response, leading Republicans insisted on a reading of article IV that not only secured equality but that protected fundamental rights of American citizens. They read article IV to say "the citizens of each state shall be entitled to all privileges and immunities of citizens of the United States in every state." For them, article IV secured absolute rights of American citizens that the state could not deny. It is not possible to show that all Republicans shared this reading. But it is indisputable that leading Republicans in 1866 read the article to protect fundamental national rights that the states could not abridge. Their colleagues did not directly contradict them on this point.

At any rate, the ambiguity was corrected by the final draft of the Fourteenth Amendment. It clearly protected national rights, not simply those under state law. In 1871 Senator Frelinghuysen emphasized that the Fourteenth Amendment protected an absolute body of national privileges from state action. In this respect it was different from the privileges and immunities clause of article IV, section 2 as construed by the courts. According to Frelinghuysen, *"Whatever may have been the intention of the framers of the Constitution,"* the courts had limited article IV, section 2 to protection against discrimination.[12]

Furthermore, it is clear that Republicans thought the Fourteenth Amendment protected freedom of speech and of the press and other basic constitutional rights.[13] Their statements on this question alone are sufficient to dispel the notion that the amendment in general and the privileges or immunities clause in particular protected only the right to equality under state law. Once this fact is recognized, one branch of the argument against application of the Bill of Rights to the states under the amendment collapses. The hypothesis that the amendment was exactly the same as the Civil Rights bill and that the bill only provided for equality in certain rights under state law is simply refuted by the evidence that Republicans thought the amendment protected absolute rights to freedom of speech, to assemble, to bear arms, and to due process that states could not abridge.

In a real sense one can never prove that the amendment was designed to apply the Bill of Rights to the states. One can simply take the hypothesis and see how well it fits the evidence. The hypothesis fits the evidence very well indeed. On the other hand, one can take the contrary hypothesis—that except for due process (without substantive content or the procedural content of the Bill of Rights) the amendment only provided for equality under state law. That hypothesis can be refuted easily and is impossible to reconcile with most of the evidence.

The great controversy is how to take the absence of evidence. One group treats the absence of statements that the Fourteenth Amendment will apply the Bill of Rights to the states as evidence that no such purpose was intended. (For this group, statements that the amendment will require states to obey all rights of citizens of the United States are not good enough.) If Republicans in the state legislatures failed to say anything about the meaning of the amendment, silence is taken as an admission that they did not intend to apply the Bill of Rights to the states. If speakers failed to discuss the meaning of section 1, the omission is treated as proof positive that no intent to apply the Bill of Rights existed. However, many speakers did not mention the due process clause of the amendment. Surely such failure cannot be taken as an acceptable basis for reading the clause out of the amendment.

One way to test the argument that silence precludes the application of the Bill of Rights to the states is to turn it on its head. The failure of Republicans to say that the amendment was not designed to apply the Bill of Rights to the states could be taken as proof that they did intend to so apply it. At first the argument may seem absurd. When one recalls, however, that there was a consensus among Republicans in the campaign of 1866 that the amendment would protect rights of American citizens, and when one recalls that leading Republicans numbered among those rights the right not to be deprived of Bill of Rights liberties by the states, the argument makes at least as much sense as its opposite.

Most Republicans believed that the states were already required to obey the Bill of Rights. They did not accept the positivist notion that the Constitution was merely what the Supreme Court of the moment said it was. For many Republicans, the amendment merely declared constitutional law properly understood. Not a single Republican in the Thirty-ninth Congress said in debate that states were not and should not be required to obey the Bill of Rights. *Barron v. Baltimore* was mentioned only when Republicans urged its repudiation.[14]

The best way to understand the Republican reading of the Thirteenth Amendment and the Civil Rights bill is to recognize that those pieces of legislation reflected the preexisting liberties of American citizens. The Thirteenth Amendment freed the slaves. As a result, Republicans thought, they were made citizens of the United States. As citizens they were protected in the basic rights of American citizens, including protection of Bill of Rights liberties from state infringement. Slavery had deformed the law and diverted it from protections of the citizens' rights. Abolition of slavery was expected to reinvigorate the Constitution as a document protecting basic liberties.

The Civil Rights bill attempted to write this understanding into law. Republicans thought that the freed slaves were citizens. The Civil Rights bill said so. They were entitled to equal protection of state law. The Civil Rights bill said so. Citizens, by Republican understanding, were also entitled to protection of their Bill of Rights liberties from state violation. By vesting blacks with the *full* and equal benefit of *all* (not just state) laws and proceedings for the security of person and of property as enjoyed by white citizens, the Civil Rights bill (according to Republican legal thought) also secured protections of the Bill of Rights to blacks.

Some scholars have relied on Republican statements that the Fourteenth Amendment was already effectively in the Constitution, or already there except for equal protection, to bolster their contention that the amendment was not intended to apply the Bill of Rights to the states.[15] By comparable logic, one might argue that the amendment did not make blacks citizens or did not require the states to accord due process because some Republicans thought the Constitution provided for these things before its amendment.

The main argument scholars have made to prove that the Fourteenth Amendment was not designed to apply the Bill of Rights to the states is that most of its supporters did not say the amendment would apply "the Bill of Rights" to the states, and that some *did* say that the Civil Rights bill contained the same principles as those set out in the amendment.[16] This insistence that supporters of the amendment should use the phrase "Bill of Rights" is curious. When Congressman Bingham used the phrase, these very scholars insist that he did not really mean the amendments to the Constitution but was using the phrase in some technical sense, never heard of before or since. In any case, advocates of section 1 did use phrases that included Bill of Rights liberties. In fact, they used phrases that were more accurate, since the rights of American citizens include, but are not limited to, those in the Bill of Rights.

Both in the Thirty-ninth Congress and in the campaign of 1866 and during ratification, supporters said that the amendment would secure: *all rights* of citizens of the United States;[17] the rights thrown around the citizen by the supreme law of the land;[18] all his rights to every citizen;[19] the privileges conferred on every citizen by the federal Constitution;[20] the full enjoyment of all constitutional rights;[21] every right guarantied by the Constitution;[22] constitutional rights;[23] individual freedom and civil liberty;[24] immunities such as freedom of speech;[25] civil liberty and civil rights;[26] protection of life, liberty, and property;[27] all the rights that the Constitution provides;[28] and the rights of citizens enumerated in the Constitution.[29] In evaluating the meaning of these broad statements, it is important to remember that they referred to constitutional limitations specifically placed on the states in the interest of liberty. Statements such as these have been rejected by some scholars as too broad. However, when Republicans mentioned particular rights in the Bill of Rights, such as freedom of speech, these same critics reject their statements as too narrow.[30]

Today, the idea that the states should be required to obey the Bill of Rights is under attack, an attack advanced in the name of history and the duty of fidelity to the intention of its framers. States, we are told, must be free to experiment.

To ignore or dismiss the argument for freeing the states from the Bill of Rights base misses the point of how the judicial system works. By a widely accepted mythology, we live in a nation where the constitutional rights of the individual are so sacred that they are protected from the power of government, even from the power of the majority. In fact, of course, the rights of the individual are protected only so long as judges hold these rights in high esteem. Shifts in political power produce shifts in judicial personnel. Such shifts regularly change the way the judges interpret the rights of the individual.

Those concerned with the maintenance of liberty have two potential devices at their command to protect individual rights. They may seek to persuade the judges and they may seek to persuade the people. In both cases the question of legitimacy is a crucial one. When the public becomes convinced that an institution, or a rule of law, is illegitimate, the institution or the rule loses much of its power. If a judge becomes convinced that a rule is not legitimate, the rule will be changed, at least if the judge is a justice of a supreme court and if he can convince a majority of his colleagues.

History provides one type of legitimacy. It can teach a decent respect for guaranties of liberty, guaranties that might otherwise be dismissed as unreasonable interferences with the necessary power of government. Many judges and many citizens will not be deflected from their philosophies or agendas by examination of the history of liberty. One can only hope that enough will consider the meaning of history to make a difference or that other criteria of legitimacy will receive sufficient acceptance to provide a basis for bolstering the law as an institution guarantying liberty and justice.

The framers of the Fourteenth Amendment had lived through thirty years of state and federal experiments with the rights in the Bill of Rights. The history of those years shows, as clearly as history shows anything, the need for strict adherence to the rights in the Bill of Rights.

As Justice Black noted in dissent, in *Adamson v. California*:

> I cannot consider the Bill of Rights to be an outworn 18th Century "strait jacket". . . . Its provisions may be thought outdated abstractions by some. And it is true that they were designed to meet ancient evils. But they are the same kind of human evils that have emerged from century to century whenever excessive power is sought by the few at the expense of the many. In my judgment the people of no nation can lose their liberty so long as a Bill of Rights like ours survives and its basic purposes are conscientiously interpreted, enforced and respected.[31]

Notes

Introduction

1 *E.g.*, Barron v. Baltimore, 32 U.S. (7 Pet.) 243 (1833); Livingston v. Moore, 32 U.S. (7 Pet.) 469 (1833).

2 *E.g.*, *compare* United States v. Cruikshank, 92 U.S. (2 Otto) 542 (1876) *and* O'Neil v. Vermont, 144 U.S. 323 (1892) *with* Chicago, Burlington, and Quincy R.R. Co. v. Chicago, 166 U.S. 226 (1897).

3 United States v. Cruikshank, 92 U.S. (2 Otto) 542 (1876).

4 Maxwell v. Dow, 176 U.S. 581 (1900).

5 Twining v. New Jersey, 211 U.S. 78 (1908).

6 *In re* Kemmler, 136 U.S. 436 (1890).

7 *See, e.g.*, cases cited in notes 4, 5, and 6 *supra*.

8 *E.g.*, J. Ely, *Democracy and Distrust* 37, 196 (1980).

9 *E.g.*, Duncan v. Louisiana, 391 U.S. 145 (1968); Benton v. Maryland, 395 U.S. 784 (1969).

10 Friendly, "The Bill of Rights as a Code of Criminal Procedure," 53 Calif. L. Rev. 929, 934–35 (1965).

11 Perry, "Interpretivism, Freedom of Expression, and Equal Protection," 42 Ohio St. L. J. 261, 286 (1981) (hereinafter cited as Perry, "Interpretivism").

12 A. Bickel, *The Least Dangerous Branch* 102 (1962).

13 Adamson v. California, 332 U.S. 46, 68–123 (1947).

14 Grey, "Do We Have an Unwritten Constitution?" 27 Stan. L. Rev. 703, 711–12 (1975).

15 Alfange, "On Judicial Policymaking and Constitutional Change: Another Look at the 'Original Intent' Theory of Constitutional Interpretation," 5 Hastings Const. L. Q. 603, 607 (1978).

16 Berger, "Incorporation of the Bill of Rights in the Fourteenth Amendment: A Nine-Lived Cat," 42 Ohio St. L. J. 435 (1981) (hereinafter cited as Berger, "Incorporation"). For a rebuttal, see Curtis, "Further Adventures of the Nine-Lived Cat: A Response to Mr. Berger on Incorporation

of the Bill of Rights," 43 Ohio St. L. J. 84 (1982) (hereinafter cited as Curtis, "Further Adventures").

17 Kurland, "The Irrelevance of the Constitution: The Religion Clauses of the First Amendment and the Supreme Court," 24 Vill. L. Rev. 3, 9–10 (1978).

18 Denvir, book review, 44 Ohio St. L. J. 139, 140 n.11 (1983) (reviewing M. Perry, *The Constitution, The Courts, and Human Rights* [1982]).

19 *E.g.,* H. Abraham, *Freedom and the Court* 40 (1982); H. Flack, *The Adoption of the Fourteenth Amendment* (1908); H. Hyman and W. Wiecek, *Equal Justice under Law* 386–438 (1982); J. James, *The Framing of the Fourteenth Amendment* (1956); Avins, "Incorporation of the Bill of Rights: The Crosskey-Fairman Debates Revisited," 6 Harv. J. on Legis. 1 (1968) (hereinafter cited as Avins); Crosskey, "Charles Fairman, 'Legislative History,' and the Constitutional Limitations on State Authority," 22 U. Chi. L. Rev. 1 (1954) (hereinafter cited as Crosskey); Curtis, "The Fourteenth Amendment and the Bill of Rights," 14 Conn. L. Rev. 237 (1982) (hereinafter cited as "The Fourteenth Amendment"); Curtis, "Further Adventures," *supra* note 16; Kaczorowski, "Searching for the Intent of the Framers of the Fourteenth Amendment," 5 Conn. L. Rev. 368 (1972) (hereinafter Kaczorowski). *Cf.* H. Graham, *Everyman's Constitution* (1968) (selective incorporation).

20 *E.g.,* Perry, *supra* note 11, at 286.

21 R. Berger, *Government by Judiciary* 413 (1977) (hereinafter cited as *Government by Judiciary*).

22 Crockett v. Sorenson, 568 F. Supp. 1422 (W. D. Va. 1983).

23 Jaffree v. Board of School Commissioners of Mobile County, 554 F. Supp. 1104 (S. D. Ala. 1983), *rev'd* Jaffree v. Wallace, 705 F.2d 1526 (11th Cir. 1983), *cert. denied,* 104 S. Ct. 1707, 80 L.Ed.2d 181 (1984).

24 Jaffree v. Wallace, *supra* note 23.

25 G. Will, "A Labored Ruling on Pornography," *Greensboro Rec.* July 21, 1982, at A-12, col. 3–6.

26 S. 3018, 97th Cong., 2d sess. (1982) (East's bill); *see, N.Y. Times,* Aug. 3, 1985, p. 7, col. 3 (Meese).

27 *See* Jaffree v. Board of School Comm'rs of Mobile County, 104 S. Ct. 1707, 80 L.Ed.2d 181 (1984).

28 *Government by Judiciary, supra* note 21, at 413.

29 The recent trend has been to narrow the scope of the protections of the Bill of Rights. *See, e.g.,* United States v. Salvucci, 448 U.S. 83 (1980), *overruling* Jones v. United States, 362 U.S. 257 (1960); Fisher v. United States, 425 U.S. 391 (1976) (essentially overruling Boyd v. United States, 116 U.S. 616 [1886]); Hudgens v. NLRB, 424 U.S. 507 (1976) (essentially overruling Amalgamated Food Employees Union Local 590 v. Logan Valley Plaza, Inc., 391 U.S. 308 [1968]); Colgrove v. Battin, 413 U.S. 149 (1973); Kastigar v. United States, 406 U.S. 441 (1972) (essentially overruling Counselman v. Hitchcock, 142 U.S. 547 [1892]). *See also* Zurcher v. Stanford Daily, 436 U.S. 547 (1978) (allowing the issue of search warrants, instead of subpoenas, to search newspaper offices for evidence of a crime).

Cf. Paul v. Davis, 424 U.S. 693 (1976) (a citizen mistakenly labeled an active shoplifter by a state government official without notice or opportunity to be heard has no federal right to protection against such conduct although remedy may be available at state law); Members of the City Council of Los Angeles v. Taxpayers for Vincent, 104 S. Ct. 2118, 80 L.Ed.2d 772 (1984); United States v. Leon, 104 S. Ct. 230, 82 L.Ed.2d 677 (1984).

30 Apodaca v. Oregon, 406 U.S. 404, 414 (1972) (Powell, J., concurring). *See* Johnson v. Louisiana, 406 U.S. 356, 366 (1972) (Powell, J., concurring).

31 Crist v. Bretz, 437 U.S. 28, 40 (1978) (Powell, J., dissenting).

32 Buckley v. Valeo, 424 U.S. 1, 291 (1976).

33 Taylor, "Whoever Is Elected, Potential Is Great for Change in High Court's Course," *N.Y. Times*, Oct. 21, 1984, § 1, at 30, col. 6.

34 Monaghan, "Our Perfect Constitution," 56 N.Y.U.L. Rev. 353, 378 (1981).

35 Fairman, "Does the Fourteenth Amendment Incorporate the Bill of Rights?" 2 Stan. L. Rev. 5 (1949) (hereinafter cited as Fairman).

36 332 U.S. 46, 68–123 (Black, J., dissenting).

37 Palko v. Connecticut, 302 U.S. 319 (1937); Twining v. New Jersey, 211 U.S. 78 (1908).

38 Adamson v. California, 332 U.S. at 68–123 (1947).

39 *Id.*

40 *Id.*

41 Fairman, *supra* note 35.

42 *Id.* at 137; Fairman, "A Reply to Professor Crosskey," 22 U. Chi. L. Rev. 144, 155 (1954).

43 Fairman, *supra* note 35, at 134–39.

44 *Id.* at 139.

45 *Id.* at 138.

46 *Id.* at 139.

47 *See, e.g.*, chapter 5 *infra*.

48 *Government by Judiciary*, *supra* note 21.

49 *See, e.g.*, *supra* notes 11, 14.

50 *See generally* Crosskey, *supra* note 19, at 125–43 and notes 146–229 to Chap. 2 *infra*.

51 Fairman, *supra* note 35, at, *e.g.*, 5–34, 81–120, 134, 136–37.

52 *Id.* at, *e.g.*, 81–120.

53 *Id.*; Crosskey, *supra* note 19, at 104.

54 *E.g.*, Cong. Globe, 39th Cong., 1st sess., 1115, 1832 (1866).

55 Dred Scott v. Sandford, 60 U.S. (19 How.) 393 (1857).

56 32 U.S. (7 Pet.) 243 (1833).

57 U.S. Constitution, art. IV, § 2.

58 *See* Cong. Globe, 39th Cong., 1st sess., 430 (Bingham); 1263 (Broomall); 1833, 1835–36 (Lawrence) (1866); 38th Cong., 1st sess. 1202 (Wilson) (1864).

59 *National Party Platforms, 1840–1956*, at 27 (K. Porter and D. Johnson eds. 1956); Cong. Globe, 37th Cong., 2d sess., 1638, 1640 (Bingham) (1862). Both sources indicate that the due process clause banned slavery

in the federal territories because slavery itself was a deprivation of liberty without due process.

60 *See* "The Fourteenth Amendment," *supra* note 19, at 250, 255–56.

61 *E.g.*, Berger, "Incorporation," *supra* note 16, at 440–42, 458.

62 Curtis, "Further Adventures," *supra* note 16 at 104–106.

63 *E.g.*, L. Levy, "The Fourteenth Amendment and the Bill of Rights," L. Levy, ed., *Judgments* 64 (1972) for an analysis of the question, including Fairman's failure to consider the antislavery background; M. Benedict, *A Compromise of Principle* (1974); C. Eaton, *The Freedom of Thought in the Old South* (1940, 1964); D. Fehrenbacher, *The Dred Scott Case* (1978); E. Foner, *Free Soil, Free Labor, Free Men* (1970); J. James, *The Framing of the Four-teenth Amendment* (1956); J. James, *The Ratification of the Fourteenth Amend-ment* (1984); E. McKitrick, *Andrew Johnson and Reconstruction* (1960); T. Morris, *Free Men All* (1974); R. Nye, *Fettered Freedom* (1972); D. Potter, *The Impending Crisis* (1976); R. Sewell, *Ballots for Freedom* (1976); P. Smith, *Trial by Fire* (1982); tenBroek, *Equal under Law* (1965); H. Trefousse, *The Radical Republicans* (1968); W. Wiecek, *The Sources of Antislavery Constitu-tionalism in America, 1760–1848* (1977); Avins, "Incorporation," *supra* note 19; Crosskey, *supra* note 19; Graham, "Our Declaratory Fourteenth Amendment," 7 Stan. L. Rev. 3 (1954); Kaczorowski, *supra* note 19; and the other articles and books cited in the text and notes. For an article that appeared about the same time as my first effort and that led me to look at the Civil Rights bill in a new light, see Soifer, "Protecting Civil Rights: A Critique of Raoul Berger's History," 54 N.Y.U.L. Rev. 651 (1979). My own thinking has been repeatedly stimulated and refreshed by the vigor-ous criticisms of Raoul Berger. For the dialogue, see Berger, "Incorporation of the Bill of Rights: A Reply to Michael Curtis' Response," 44 Ohio St. L. J. 1 (1983) (hereinafter cited as Berger, "A Reply"). The reply was a response to Curtis, "Further Adventures," *supra* note 16, which in turn responded to Berger's "Incorporation," *supra* note 16, which in turn responded to Curtis, "The Bill of Rights as a Limitation on State Authority: A Reply to Professor Berger," 16 Wake Forest L. Rev. 45 (1980) (hereinafter cited as Curtis, "The Bill of Rights"), which in turn responded to R. Berger, *Government by Judiciary* (1977). Finally, the work of Charles Fairman has been a great benefit in clarifying my thinking. That I strongly disagree with Fairman and Berger does not diminish my debt to them. Most of all perhaps my thinking has been influenced by two sources —Crosskey's article and the speeches of Republicans in the *Congressional Globe* and elsewhere. Although my ideas have been shaped or confirmed by others, the limitations in the theory espoused and the mistakes I make are my own responsibility.

On other topics of Fourteenth Amendment interest, see Bickel, "The Original Understanding and the Segregation Decision," 69 Harv. L. Rev. 1 (1955) (hereinafter cited as Bickel); Dimond, "Strict Construction and Judicial Review of Racial Discrimination under the Equal Protection Clause: Meeting Raoul Berger on Interpretivist Grounds," 80 Mich. L. Rev. 462 (1982) (hereinafter cited as Dimond); Frank and Munro, "The

Original Understanding of 'Equal Protection of the Law,'" 50 Colum. L. Rev. 131 (1950) (hereinafter cited as Frank and Munro).

64 Crosskey, *supra* note 19, at 11–21.

65 TenBroek, *Equal under Law* (1965).

66 *See* note 63 *supra*.

67 H. Hyman and W. Wiecek, *Equal Justice under Law: Constitutional Development 1835–75. Cf.* Faber and Muench, "Ideological Origins of the Fourteenth Amendment," 1 Const. Commentaries 235 (1984). For another scholar citing Crosskey with approval, *see* J. Ely, *Democracy and Distrust* (1980).

68 Linde, "Judges, Critics, and the Realist Tradition," 82 Yale L. J. 227, 254 (1972).

69 *Cf. id.* On legitimacy generally, see L. Lusky, *By What Right* (1975).

70 C. Woodward, *American Attitudes toward History* 1–20 (Oxford 1968), reprinted in *Historian as Detective* 24–38 (1981).

71 *See, e.g.,* Perry, *supra* note 11; Brest, "The Misconceived Quest for the Original Understanding," 60 B.U.L. Rev. 204 (1980) (hereinafter cited as Brest).

72 *See, e.g.,* Gillers, book review, 92 Yale L. J. 731 (1983) (reviewing R. Berger, *Death Penalties: The Supreme Court's Obstacle Course* [1982]).

73 *Compare Government by Judiciary, supra* note 21, *with* Perry, *supra* note 11, *and* Brest, *supra* note 71. *See* Lusky, *supra* note 69; Van Alstyne, "Interpreting *This* Constitution: The Unhelpful Contributions of Special Theories of Judicial Review," 35 U. Fla. L. Rev. 209 (1983).

74 *Government by Judiciary, supra* note 21; for very different historical approaches, *see* Bickel, *supra* note 63; Dimond, *supra* note 63; Frank and Munro, *supra* note 63.

75 *Cf.* Brest, *supra* note 71, and Perry, *supra* note 11.

76 C. Miller, *The Supreme Court and the Uses of History* 50 (1969) (hereinafter cited as Miller).

77 Dred Scott v. Sandford, 60 U.S. (19 How.) 393, 426 (1857).

78 D. Fehrenbacher, *The Dred Scott Case* (1978) (hereinafter cited as Fehrenbacher).

79 Miller, *supra* note 76, at 81; B. Schwartz, *The Bill of Rights: A Documentary History* 1030 (1971).

80 *E.g.,* Mapp v. Ohio, 367 U.S. 643, 647 (1961).

81 *See* Maxwell v. Dow, 176 U.S. 581, 601 (1900).

82 *Cf.* United States v. Wong Kim Ark, 169 U.S. 649, 699 (1898).

83 169 U.S. 649 (1898).

84 *Id.* at 699.

85 Maxwell v. Dow, *supra* note 81, at 602.

86 Monaghan, *supra* note 34, at 375.

87 *See* Cong. Globe, 39th Cong., 1st sess., 1010 (Clarke); 282 (Thayer) (1866).

88 *Id.* at 38th Cong., 1st sess., 2978–79 (Farnsworth) (1864).

89 2 *Collected Works of Abraham Lincoln* 405–406 (R. Blaser ed. 1953).

Chapter 1

1 B. Bailyn, *The Ideological Origins of the American Revolution* 27, 34–35, 77–81 (1967) (hereinafter cited as Bailyn).

2 *See id.* at 47–54.

3 *Id.* at 57.

4 B. Schwartz ed., *The Bill of Rights, A Documentary History* 222 (1971) (hereinafter cited as Schwartz).

5 *See id.* at 222–26 (Address to Inhabitants of Quebec), 201–10 (Rights of the Colonists and a List of Infringements and Violations of Rights, 1772), 256–313 (Revolutionary Constitutions and Declarations of Rights), 251–3 (Declaration of Independence); Bailyn, *supra* note 1 at 181–92, 105–108, 74.

6 W. Wiecek, *The Sources of Antislavery Constitutionalism in America, 1760–1848* 76 (1976) (hereinafter cited as Wiecek).

7 U.S. Constitution, Art. IV, § 2, clause 3.

8 Wiecek, *supra* note 6, at 82.

9 *Id.* at 74.

10 *Id.* at 76.

11 Schwartz, *supra* note 4, at 444.

12 *Id.* at 606.

13 *Id.* at 607.

14 *Id.* at 616.

15 *Id.* at 620.

16 *Id.* at 621.

17 *Id.* at 2: 1027.

18 *Id.* at 1030.

19 *Id.* at 1030–31.

20 *Id.* at 1031.

21 32 U.S. (7 Pet.) 243 (1833).

22 *See* Crosskey, "Charles Fairman, 'Legislative History,' and the Constitutional Limitations on State Authority," 22 U. Chi. L. Rev. 1, 125–43 and authorities cited (1954) (hereinafter cited as Crosskey).

23 32 U.S. (7 Pet.) 243, at 249.

24 *See, e.g.,* J. Ely, *Democracy and Distrust* 196 (1980); L. Levy, "The Fourteenth Amendment and the Bill of Rights" in L. Levy, ed., *Judgments* 67 (1972).

25 Fletcher v. Peck, 10 U.S. (6 Cranch) 87, 139 (1816).

26 Fehrenbacher, *The Dred Scott Case* 117 (1978) (hereinafter cited as Fehrenbacher).

27 *Id.* at 120.

28 Livingston v. Moore, 32 U.S. (7 Pet.) 469 at 550–52 (1833).

29 44 U.S. (3 How.) 589 (1845).

30 *Id.* at 609.

31 1 Ga. 243 (1846). *See also* W. Rawle, *A View of the Constitution* 125–56 (1829); Cockrun v. State, 24 Tex. 394 (1859). See J. Featherstone, "The Second Amendment ... Guaranties on Individual Right to Keep and

Bear Arms" in *Report of the Subcommittee on the Constitution of the Committee of the Judiciary 97th Cong. 2d sess.* (1982).

32 Nunn v. Georgia, 1 Ga. 243, 249 (1846).

33 *Id.* at 250.

34 *Id.*

35 Rinehart v. Schuyler, 7 Ill. 473, 522 (1846).

36 Boring v. Williams, 17 Ala. 510, 516 (1850); Noles v. State, 24 Ala. 672, 677, 690 (1854); Colt v. Eves, 12 Conn. 242, 250, 252 (1837); Boyd v. Ellis, 11 Iowa 97, 99 (1860); State v. Barnett, 3 Kans. 250, 251, 253 (1865); State v. Keyes, 8 Vt. 57, 61, 62 (1836); Commonwealth v. Hitchings, 5 Gray (Mass.) 482, 483, 485 (1855); Jones v. Robbins, 8 Gray (Mass.) 329, 346 (1857); State v. Schricker, 29 Mo. 265, 266 (1860); Raleigh & G. R. Co. v. David, 19 N.C. 451, 459 (1837); State v. Newsom, 27 N.C. 250, 251 (1844); State v. Glen, 52 N.C. 321, 331 (1859); State v. Paul, 5 R.I. 185, 187, 196 (1858); State v. Shumpert, 1 S.C. 85, 86 (1868); Woodfolk v. Nashville & C. R. Co., 32 Tenn. 422, 431 (1852); Rhinehart v. Schuyler, 2 Gil. (Ill.) 473, 522 (1845); Campbell v. State, 11 Ga. 353 (1852); Cockrun v. State, 24 Tex. 394 (1859); *cf.* State v. Keith, 63 N.C. 141 (1869). Most of these cases were collected by W. W. Crosskey, *supra* note 19 at 142 n.266.

37 Fehrenbacher, *supra* note 26, at 522.

38 *See id.* at 474.

Chapter 2

1 *See generally* C. Swisher, *American Constitutional Development* 230–348 (2d ed. 1954); J. James, *The Framing of the Fourteenth Amendment* (1956) (hereinafter cited as James).

2 R. Sewell, *Ballots for Freedom* 7 (1976) (hereinafter cited as Sewell); Fehrenbacher, *The Dred Scott Case* 87 (1978) (hereinafter cited as Fehrenbacher).

3 Fehrenbacher, *supra* note 2, at 166–67.

4 *Id.* at 184.

5 *Id.* at 188, 192.

6 *Id.* at 474.

7 *Id.* at 453.

8 *Id.* at 192.

9 2 *Complete Works of Abraham Lincoln* 461 (House Divided Speech) (R. Blaser. ed. 1953) (hereinafter cited as *Works of Lincoln*).

10 E. Foner, *Free Soil, Free Labor, Free Men* 122, 207–209 (1970) (hereinafter cited as Foner).

11 *Id.* at 122.

12 *Id.* at 311.

13 *Id.*

14 *Id.* at 314–15.

15 L. Litwack, *North of Slavery* 93 (1961).

16 *Id.* at 66.

17 *E.g.*, Cong. Globe, 35th Cong., 1st sess., 1964 (Fessenden), 1967 (Wilson) (1858).

18 *Id.* at 1964–65 (Trumbull).
19 Abraham Lincoln, for example. *See Created Equal? The Complete Lincoln-Douglas Debates of 1858*, at 116 (P. Angle ed. 1958) (hereinafter cited as *Created Equal*).
20 3 *Works of Lincoln, supra* note 9, at 500; H. Belz, *Emancipation and Equal Rights* 44 (1978) (hereinafter cited as Belz).
21 *E.g.*, Foner, *supra* note 10, at 263–64.
22 Act of April 19, 1866, 14 Stat. 27.
23 32 U.S. (7 Pet.) 243 (1833).
24 W. Wiecek, *The Sources of Antislavery Constitutionalism in America, 1760–1848*, at 174–77 (1977) (hereinafter cited as Wiecek).
25 *Id.* at 174–75.
26 *Id.* at 175–77.
27 *Id.* Sen. Calhoun's bill was defeated.
28 *Id.* at 179–80.
29 *Id.* at 181–82.
30 C. Eaton, *The Freedom of Thought in the Old South* 118 (1964) (hereinafter cited as Eaton).
31 *Id.* at 127.
32 *Id.*
33 *Id.* at 129.
34 *Id.* at 118–43.
35 R. Nye, *Fettered Freedom* 174–218 (1972) (hereinafter cited as Nye).
36 Eaton, *supra* note 30 at 244. D. Potter, *The Impending Crisis*, 386–87 (1976).
37 Eaton, *supra* note 30 at 245.
38 State v. Worth, 52 N.C. (7 Jones) 488, 492 (1860).
39 Eaton, *supra* note 30, at 199.
40 *Id.* at 209, 211–12.
41 *Id.* at 176–77; Nye, *supra* note 35, at 174–218.
42 Eaton, *supra* note 30, at 176–77; Nye, *supra* note 35, at 174–218.
43 Eaton, *supra* note 30, at 185.
44 *Created Equal, supra* note 19, at 290–91, 300.
45 H. Trefousse, *The Radical Republicans* (1968) (hereinafter cited as Trefousse).
46 Sewell, *supra* note 2, at 284.
47 Fehrenbacher, *supra* note 2, at 193; *Encyclopedia of American History* 218–19 (R. Morris ed. 1953).
48 *Id.*
49 *National Party Platforms 1840–1956*, at 27 (K. Porter and D. Johnson eds. 1956) (hereinafter cited as *Party Platforms*).
50 *Id.* at 28.
51 Cong. Globe, 34th Cong., 1st sess. 122–27 appendix (1856).
52 *Id.*
53 *Id.* at 124.
54 *Id.*
55 *Id.*

56 *Id.*

57 Debates prior to the framing of the Fourteenth Amendment also show
   that Republicans were dissatisfied with state treatment of individual
   liberties. Republican congressmen repeatedly cited denial of individual
   liberty in southern states and elsewhere as a grave political evil. *See* notes
   58–100 *infra.*

58 *Party Platforms, supra* note 49, at 35.

59 M. Benedict, *A Compromise of Principle* 486 (1974) (hereinafter cited as
   Benedict).

60 Belz, *supra* note 20, at 28. *See* Trefousse, *supra* note 45, at 249.

61 *See generally* James, *supra* note 1; E. McKitrick, *Andrew Johnson and Reconstruction* (1960).

62 J. Randall and D. Donald, *The Civil War and Reconstruction* 573–74 (1961);
   K. Stampp, *The Era of Reconstruction* 80 (1965).

63 6 C. Fairman, *History of the Supreme Court of the United States, Reconstruction
   and Reunion (1864–1888),* at 113–14 (1971).

64 James, *supra* note 1, at 21–22 (1956).

65 Fehrenbacher, *supra* note 2, at 511–12.

66 Cong. Globe, 39th Cong., 1st sess., 6–7 (1865).

67 *See, e.g.,* Cong. Globe, 38th Cong., 1st sess., 114 (Arnold), 261 (resolution
   introduced by Smith), 1202 (Wilson), 2102 (Boutwell) (1864).

68 *Biographical Directory of the American Congress* 1549 (1971) (hereinafter
   cited as BDAC).

69 Cong. Globe, 39th Cong., 1st sess., 1013 (1866).

70 *Id.* The Court in Dred Scott v. Sandford, 60 U.S. (19 How.) 393 (1857),
   held that blacks were not citizens of the United States, were not entitled
   to any of the rights, privileges, and immunities of citizens of the United
   States, and were not entitled to sue in federal court. In addition, the
   Court suggested that laws of Congress banning slavery from the territories were unconstitutional. *Id.* at 448–52.

71 Cong. Globe, 39th Cong., 1st sess., 1013 (1866).

72 Benedict, *supra* note 59, at 348–51, especially 350.

73 2 *Works of Lincoln, supra* note 9, at 461, 466–67.

74 1 *Dictionary of American Biography* 368–69 (1927) (hereinafter cited as
   DAB).

75 Benedict, *supra* note 59, at 342, 346.

76 Cong. Globe, 38th Cong., 1st sess., 114 (1864).

77 Benedict, *supra* note 59, at 31.

78 Cong. Globe, 38th Cong., 1st sess., 1202 (1864).

79 *Id.*

80 *Id.*

81 Benedict, *supra* note 59, at 341, 349. 10 DAB, *supra* note 74, at 260–61.

82 Cong. Globe, 38th Cong., 2d sess., 193 (1865).

83 *Id.*

84 *Id.*

85 *Id.*

86 Nye, *supra* note 35, at 117–73.

87 6 DAB, *supra* note 74, at 284–85.

88 Benedict, *supra* note 59, at 342, 345, 350.

89 Cong. Globe, 38th Cong., 1st sess., 2979 (1864).

90 Benedict, *supra* note 59, at 350; Cong. Globe, 38th Cong., 1st sess., 2979 (1864).

91 Cong. Globe, 38th Cong., 1st sess., at 1369 (1864).

92 *See, e.g., id.* at 1313 (Trumbull), 1439 (Harlan), 2615 (Morris). *See also* Cong. Globe, 38th Cong., 2d sess., 138 (Ashley), 237 (Smith) (1865).

93 Eaton, *supra* note 30, at 118, 128–29.

94 Eaton, *supra* note 30, at 199, 209, 211–12. *See* Wiecek, *supra* note 24, at 178; Cong. Globe, 38th Cong., 1st sess., 2979 (Farnsworth) (1864).

95 Nye, *supra* note 35, at 15, 174–218. *See* Eaton, *supra* note 30, at 185.

96 *Created Equal, supra* note 19, at 290–91.

97 T. Morris, *Free Men All* 5–6, 24, 96, 101–102, 104 (1974) (hereinafter cited as Morris).

98 Fugitive Slave Act, ch. 60, §§ 1–10, 9 Stat. 462 (1850).

99 Morris, *supra* note 97, at 146. *See* S. Campbell, *The Slave Catchers*, 26–28 (1970).

100 Fehrenbacher, *supra* note 2 at 44.

101 Morris, *supra* note 97, at 146. Northern personal liberty laws had been seriously crippled by the decision in Prigg v. Pennsylvania, 41 U.S. (16 Pet.) 539 (1842).

102 Morris, *supra* note 97, at 146. The explanation was that more paperwork was required.

103 P. Paludan, *A Covenant with Death* 149 (1975) (hereinafter cited as Paludan).

104 *Id.*

105 M. Krug, *Lyman Trumbull* 207–208 (1965).

106 Belz, *supra* note 20, at 12–13.

107 *See, e.g.*, Cong. Globe, 39th Cong., 1st sess., 728 (Henderson), 1757–58 (Trumbull), 1832–33 (Lawrence), 2904 (Bromwell) (1866).

108 *Id.* at 1072.

109 *Id.* at 304; *see id.* at 237 (Kasson—right of exercising personal conscience is a natural right).

110 *Id.* at 1089 (Bingham), 2904 (Bromwell).

111 *Id.* at 1292 (Bingham); 1832–33 (Lawrence), 99 appendix (Yates).

112 *Id.* at 1088 (Woodbridge), 99 app. (Yates), 257 appendix (Baker). For Republican attachment to federalism, see generally Belz, *supra* note 20; Paludan, *supra* note 103.

113 Cong. Globe, 39th Cong., 1st sess., 1825 (Baldwin), 1839 (Clarke), 144 app. (Loan). *See also* Cong. Globe, 35th Cong., 1st sess., 1964 (1859) (Fessenden). "Why," Sen. Nye asked, "do you not talk about State wrongs?" Cong. Globe, 39th Cong., 1st sess., 2526 (1866).

114 Cong. Globe, 39th Cong., 1st sess., 123, 158 (Bingham), 1781 (Trumbull), 2405 (Ingersoll), 67 appendix (Garfield), 99 appendix (Yates) (1866).

115 32 U.S. (7 Pet.) 243 (1833).

116 60 U.S. (19 How.) 393 (1857).

117 *Id.* at 404–10. *See also* Crosskey, "Charles Fairman, 'Legislative History,'

and the Constitutional Limitations on State Authority," 22 U. Chi. L. Rev. 1, 5–10 (1954) (hereinafter cited as Crosskey). For a brilliant analysis of Dred Scott, see Fehrenbacher, *supra* note 2.

118 Sewell, *supra* note 2, at 49.

119 *Id.* at 50.

120 J. tenBroek, *Equal under Law* 69–71 (1965) (hereinafter cited as tenBroek).

121 Wiecek, *supra* note 24, at 259.

122 J. Tiffany, *A Treatise on the Unconstitutionality of American Slavery* 84–95 (1849) (hereinafter cited as Tiffany).

123 Cong. Globe, 38th Cong., 2d sess., 243 (Woodbridge), 265 (Stevens) (1865); 38th Cong., 1st sess., 1461 (Henderson) (1864). For the minority view that the due process clause prohibited slavery in the states, see Cong. Globe, 38th Cong., 2d sess., 138 (Ashley), 486 (Morris) (1865); 38th Cong., 1st sess., 1479 (Sumner), 2978 (Farnsworth) (1864).

124 Tiffany, *supra* note 122, at 55–57, 84–97.

125 *Id.* at 55.

126 *Id.* at 56.

127 *Id.* at 56.

128 *Id.* at 57–58.

129 *Id.* at 97.

130 *Id.* at 99.

131 *Id.* at 139–40.

132 *Id.* at 56 (emphasis omitted).

133 *Id.* at 97–99.

134 60 U.S. (19 How.) at 403.

135 *Id.* at 449.

136 5 Wiecek, *supra* note 24, at 239; Sewell, *supra* note 2, at 20, 30. Others have noted that these categories can oversimplify reality. *See* Soifer, book review, 67 Geo. L. J. 1281 (1979); M. Dillon, *The Abolitionists*, 144–47 (1974).

137 Sewell, *supra* note 2, at 39.

138 Wiecek, *supra* note 24, at 239.

139 *Id.* at 244.

140 *Id.* at 245; W. Phillips, *The Constitution, A Pro-Slavery Compact* 96–97 (1844, reprinted 1969).

141 Foner, *supra* note 10, at 86; Wiecek, *supra* note 24, at 240.

142 Wiecek, *supra* note 24, at 242.

143 Fehrenbacher, *supra* note 2, at 27.

144 Note 123 *supra*; Foner, *supra* note 10, at 75–87.

145 *Cf., e.g.*, Foner, *supra* note 10, at 302.

146 *See, e.g.*, Cong. Globe, 39th Cong., 1st sess., 574 (Trumbull), 1115 (Wilson), 1832 (Lawrence) (1866).

147 *See generally Party Platforms, supra* note 49, at 27.

148 60 U.S. (19 How.) at 450.

149 *See* note 147 *supra*.

150 Cong. Globe, 37th Cong., 2d sess., 1638 (1862) (Bingham—on abolition in District of Columbia).

151 *Party Platforms, supra* note 49, at 27.

152 *Id.* at 5, 13, 32–33.

153 Fehrenbacher, *supra* note 2, at 122, 476–77.

154 Cong. Globe, 37th Cong., 2d sess., 1638 (1862).

155 *Id.* at 1639.

156 *Id.* at 1640.

157 *See, e.g.,* Cong. Globe, 39th Cong., 1st sess., 430 (Bingham), 1263 (Broomall), 1833, 1835–36 (Lawrence) (1866); 38th Cong., 1st sess., 1202 (1864) (Wilson).

158 60 U.S. (19 How.) at 422–23.

159 *See* notes 170–202 *infra* and accompanying text.

160 32 U.S. (7 Pet.) 243 (1833). *See* notes 170–202 *infra* and accompanying text.

161 Cong. Globe, 39th Cong., 1st sess., 163 (1866).

162 *Id.* at 1478. See Benedict, *supra* note 59, at 350.

163 U.S. Constitution, amend. XIII.

164 Cong. Globe, 39th Cong., 1st sess., 1780 (1866).

165 *Id.* at 513.

166 *Id.* at 602.

167 *Id.* at 475. Trumbull said civil rights included the right to make and enforce contracts, to sue, to give evidence, to acquire property, and to enjoy full and equal benefit of all laws and proceedings for security of person or property.

168 *Id.*

169 *Reprinted in id.* at 1843.

170 *See* Cong. Globe, 39th Cong., 1st sess., 1266 (1866) (Raymond).

171 *Id.* at 1089–90, 2765–66.

172 Cong. Globe, 38th Cong., 1st sess., 1202 (1864).

173 *Id.*

174 *Id.*

175 Cong. Globe, 38th Cong., 2d sess., 193 (1865).

176 Cong. Globe, 38th Cong., 1st sess., 20 (1864).

177 Nye, *supra* note 35, at 144–49.

178 E. Magdol, *Owen Lovejoy, Abolitionist in Congress* 60 (1967).

179 *E.g., id.* at 238.

180 Cong. Globe, 38th Cong., 1st sess., at 114–15, 1197 (1864).

181 *Id.* 1971–72.

182 11 *National Cyclopedia of American Biography* 511 (1909) (hereinafter cited as NCAB); Benedict, *supra* note 59, at 350.

183 Cong. Globe, 38th Cong., 2d sess., 479 (1865). For other Republican complaints about violations of the Bill of Rights in the southern states, see Cong. Globe, 38th Cong., 1st sess., 951 (Baldwin—slavery "organized despotism and defiance of constitutional rights in every community subject to its sway"), 1313 (Trumbull—freedom of speech), 1439 (Harlan — freedom of speech), 2615 (Morris — freedom of speech) (1864). *See* Cong. Globe, 38th Cong., 2d sess., 237 (1865) (Smith). *See also* Cong. Globe, 39th Cong., 1st sess., 167 (Howe), 783

(Ward), 1617 (Moulton), 142 appendix (Wilson) (1866).

184 Cong. Globe, 39th Cong., 1st sess., 340 (1866).

185 *Id.*

186 Benedict, *supra* note 59, at 351.

187 Cong. Globe, 39th Cong., 1st sess., 340 (1866).

188 *Id.* at 67 appendix.

189 7 DAB, *supra* note 74, at 145; Benedict, *supra* note 59, at 351, 354, 358.

190 8 DAB, *supra* note 74, at 54; Benedict, *supra* note 59, at 353.

191 Cong. Globe, 39th Cong., 1st sess., at 1183.

192 *Id.*

193 *Id.* For Henry Wilson's views, see *id.* at 1255.

194 BDAC, *supra* note 68, at 644; Benedict, *supra* note 59, at 351.

195 Cong. Globe, 39th Cong., 1st sess., at 1263 (1866).

196 *Id.* at 1628. BDAC, *supra* note 68, at 1081.

197 Cong. Globe, 39th Cong., 1st sess., 1629 (1866). For Lawrence's views, *see id.* at 1833.

198 *Id.* at 1847.

199 *Id.* at 1837–38.

200 7 DAB, *supra* note 74, at 600.

201 Cong. Globe, 39th Cong., 1st sess., 1072 (1866). Several Republicans, of course, believed a constitutional amendment was required to correct Barron v. Baltimore.

202 Cong. Globe, 39th Cong., 1st sess., 1075 (1866).

203 *Id.* at 5.

204 *Id.* at 111.

205 *Id.* at 207.

206 *Id.* at 263. *See also id.* at 667, 911 (protection of blacks in natural and civil rights).

207 *Id.* at 566 (Brown), 741 (Lane).

208 *Id.* at 868 (Newell).

209 *Id.* at 1032 (McClurg).

210 *Id.* at 1295 (Wilson).

211 *Id.* at 1182 (Pomeroy).

212 *Id.* at 1074. Narrower goals were less frequently mentioned. *See id.* at 111 (Stewart), 508 (Kasson).

213 *See, e.g., id.* at 123 (Bingham), 67 appendix (Garfield). Republican concern for rights in the Bill of Rights was a long-standing concern that had been expressed in party platforms. *See Party Platforms, supra* note 49, at 27–28; Sewell, *supra* note 2, at 284.

214 Cong. Globe, 39th Cong., 1st sess., 155 appendix (1866).

215 20 DAB, *supra* note 74, at 600; Benedict, *supra* note 59, at 303.

216 Cong Globe, 39th Cong., 1st sess., at 99 appendix (1866).

217 *See, e.g., id.* at 783 (Ward), 1072 (Nye), 1183 (Pomeroy), 1262 (Broomall), 1291 (Bingham), 1617 (Moulton–specifically mentioning outrages against Union men and lack of protection for freedom of speech, press, and life, liberty or property), 1629 (Hart), 1837 (Clarke), 67 appendix (Garfield), 142 appendix (Wilson). *See also id.* at 237 (Kasson), 462 (Baker).

218 *Id.* at 566.

219 2 DAB, *supra* note 74, at 105–106.

220 5 DAB, *supra* note 74, at 369–71; Benedict, *supra* note 59, at 351.

221 Cong. Globe, 39th Cong., 1st sess., at 586 (1866).

222 *Id.* at 1032, 2724.

223 Cong. Globe, 39th Cong., 1st sess., 1821 (1866).

224 *Id.* at 1319.

225 *Id.* at 1625.

226 *Id.* at 1627.

227 *Id.* at 337.

228 *Id.* at 436.

229 *Id.* at 494.

Chapter 3

1 Cong. Globe, 39th Cong., 1st sess., 6–7 (1865).

2 *Id.*

3 J. James, *The Framing of the Fourteenth Amendment* 37–54 (1965) (hereinafter cited as James); J. Randall and D. Donald, *The Civil War and Reconstruction* 575 (1961).

4 James, *supra* note 3, at 81; Cong. Globe, 39th Cong., 1st sess., 14 (1865).

5 Cong. Globe, 39th Cong., 1st sess., 77 (1865).

6 *Id.*

7 James, *supra* note 3, at 50.

8 James, *supra* note 3, at 97.

9 *See* B. Kendrick, *The Journal of the Joint Committee of Fifteen on Reconstruction* 61 (1914) (hereinafter cited as Kendrick).

10 Cong. Globe, 39th Cong., 1st sess., 806, 2033, 1095 (1866).

11 James, *supra* note 3, at 97.

12 *Id.* at 99.

13 Kendrick, *supra* note 9, at 106.

14 *Id.*

15 Cong. Globe, 39th Cong., 1st sess., 3042 (Senate), 3149 (House) (1866).

16 Cong. Globe, 39th Cong., 1st sess., at 1 appendix (1866).

17 *Id.* at 1, 5 appendix.

18 2 *Dictionary of American Biography* 277–78 (1927) (hereinafter cited as DAB); *N.Y. Times*, March 10, 1866, at 1, col. 2; M. Benedict, *A Compromise of Principle* 350, 354 (1974) (hereinafter cited as Benedict).

19 *See* Cong. Globe, 34th Cong., 1st sess., 122–27 appendix (1856).

20 James, *supra* note 3, at 81.

21 Cong. Globe, 39th Cong., 1st sess., 157–58 (1866). As this quote indicates, Bingham believed there was an ellipsis implied in the language of article IV, section 2.

22 Cong. Globe, 35th Cong., 2d sess., 974 (1859).

23 R. Sewell, *Ballots for Freedom* 331–32 (1976).

24 Cong. Globe, 35th Cong., 2d sess., 984 (1859).

25 *Id.* at 982.

26 *Id.*

27 *Id.* at 983.

28 *Id.* at 984.

29 *Id.*

30 *Id.* at 983.

31 *Id.; see also* Crosskey, "Charles Fairman, 'Legislative History,' and the Constitutional Limitations on State Authority," 22 U. Chi. L. Rev. 1 (1954) (hereinafter cited as Crosskey).

32 *See, e.g.,* Cong. Globe, 39th Cong., 1st sess., 1089–90, 1292 (1866).

33 *Id.* at 429, 1034.

34 *Id.* at 429.

35 *Id.* at 432.

36 *Id.*

37 *Id.* at 1013 (Plants).

38 *Id.* at 586.

39 James, *supra* note 3, at 82.

40 Kendrick, *supra* note 9, at 61.

41 Cong. Globe, 39th Cong., 1st sess., 813 (1866).

42 *Id.* at 1033–34.

43 Crosskey, *supra* note 31, at 20.

44 *See, e.g.,* notes 157 and 159 in chapter 2 *supra* and accompanying text. For Congressman Lawrence the clause seems both to have protected fundamental rights of all citizens, such as those contained in the due process clause, and to have ensured equality in certain rights with citizens of a state. Cong. Globe, 39th Cong., 1st sess., 1833–35 (1866). For other comments on the clause, *see id.* at 474 (Trumbull), 867 (Newell), 899 (Cook—emphasizing equality of rights of a citizen of one state with citizens of a state to which he goes).

45 For Fessenden's repudiation of Dred Scott, *see* Cong. Globe, 35th Cong., 1st sess., 1964 (1858).

46 Cong. Globe, 39th Cong., 1st sess., 1034 (1866).

47 *Id. See also* Tiffany, *A Treatise on the Unconstitutionality of Slavery* 71 (1849) (hereinafter cited as Tiffany). Tiffany did not accept the positivist view that the law was whatever the Supreme Court said it was. He believed that court decisions were not law, but only evidence of what the law had been held to be on a particular occasion. Tiffany's approach explained why decisions could be corrected when found to be mistaken.

48 65 U.S. (24 How.) 66 (1861).

49 *Id.* at 107–10. In Prigg v. Pennsylvania, 41 U.S. (16 Pet.) 539, 615–16 (1842), the Court held that the fugitive slave clause (also in art. IV, § 2) could be enforced by congressional legislation, but the Court suggested that state officers could not be compelled to enforce the provisions of the clause.

50 E. Foner, *Free Soil, Free Labor, Free Men* 77 (1970).

51 *See* note 157 to chapter 2, *supra.*

52 Cong. Globe, 39th Cong., 1st sess., 430 (1866). The Supreme Court, on several occasions, has referred to the rights in the Bill of Rights as privi-

leges or immunities of citizens. Palko v. Connecticut, 302 U.S. 319, 325–26 (1937); Boyd v. United States, 116 U.S. 616, 618 (1886). The Fourth and Fifth Amendment question raised in *Boyd* was described as "a very grave question of constitutional law, involving the personal security, and privileges and immunities of the citizen." *Id. See also* Shuttlesworth v. Birmingham, 394 U.S. 147, 152 (1969) (use of streets for assembly and free speech "'has, from ancient times, been a part of the privileges, immunities, rights, and liberties of citizens'"). Oddly enough, use of the same phrase by Bingham and his colleagues to refer to the rights in the Bill of Rights has never been considered adequate.

53 1 W. Blackstone, *Commentaries on the Laws of England* *129 (1765) (Asterisk indicates page number in original edition) (hereinafter cited as Blackstone).

54 *Id.*

55 A. Howard, *The Road from Runnymede: Magna Carta and Constitutionalism in America* 412–25 (1968) (hereinafter cited as Howard).

56 *Id.* at 142.

57 *Id.* at 143 (emphasis omitted).

58 *Id.* at 141–43.

59 *Id.* at 174 (emphasis omitted).

60 *Id.* at 175.

61 *Id.* at 179–80, 182.

62 P. Smith, *The Constitution, A Documentary and Narrative History*, 73–74 (1978).

63 75 U.S. (8 Wall.) 168 (1869).

64 Antieau, "Paul's Perverted Privileges or the True Meaning of the Privileges and Immunities Clause of Article Four," 9 Wm. & Mary L. Rev. 1, 5 (1967).

65 *Id.* at 8–15. *Cf.* Conner v. Eliot, 59 U.S. (18 How.) 591 (1856).

66 Conant, "Antimonopoly Tradition under the Ninth and Fourteenth Amendments: Slaughter-House Cases Re-Examined," 31 Emory L. J. 785 (1982).

67 *E.g.*, Conner v. Eliot, 59 U.S. (18 How.) 591 (1856).

68 6 F. Cas. 546 (C.C.E.D. Pa. 1823) (No. 3230).

69 *Id.* at 551–52.

70 Nelson, "The Impact of the Antislavery Movement upon Styles of Judicial Reasoning in Nineteenth Century America," 87 Harv. L. Rev. 513, 552 (1974).

71 *Id.* at 554.

72 307 U.S. 496 (1939).

73 *Id.* at 511.

74 3 Story, *Commentaries on the Constitution of the United States* (1833).

75 C. Fairman, *History of the Supreme Court of the United States, Reconstruction and Reunion (1864–1888)* 334 (1971).

76 60 U.S. (19 How.) 393, 422 (1857).

77 *E.g.*, Cong. Globe, 39th Cong., 1st sess., 1269 (1866).

78 *Id.* at 867, 899.

79 *Id.* at 1057 (1866).

80 *Id.* at 1062–63.

81 6 *National Cyclopedia of American Biography* 140 (1892) (hereinafter cited as NCAB).

82 Benedict, *supra* note 18, at 351.

83 *Biographical Directory of the American Congress* 1115 (1971).

84 Cong. Globe, 39th Cong., 1st sess., 1054 (1866).

85 *Id.* at 1088 (emphasis added).

86 Benedict, *supra* note 18, at 349.

87 Cong. Globe, 39th Cong., 1st sess., 1063–65 (1866).

88 *Id.* at 1063–64.

89 *Id.* at 1064–65.

90 *Id.* at 1064.

91 *Id.*

92 *Id.* at 1065.

93 *Id.*

94 R. Berger, *Government by Judiciary* 153–54, 178 n.47 (1977) (hereinafter cited as *Government by Judiciary*); Fairman, "Does the Fourteenth Amendment Incorporate the Bill of Rights?" 2 Stan. L. Rev. 5, 29–32 (1949) (hereinafter cited as Fairman).

95 *Government by Judiciary, supra* note 94, at 153–54, 178 n.47.

96 Cong. Globe, 39th Cong., 1st sess., 1064–65 (1866).

97 *Id.* at 1065.

98 *Id.* at 1082.

99 *Id.*

100 *Id.* at 1088.

101 *Id.* at 1089.

102 32 U.S. (7 Pet.) 243, 247–48 (1833).

103 32 U.S. (7 Pet.) 469 (1833).

104 Cong. Globe, 39th Cong., 1st sess., 1089–90 (1866).

105 *Id.* at 1090.

106 *Id.* at 1095.

107 *Id.* For similar objections, *see id.* at 1064 (Hale), 1082 (Stewart).

108 *Id.* at 1095.

109 Act. of April 9, 1866, ch. 31, § 1, 14 Stat. 27 (emphasis added), *reprinted* in R. Carr, *Federal Protection of Civil Rights* 211 (appendix 1) (1947).

110 *See Government by Judiciary, supra* note 94, at 150–52, 36, 413. Berger's book was greeted with widespread interest and attention; Fairman, *supra* note 94 at 60–67.

111 Tiffany, *supra* note 47 at 99. *Cf.* Soifer, "Protecting Civil Rights: A Critique of Raoul Berger's History," 54 N.Y.U.L. Rev. 651, 684 (1979).

112 60 U.S. (19 How.) at 449–50.

113 *Id.* at 450.

114 116 U.S. 616 (1886).

115 *Id.* at 635.

116 Cong. Globe, 39th Cong., 1st sess., 654, 743, 1292 (1866) (Bingham's speech sets out the pertinent portion of the text of the Freedman's Bureau

bill) (emphasis added). The phrase "including the constitutional right of bearing arms" had been added by an amendment that Trumbull said did not change the meaning of the section.

117 *See, e.g.*, notes 170–202, chapter 2 *supra* and accompanying text.

118 *See* notes 163–70 to chapter 2, *supra* and accompanying text. *See also* Cong. Globe, 39th Cong., 1st sess., 1266 (1866) (Raymond). Congressman Raymond proposed to make blacks citizens "and thus secure to them whatever rights, immunities, privileges, and powers belong as of right to all citizens of the United States." *Id.* If blacks were made citizens, Raymond said, they would have the right of free passage from one state to another, the right to testify in federal courts, and the right to bear arms. *Id.*

119 Cong. Globe, 39th Cong., 1st sess., 1291 (1866). *See also id.* at 1294 (Wilson).

120 Benedict, *supra* note 18, at 33.

121 19 DAB *supra* note 18, at 19.

122 Benedict, *supra* note 18, at 353, 360.

123 Cong. Globe, 39th Cong., 1st sess., 574 (1866).

124 *Id.* at 599.

125 *Id.* (emphasis added).

126 *Id.* at 600.

127 *Id.* at 1760 (emphasis added).

128 *Id.* at 1757.

129 *Id.*

130 *Id.* at 475.

131 *Id.* at 474–75.

132 6 F. Cas. 546 (C.C.E.D. Pa. 1823) (No. 3230).

133 *Id.* at 551.

134 *Id.* at 551–52. Particular privileges mentioned by Washington (a list he said was not exclusive) included the right to pass through and reside in a state, to institute court actions, to hold and dispose of property, and to enjoy the benefits of the writ of habeas corpus. These and many others that might be mentioned, Washington said, were privileges and immunities. *Id.* at 552.

135 20 DAB, *supra* note 18, at 332.

136 Benedict, *supra* note 18, at 351, 31.

137 Cong. Globe, 39th Cong., 1st sess., 1118 (1866) (emphasis added).

138 *Id.*

139 *Id.* at 1118–19 (emphasis added).

140 *Id.* at 1118.

141 W. Blackstone, *supra* note 53 at *123. (Asterisk indicates pages of original edition.)

142 *Id.* at *123–24; *127–28.

143 B. Schwartz, *The Bill of Rights* 17–19, 20–21 (1971) (hereinafter cited as Schwartz).

144 *Id.* at 40–41, 42–43.

145 Blackstone, *supra* note 53, at *125–29. My law partner Charles Lloyd

directed my attention to Blackstone's use of *privileges* and *immunities*.

146 11 DAB, *supra* note 18, at 52; Benedict, *supra* note 18, at 350.

147 Cong. Globe, 39th Cong., 1st sess., 1832 (1866).

148 *Id.* at 1835.

149 *Id.* at 1832–33.

150 *Id.* at 1833.

151 *Id.*

152 *Id.* at 1835.

153 *Id.* at 1836.

154 *Id.* at 1293.

155 *Id. See id.* at 1064.

156 Supreme Court Proceedings, "In Memoriam, Morrison R. Waite," 126 U.S. 585, 599–600 (1888).

157 10 NCAB, *supra* note 81, at 148; Benedict, *supra* note 18, at 350. For a fine discussion of the Civil Rights bill debates *see* Crosskey, *supra* note 31, at 44–50.

158 Cong. Globe, 39th Cong., 1st sess., 1152 (1866).

159 *Id.* at 1151.

160 *Id.* at 1152.

161 *Id.* at 1151.

162 *Id.*

163 *Id.*

164 *Id.* at 1153.

165 *Id.* at 1270.

166 *Id.* at 1294.

167 *Id.* at 1292 (Bingham), 1294 (Wilson).

168 *Id.* at 1294.

169 *Id.*

170 14 U.S. (16 Pet.) 539 (1842).

171 *Id.*

172 Tiffany, *supra* note 47, at 99–100.

173 Cong. Globe, 39th Cong., 1st sess., 1294 (1866). Other Congressmen apparently followed Wilson's analogy. *See id.* at 1153, 1270 (Lawrence), 1833 (Thayer). For a contrary reading, see Berger, "Incorporation of the Bill of Rights in the Fourteenth Amendment: A Nine-Lived Cat," 42 Ohio St. L. J. 435, 453–56 (1981) (hereinafter cited as Berger, "Incorporation").

174 *See* Cong. Globe, 39th Cong., 1st sess., 2081 (1866). Nicholson suggested that states should be free to impose harsher penalties on blacks because of their "brutal, sensual nature." and warned that "the negro's idea of freedom is to do nothing but bask in the sunshine."

175 *Id.* at 1260. For Democratic views, *see id.* at 1122–23, 1156 (Thirteenth Amendment), 1270 (Kerr—Bill of Rights), 3212 (Niblack—privileges and immunities). *But see id.* at 530, 766 (Johnson), 1157 (Thornton).

176 Cong. Globe, 39th Cong., 1st sess., 1122–23, 1156 (1866).

177 *Id.* at 1269.

178 *Id.* at 1270.

179 *Id.* at 1291.

180 *Id.*

181 *Id.*

182 *Id.* at 1292.

183 *Id.* at 1291.

184 *Id.*

185 *Id.* at 1367 (Bingham voting against passage).

186 *Id.* at 1294.

187 *Id.*

188 *Id.* at 1366.

189 *See, e.g., id.* at 99 appendix, 2765–66, 1072; *see* 42d Cong., 2d sess., 843.

190 Cong. Globe, 39th Cong., 1st sess., at 1115.

191 *Id.* at 1072.

192 *Id.* at 866.

193 *Id.* at 1468 (Hill); 38th Cong., 2d sess., 142 (1865) (Orth); 38th Cong., 1st sess., 2615 (1864) (Morris).

194 *See, e.g.,* Cong. Globe, 39th Cong., 1st sess., 1120, 1270 (1866).

195 Kendrick, *supra* note 9, at 83.

196 *Id.* at 87.

197 *Id.* at 98; for an attempt to make sense out of the shifting votes in the committee, *see* Maltz, "The Fourteenth Amendment as a Political Compromise—Section One in the Joint Committee on Reconstruction," 45 Ohio St. L. J. 933 (1985).

198 Berger, "Incorporation," *supra* note 173 at 454.

199 Kendrick, *supra* note 9, at 83, 85.

200 *Id.* at 87.

201 Cong. Globe, 39th Cong., 1st sess., 2265 (1866); Howard, *supra* note 66, at 335; Howe, "The Meaning of 'Due Process of Law' Prior to the Adoption of the Fourteenth Amendment," 18 Cal. L. Rev. 583 (1930).

202 Cong. Globe, 39th Cong., 1st sess., 2265, 2286 (1866).

203 *Id.* at 2286.

204 Benedict, *supra* note 18, at 351.

205 17 DAB, *supra* note 18, at 622.

206 Cong. Globe, 39th Cong., 1st sess., 2459 (1866). Rep. Garfield was "glad to see this first section here which proposes to hold over every American citizen without regard to color, the protecting shield of law." Garfield thought that the amendment put the Civil Rights bill beyond partisan strife, which it undoubtedly did. He believed that the bill was constitutional even without the amendment. *Id.* at 2462.

207 *Id.* at 2459.

208 *Id.* at 2465.

209 *Id.* at 1151–53. *See also id.* at 1833 (Lawrence).

210 *Id.* at 1152.

211 *Id.* at 2498 (Broomall), 2511 (Eliot). Congressman Broomall said the Fourteenth Amendment gave "power to the Government of the United States to protect its own citizens within the States, within its own jurisdiction." *Id.* at 2498.

212 *See, e.g., id.* at 2883 (Latham), 3069 (Van Aernam). Latham treated § 1

as meaning that no state could discriminate on account of race or color with respect to the civil rights of its citizens. And he said that as long as civil rights did not include political rights, the section "probably includes nothing more than the Constitution originally intended." *Id.* at 2883. Either Latham was reading the due process clause out of the amendment, or he thought the Constitution was originally intended to apply the clause to the states contrary to the conclusion reached in Barron v. Baltimore.

213 *Id.* at 2468 (Kelley), 2539 (Farnsworth).

214 *Id.* at 2542.

215 *Id.*

216 *Id.* Cruel and unusual punishments, of course, violate the Eighth Amendment, one of the guaranties in the Bill of Rights.

217 *See id.* at 2764–70.

218 9 DAB, *supra* note 18, at 278; Benedict, *supra* note 18, at 38.

219 Cong. Globe, 39th Cong., 1st sess., 2765 (1866).

220 *Id.* at 2765–66. For news accounts of Howard's speech, *see, e.g., N.Y. Times*, May 24, 1866, at 1, col. 5–6; *Philadelphia Inquirer*, May 24, 1866, at 8, col. 2.

221 Cong. Globe, 39th Cong., 1st sess., 2768, 2890 (1866).

222 *Id.* at 3031.

223 Fairman, "Does the Fourteenth Amendment Incorporate the Bill of Rights?" 2 Stan L. Rev. 5, 63 (1949).

224 Schwartz, *supra* note 143, at 840. The first quotation is from the preface to the resolution for a bill of rights introduced in the Virginia convention called to ratify the federal Constitution. Virginia considered civil and criminal juries as among the essential and inalienable rights of the people. *Id.* at 841. The second quotation is from James Madison speaking in Congress on behalf of the Bill of Rights. He was referring specifically to trial by jury. *Id.* at 1029.

225 20 DAB, *supra* note 18, at 599–600; Benedict, *supra* note 18, at 353.

226 Cong. Globe, 39th Cong., 1st sess., 3038 (1866). In fact, under *Dred Scott* the rights in the Bill of Rights were rights of citizens of the United States only and did not extend to blacks who could be citizens of a state but not of the United States. 2 W. Crosskey, *Politics and the Constitution* 1089–95 (1953).

227 Cong. Globe, 39th Cong., 1st sess., 3167 (1866). *See generally* E. McKitrick, *Andrew Johnson and Reconstruction* (1960).

228 Cong. Globe, 39th Cong., 1st sess., 3167 (1866).

229 *Id.* at 3201.

230 *Id.* at 210 appendix. *See also id.* at 227 appendix (Defrees).

231 *Id.* at 2510.

232 *Id.* at 2964.

233 *Id.* at 3242.

234 *Id.* at 2961 (emphasis added).

235 *Id.* at 255–56 appendix.

236 *Id.*

Chapter 4

1 Fairman, "Does the Fourteenth Amendment Incorporate the Bill of Rights?" 2 Stan. L. Rev. 5 (1949). For a reply to which I am indebted throughout this chapter and elsewhere, *see* Crosskey, "Charles Fairman, 'Legislative History,' and the Constitutional Limitations on State Authority," 22 U. Chi. L. Rev. 1 (1954) (hereinafter cited as Crosskey).

2 Adamson v. California, 332 U.S. 46, 71 (1947) (Black, J., dissenting).

3 Fairman, *supra* note 1, at 134.

4 Duncan v. Louisiana, 391 U.S. 145 at 510 (Harlan, J., dissenting).

5 *E.g.*, Grey, "Do We Have an Unwritten Constitution?" 27 Stan. L. Rev. 703, 711–12 (1975).

6 J. tenBroek, *The Antislavery Origins of the Fourteenth Amendment* (1951); Graham, "Our Declaratory Fourteenth Amendment," 7 Stan. L. Rev. 3 (1954); Graham, "The Early Antislavery Backgrounds of the Fourteenth Amendment" (1950), Wisc. L. Rev. 479.

7 Fairman, *supra* note 1, at 11–12.

8 *Id.* at 12.

9 *Id.* at 42–50, 72–73.

10 *Id.* at 15–16.

11 C. Fairman, VI *History of the Supreme Court of the United States: Reconstruction and Reunion 1886–88* Part One 335 (1971).

12 Fairman, *supra* note 1, at 17.

13 *Id.* at 22.

14 *Id.* at 25–26.

15 *Id.* at 25.

16 *Id.*

17 *Id.* at 25.

18 *Id.* at 26.

19 *Id.* at 26.

20 *Id.* at 27–28.

21 *Id.* at 29 (Kelly), 29–32 (Bingham and Hale). Fairman's claim that Bingham believed that "the bill of rights" had been part of the Constitution since 1789 (used once again to suggest that Bingham was not talking about *the* Bill of Rights) is in error. Bingham actually said that the word *property* had been in the Bill of Rights since 1789, a correct statement since the Bill of Rights was proposed by Congress in that year. *Id.* at 30–31.

22 *Id.* at 32.

23 *Id.* at 33.

24 *Id.* at 33.

25 *Id.* at 33–34.

26 *Id.* at 35–36.

27 *Id.* at 38.

28 *Id.*

29 Cong. Globe, 39th Cong., 1st sess., 1294 (Wilson); *see also* 1835–36 (Lawrence) and 474 (Trumbull).

30 Fairman, *supra* note 1, at 39.
31 *Id.*
32 *Id.*
33 *Id.* at 40.
34 *Id.* at 41.
35 *Id.* at 42.
36 *Id.* at 43.
37 *Id.* at 44.
38 *Id.* at 45.
39 *Id.* at 46.
40 *Id.* at 44.
41 *Id.* at 45. See Cong. Globe, 39th Cong., 1st sess., 432, 813, 816 (prototypes); see 430 (1866).
42 Fairman, *supra* note 1, at 47.
43 *Id.* at 29 (Hale), 47 (Raymond), 50 (Farnsworth), 61 (Poland), 64 (Johnson).
44 *Id.* at 50–51.
45 *Id.* at 51–55.
46 *Id.* at 58.
47 *Id.* at 63.
48 *Id.*
49 *Id.* at 65.
50 *Id.* at 74.
51 *Id.*
52 *Id.* at 75–76.
53 *Id.*
54 *Id.* at 77.
55 *Id.* at 97.
56 *Id.* at 139.
57 *Id.*
58 *Id.* at 26–27.
59 *Id.* at 25–26, 32 (Bingham), *cf.* 17 (Trumbull), 39 (Thayer) "an easy target."
60 Cong. Globe, 39th Cong., 1st sess., 1064 (1866); *see* Crosskey, *supra* note 1, at 30–33.
61 Cong. Globe, 39th Cong., 1st sess., at 1089.
62 *Compare id.* at 1089 with 1095.
63 Fairman, *supra* note 1, at 27.
64 Cong. Globe, 39th Cong., 1st sess., 1090 (1866).
65 *Id.*
66 *Id.*
67 *Id.*
68 *Id.*
69 *Id.*
70 *Id.*
71 *Id.* at 1065.
72 *Id.* at 1089.
73 *Id.* at 1294.

74 *Id.* at 2883.

75 *Id.* at 2459.

76 *E.g., id.* at 3069 (principles of Civil Rights bill protected by the amendment), 2498 (power to pass bill given by amendment); 2545 (Bingham on need for amendment to give power to pass bill).

77 *Id.* at 2883.

78 *Id.* at 1266 (Raymond), 1153 (Thayer).

79 *Id.* at *e.g.,* 340 (Cowan), 1183 (Garfield), 1263 (Broomall), 1629 (Hart), 1838 (Clarke), 1072 (Nye).

80 *Id.* at 1153.

81 *See* note 79 *supra.*

82 Cong. Globe, 39th Cong., 1st sess., 654, 743, 1292 (1866).

83 *Id.* at 743.

84 *See* note 79 *supra.*

85 60 U.S. (19 How.) 393 (1857).

86 *Id.* at 404–409.

87 Notes 82 and 83 *supra.*

88 *See* chapter 5 *infra.*

89 Fairman, *supra* note 1, at 137.

90 Fairman, "A Reply to Professor Crosskey," 22 U. Chi. L. Rev. 144, 155 (1954).

91 *See generally,* T. Morris, *Free Men All,* at chapters 10–12 (1974) (hereinafter cited as Morris).

92 *Id.* at 77–78. *See also id.* at 90–92, 137–38.

93 *Id.* at 8–9, 77.

94 *Id.* at 74.

95 *Id.* at 71–93.

96 41 U.S. (16 Pet.) 539 (1842).

97 *Id.* at 622.

98 S. Campbell, *The Slave Catchers,* at 32–46 (1968). For discussions of the Fugitive Slave Act, chapter 60, §§ 1–10, 9 Stat. 462 (1850), *see* Morris, *supra* note 91, at 130–47. *See also* Campbell, *supra,* at 3–48.

99 Morris, *supra* note 91, at 78.

100 *Id.*

101 *Id.* at 137.

102 *Id.* at 138.

103 Cong. Globe, 38th Cong., 1st sess., 2919 (1864) (Morris). At least some southern states had denied slaves the right to trial by jury. *See* State v. Dick, 4 La. Ann. 182 (1849); Avins, "Incorporation of the Bill of Rights: The Crosskey-Fairman Debates Revisited," 6 Harv. J. Legis. 1 (1968).

104 II *Legal Papers of John Adams* 200–201, 207 (L. Wroth and H. Zobel eds. 1965). D. Fehrenbacher, *The Dred Scott Case* 122 (1978).

105 A. Howard, *The Road from Runnymede* 341 (1968).

106 Fairman, *supra* note 1, at 59.

107 *National Party Platforms* 27, 32–33 (D. Johnson ed. 1956). *See* Cong. Globe, 37th Cong., 2d sess., 1638–39 (1862).

108 Cong. Globe, 39th Cong., 1st sess., 1090 (1866).

109 *Id.* at 1115, 1294.

110 *Id.* at 1291–92.

111 C. Fairman, *Reconstruction and Reunion* (6 *History of the Supreme Court of the United States* [1971]) (hereinafter cited as Fairman, *Reconstruction*) at 1141, 1129.

112 Cong. Globe, 38th Cong., 1st sess., 1202 (Wilson) (1864).

113 *Id.* at 39th Cong., 1st sess., 430, 1034 (Bingham).

114 Fairman, *Reconstruction, supra* note 111, at 1156.

115 *Id.* at 1157.

116 Cong. Globe, 39th Cong., 1st sess., 1118–19, 1294 (Wilson), 1153, 1270 (Thayer), 1291 (Bingham).

117 Fairman, *Reconstruction, supra* note 111, at 1159.

118 *Id.* at 1286.

119 *Id.* at 1124–25.

120 *Id.* at 1277.

121 *Id.* at 461, 462.

122 *Id.* at 1288–1289.

123 *Id.* at 1291.

124 TenBroek, *Equal under Law* 214 (1965; original ed. 1951) (hereinafter cited as tenBroek).

125 Cong. Globe, 42d Cong., 1st sess., appendix 84 (1871).

126 TenBroek, *supra* note 124, at 238.

127 *Id.* at 239.

128 *E.g.,* Cong. Globe, 39th Cong., 1st sess., 340, appendix 67, 1183, 1628–29, 1072, 654, 743, 1292, 1266, 1294.

129 Graham, "Our Declaratory Fourteenth Amendment," 7 Stan. L. Rev. 3 (1954) (hereinafter cited as Graham).

130 *Id.* at 19 n.80.

131 Cong. Globe, 39th Cong., 1st sess., 2765–66 (1866). Emphasis added.

132 Graham, *supra* note 129, at 18 n.80; note 131 *supra.*

133 Graham, *supra* note 129.

134 Friendly, "The Bill of Rights as a Code of Criminal Procedure," 53 Cal. L. Rev. 929, 934–35 (1965).

135 *Id.*

136 *E.g.,* see notes 183–202, chapter 2 *supra.*

137 M. Conant, "Antimonopoly Tradition under the Ninth and Fourteenth Amendments: Slaughter-House Cases Re-Examined," 31 Emory L. J. 785, 817 (1982).

138 Cong. Globe, 39th Cong., 1st sess., 2765–66 (1866).

139 Berger, "Incorporation of the Bill of Rights in the Fourteenth Amendment: A Nine-Lived Cat," 42 Ohio St. L. J. 435 (1981) (hereinafter cited as Berger, "Incorporation").

140 In addition to Crosskey, "Charles Fairman, 'Legislative History,' and the Constitutional Limitations on State Authority," 22 U. Chi. L. Rev. 1 (1954) (hereinafter cited as Crosskey), *see, e.g.,* H. Abraham, *Freedom and the Court* 45–46 (1977); I. Brant, *The Bill of Rights* 302–59 (1967); H. Flack, *The Adoption of the Fourteenth Amendment* (1908); J. James, *The Framing of*

the Fourteenth Amendment 85, 130 (1965); H. Hyman and W. Wiecek, *Equal Justice under Law, Constitutional Development 1835–1875*, chapter 11 (1982). For balanced appraisal of Crosskey's work, *see* C. Pritchett, *The American Constitution* 376–82 (1959). *See also* C. Swisher, *American Constitutional Development* 329–34 (1954). For an article (which I initially overlooked) rejecting Fairman's analysis, see Avins, "Incorporation of the Bill of Rights: The Crosskey-Fairman Debates Revisited," 6 Harv. J. Legis. 1 (1968). For another article rejecting Fairman's analysis, see Kaczorowski, "Searching for the Intent of the Framers of the Fourteenth Amendment," 5 Conn. L. Rev. 368 (1972). Citation of these articles does not, of course, indicate agreement with every assertion made in them.

141 Fairman, "Does the Fourteenth Amendment Incorporate the Bill of Rights?" 2 Stan. L. Rev. 5 (1949) (hereinafter cited as Fairman).

142 Berger, "Incorporation," *supra* note 139.

143 Fairman, *supra* note 141.

144 *See* chapter 2, *supra*.

145 *Id.*

146 Berger, "Incorporation," *supra* note 139, at 441–42. *See*, Fairman, *Reconstruction, supra* note 111, at 335.

147 Berger, *Government by Judiciary*, at 39 *passim* (1977) (hereinafter cited as *Government by Judiciary*).

148 *Government by Judiciary, supra* note 147, at 40; Dred Scott v. Sandford, 60 U.S. (19 How.) 393, 422 (1857).

149 *Government by Judiciary, supra* note 147, at 40.

150 *Id.* at 39–40.

151 Barron v. Baltimore, 32 U.S. (7 Pet.) 243, 247 (1833).

152 6 F. Cas. (No. 3230) 546 (C.C.E.D. Pa. 1823).

153 *Government by Judiciary, supra* note 147, at 22, 36, 41, 43.

154 *See id.* Soifer has come, independently, to some remarkably similar conclusions as to Berger's treatment of the privileges and immunities question. "Protecting Civil Rights: A Critique of Raoul Berger's History," 54 N.Y. U. L. Rev. 651 (1979). His article is not directed at the question of incorporation of the Bill of Rights as a limit on the states.

155 *Government by Judiciary, supra* note 147, at 42, citing Cong. Globe, 39th Cong., 1st sess., 1757 (1866) (emphasis added).

156 6 F. Cas. at 551.

157 *Id.* at 551–52.

158 *Id.* at 551.

159 *Id.* at 551–52.

160 Fairman, *Reconstruction, supra* note 111, at 1121.

161 *Government by Judiciary, supra* note 147, at 38.

162 Cong. Globe, 38th Cong., 2d sess., 193 (1865); *see also* Cong. Globe, 39th Cong., 1st sess., 1263 (1866) (Broomall)—specifically citing rights of speech, petition, due process, and the right to be free from illegal arrest. Howard may not have accepted this view. *See* notes 74–92, chapter 2 *supra*.

163 *Government by Judiciary, supra* note 147, at 38.

164 *Compare id.* at 38 with *id.* at 148.
165 Cong. Globe, 39th Cong., 1st sess., 158, 1117, 1757, 1833 (1866). For the orthodox judicial view *see* Dred Scott v. Sandford, 60 U.S. (19 How.) 393, 422–23 (1857).
166 Cong. Globe, 39th Cong., 1st sess., 1757 (1866).
167 Corfield v. Coryell, 6 F. Cas. 546, 551 (C.C.E.D. Pa. 1823) (No. 3,230).
168 Cong. Globe, 39th Cong., 1st sess., at 2765–66.
169 *See Government by Judiciary, supra* note 147, at 41–42, 44.
170 *Id.* at 45. If Mr. Berger believes that an unorthodox reading of the clause was relied on by Republicans, then citations suggesting that the privileges or immunities clause of the amendment was absolutely identical to art. IV, § 2, are clearly beside the point.
171 *See, e.g.,* Cong. Globe, 39th Cong., 1st sess., 1833 (1866).
172 *See* Berger, "Incorporation," *supra* note 139, at 442, 455.
173 *Id.* at 442–43 (emphasis in original).
174 Cong. Globe, 42d Cong., 1st sess., 577 (1871).
175 *Government by Judiciary, supra* note 147, at 49–50.
176 *Id.* at 51.
177 *Id.* at 49–51.
178 Berger, "Incorporation," *supra* note 139, at 442.
179 *Id.*
180 Cong. Globe, 39th Cong., 1st sess., 599 (1866).
181 *Id.* at 1757.
182 *Id.* at 475.
183 *Id.* at 1760 (emphasis added).
184 Fairman, *supra* note 1, at 134–35, 138.
185 *Id.* at *e.g.* 44, 77.
186 *Id.* at 134–39.
187 *Government by Judiciary, supra* note 147, at 205.
188 *Id.* at 233.
189 *Government by Judiciary, supra* note 147, at 182 n.65.
190 *Id.* at 233.
191 Cong. Globe, 39th Cong., 1st sess., 1837 (1866).
192 Berger, "Incorporation of the Bill of Rights: A Reply to Michael Curtis' Response," 44 Ohio St. L. J. 1, 3 (1983) (hereinafter cited as Berger, "A Reply").
193 Cong. Globe, 39th Cong., 1st sess., 1837 (1866).
194 Berger, "A Reply," *supra* note 192, at 4.
195 *Id.* at 5.
196 Cong. Globe, 39th Cong., 1st sess., 1118, 1747, 2565–66.
197 *Id.* at 1757.
198 *Id.* at 1118.
199 *Id.* at 1117.
200 *Id.* at 157–58.
201 *Id.* at 1833.
202 *Id.* at 2765–66.
203 *E.g., id.* at 2542.

204 Curtis, "The Fourteenth Amendment and The Bill of Rights," 14 Conn. L. Rev. 237, 242–46 (1982).

205 *E.g.*, Cong. Globe, 39th Cong., 1st sess., 1153, 1270 (Thayer) (1866).

206 *Government by Judiciary, supra* note 147, at 136–37.

207 *Id.* at 137.

208 *Id.* at 145.

209 *Id.* at 219.

210 Berger, "Incorporation," *supra* note 139, at 445.

211 *Id.* at 452.

212 *N.Y. Times*, March 10, 1866, at 1, col. 2. The following is a brief biography of Bingham prepared for Congress: "BINGHAM, John Armor, a representative from Ohio; born in Mercer, Mercer County, Pa., January 21, 1815; pursued academic studies; apprentice in a printing office for two years; attended Franklin College, Ohio; studied law; was admitted to the bar in 1840 and commenced practice in New Philadelphia, Tuscarawas County, Ohio; district attorney for Tuscarawas County, Ohio, 1846–1849; elected as a Republican to the Thirty-fourth and to the three succeeding Congresses (March 4, 1855–March 3, 1863); unsuccessful candidate for reelection in 1862 to the Thirty-eighth Congress; appointed by President Lincoln as judge advocate of the Union Army with the rank of major in 1864; later appointed solicitor of the court of claims; special judge advocate in the trial of the conspirators against the life of President Lincoln; elected to the Thirty-ninth and to the three succeeding Congresses (March 4, 1865–March 3, 1873); unsuccessful candidate for renomination in 1872; one of the managers appointed by the House of Representatives in 1862 to conduct the impeachment proceedings against West H. Humphreys, United States judge for the several districts of Tennessee, and in 1868 in the proceedings against Andrew Johnson, President of the United States; appointed Minister to Japan and served from May 31, 1873, until July 2, 1885; died in Cadiz, Harrison County, Ohio, March 19, 1900; interment in Cadiz Cemetery." *Biographical Directory of the American Congress 1774–1971*, 92d Cong., 1st sess. (1971).

213 J. James, *The Framing of the Fourteenth Amendment* 86 (1965) (hereinafter cited as James).

214 *Reconstruction and Reunion, supra* note 111, at 461.

215 *Id.*

216 *Id.* at 1289.

217 *Government by Judiciary, supra* note 147, at 143.

218 *Id.*

219 *Id.*

220 *Id.* at 143–44.

221 Cong. Globe, 39th Cong., 1st sess., 1034 (1866).

222 *Id.* at 1089.

223 *Compare* Cong. Globe, 38th Cong., 1st sess., 1202 (1864) with *id.* at 39th Cong., 1st sess., 1294 (Wilson); *id.* at 1153, 1270 (Thayer).

224 Berger, "Incorporation," *supra* note 139, at 450.

225 *Id.*

226 As Bingham understood art. IV, § 2, it meant that "the citizens of each
State (being ipso facto citizens of the United States) shall be entitled to all
privileges and immunities (supplying the ellipsis 'of the United States') in
the several States." Cong. Globe, 39th Cong., 1st sess., 158 (1866). *See*
note 68 *supra.*

227 *Id.* at 1089.

228 *Id.* at 158.

229 Berger, "Incorporation," *supra* note 139, at 450.

230 *Id.*

231 *Government by Judiciary, supra* note 9, at 143−44.

232 *See* Cong. Globe, 39th Cong., 1st sess., 1089−90 (1866).

233 *Id.* at 1034.

234 *Government by Judiciary, supra* note 147, at 143−44.

235 Berger, "Incorporation," *supra* note 139, at 451.

236 Cong. Globe, 39th Cong., 1st sess., 1292 (1866) (emphasis added).

237 *See* Berger, "Incorporation," *supra* note 139, at 463. I do not believe that
Berger "'edited' and omitted in order to make a case." *Id.* However, I
believe that his omissions occurred based on a mistaken assumption that
the omitted portion was insignificant, a mistake that assisted his case.

238 Berger, "Incorporation," *supra* note 139, at 451 (quoting Cong. Globe,
39th Cong., 1st sess., 1292 (Bingham) (1866).

239 Cong. Globe, 39th Cong., 1st sess., 1292 (1866).

240 *Government by Judiciary, supra* note 147, at 141.

241 *Id.* at 142.

242 *Id.* at 144−45.

243 *Id.* at 140−41.

244 *Compare id.* at 43 with *id.* at 142−43.

245 *See* notes 170−202 to chapter 2, *supra.*

246 *Government by Judiciary, supra* note 9, at 142−43.

247 Cong. Globe, 39th Cong., 1st sess., 2542−43 (1866).

248 *Id.*

249 *Id.* at 2542.

250 *E.g.*, Berger, "Incorporation," *supra* note 139, at 463. Fairman, *supra* note
1, at 45.

251 *See* Crosskey, *supra* note 140, at 27.

252 Cong. Globe, at 39th Cong., 1st sess., 432 (1866).

253 *Id.* at 813.

254 *Id.* at 430.

255 Berger, "Incorporation," *supra* note 139, at 453.

256 Cong. Globe, 39th Cong., 1st sess., at 1120 (1866); *Government by Judiciary, supra* note 147, at 143.

257 *Government by Judiciary, supra* note 147, at 143.

258 Cong. Globe, 38th Cong., 2d sess., 1202 (1864).

259 Cong. Globe, 39th Cong., 1st sess., 2539 (1866).

260 32 U.S. (7 Pet.) 243 (1833).

261 Farnsworth was a political supporter of the abolitionist-Republican Owen
Lovejoy. 3 *Dictionary of American Biography* 284 (1959).

262 Cong. Globe, 38th Cong., 1st sess., 2978 (1864).

263 *Government by Judiciary, supra* note 147, at 142.

264 *Id.*

265 Cong. Globe, 39th Cong., 1st sess., 1294 (1866); *see id.* 38th Cong., 1st sess., 1202 (1864).

266 *E.g.,* Cong. Globe, 39th Cong., 1st sess., 2539, *see* 1054, 1057, 1294 (1866).

267 *Id.*

268 *Government by Judiciary, supra* note 147, at 147.

269 *Id.*

270 Cong. Globe, 39th Cong., 1st sess., 2539–40 (Farnsworth), 2058 (Boutwell), 2462 (Garfield) (1866). This statement applies, of course, only to Republicans; Democrats opposed black suffrage. *E.g., id.* at 2538 (Rogers).

271 6 F. Cas. (No. 3230) 546 (C.C.E.D. Pa. 1823).

272 *Government by Judiciary, supra* note 147, at 148 (quoting Cong. Globe, 39th Cong., 1st sess., 2764–65 [1866]).

273 *Id.*

274 Cong. Globe, 39th Cong., 1st sess., 2765 (1866).

275 *Government by Judiciary, supra* note 147, at 148–49; Fairman, *supra* note 1, at 60–61.

276 Cong. Globe, 39th Cong., 1st sess., 2961 (1866); *see* Curtis, "The Bill of Rights as a Limitation on State Authority: A Reply to Professor Berger," 16 Wake Forest L. Rev. 45, 188 (1980).

277 *Government by Judiciary, supra* note 147, at 149.

278 Cong. Globe, 39th Cong., 1st sess., 3042 (1866).

279 *Cf. Government by Judiciary, supra* note 147, at 157, 149.

280 *Id.* at 148 n.66. On this point Berger cites Fairman. *But see* "Does the Fourteenth Amendment Incorporate the Bill of Rights?" *supra* note 1, at 68.

281 *N.Y. Times,* May 24, 1866, at 1, col. 6. *See also* Crossley, *supra* note 140, at 102–103.

282 *N.Y. Times,* May 24, 1866, at 1, col. 6.

283 *Id.,* March 1, 1866, at 5, col. 2. *See also id.* March 2, 1866, at 2, col. 5.

284 *Government by Judiciary, supra* note 147, at 148 n.66 and 153.

285 *Id.* at 221–29.

286 *Id.* at 228.

287 Cong. Globe, 39th Cong., 1st sess., 1095 (1866).

288 *Id.*

289 *Id.* at 1095.

290 *See* B. Kendrick, *The Journal of the Joint Committee of Fifteen on Reconstruction* 61 (1914) (hereinafter cited as Kendrick).

291 James, *supra* note 213, at 120; Cong. Globe, 39th Cong., 1st sess., 7286 (1866).

292 Cong. Globe, 39th Cong., 1st sess., 429, 432, 813, 1034, 1064, 1088–90 (Bingham), 2765–66 (Howard) (1866).

293 *Id.* at 566 (Brown), 741 (Lane), 868 (Newell), 1032 (McClurg), and

586 (Donnelly) (1866).

294   *Id.* at 2765–66 (Howard), 1090 (Bingham).

295   Cong. Globe, 39th Cong., 1st sess., 2462 (Garfield—referring to the principles of the Civil Rights bill), 2896 (Howard—rights of citizens under the Civil Rights bill put beyond mere legislative power) (1866).

296   *See* Cong. Globe, 38th Cong., 1st sess., 1480 (Sumner) (1864). To deprive free persons of rights in the Bill of Rights without conviction of a crime was, Judge Davis believed, a badge of slavery. *Proceedings of the Republican Union State Convention* 35 (Sept. 5, 1866).

297   Cong. Globe, 38th Cong., 1st sess., 1480 (Sumner) (1864).

298   Crosskey, *supra* note 140, at 6–7 (citing Murray's Lessee v. Hoboken Land & Improvement Co., 59 U.S. (18 How.) 272 (1856).

Chapter 5

1   *Galena* (Ill.) *Weekly Gazette*, Sept. 25, 1866, at 2, col. 4. The address seems to have been carried in virtually every Republican paper.

2   *Burlington* (Iowa) *Hawk Eye*, Sept. 28, 1866, at 1, col. 2; (Springfield) *Daily Ill. St. J.*, Sept. 28, 1866, at 1, col. 4.

3   *Galena* (Ill.) *Weekly Gazette*, Aug. 21, 1866, at 1, col. 6.

4   Fairman, "Does the Fourteenth Amendment Incorporate the Bill of Rights?" 2 Stan. L. Rev. 70–71 (1949) (hereinafter cited as Fairman).

5   *Dubuque Daily Times*, Nov. 21, 1866, at 2, col. 1.

6   *See, e.g.*, notes 118–121 and 124–148, *supra* chapter 2, and accompanying text.

7   *Reprinted* in *Dubuque Daily Times*, Dec. 3, 1866, at 2, col. 2.

8   *Id.* Compare Kelley's remarks on Bingham's prototype of the Fourteenth Amendment. Cong. Globe, 39th Cong., 1st sess., 1063 (1866).

9   *See, e.g., Daily Territorial Enterprise*, Sept. 20, 1866, at 1, col. 2 (Butler); *id.*, Sept. 16, 1866, at 1, col. 3 (Sen. Stewart); *Dubuque Daily Times*, Sept. 8, 1866, at 1, col. 3.

10   *N.Y. Daily Tribune*, Sept. 4, 1866, at 1, col. 4.

11   *Philadelphia Inquirer*, Aug. 25, 1866, at 2, cols. 1–2.

12   C. Fairman, *Reconstruction and Reunion (1864–88)* 180 (1971); 4 *National Cyclopedia of American Biography* 472 (1897) (hereinafter cited as NCAB); *N.Y. Tribune*, Sept. 4, 1866, at 1, col. 3.

13   4 *Dictionary of American Biography* 183 (1946) (hereinafter cited as DAB).

14   Note 30 *supra*.

15   *N.Y. Tribune*, Sept. 4, 1866, at 1, col. 3.

16   *Illinois State Journal*, Sept. 3, 1866, at 1, col. 6.

17   *See, e.g., Fairfield* (Iowa) *Ledger*, Sept. 20, 1866, at 1, col. 3; *Philadelphia Press*, Sept. 7, 1866, at 1, col. 2.

18   *Newark Daily Advertiser*, Sept. 7, 1866, at 1, col. 7.

19   *N.Y. Daily Tribune*, Sept. 7, 1866, at 1, col. 4.

20   *Id.*

21   *Washington* (D.C.) *Evening Chron.*, Sept. 9, 1866, at 1, col. 4.

22   *Id.* at col. 7.

23 *Id.* at col. 5.

24 P. Smith, *Trial by Fire*, 707–708 (1982) (hereinafter cited as Smith).

25 *Id.*; M. Benedict, *A Compromise of Principle*, 205–206 (1974) (hereinafter cited as Benedict).

26 Smith, *supra* note 24, at 707–708; Benedict, *supra* note 25, at 205–206.

27 *Washington* (D.C.) *Evening Chron.*, Sept. 9, 1866, at 1, col. 5.

28 *Id.*

29 *Id.* at cols. 5–6.

30 *N.Y. Daily Tribune*, Sept. 11, 1866, at 5, cols. 1–2.

31 *Philadelphia Inquirer*, Sept. 5, 1866, at 8, col. 3.

32 (Springfield) *Daily Ill. St. J.*, Sept. 21, 1866, at 2, col. 6.

33 *Id.*, Oct. 12, 1866, at 4, col. 4.

34 *Id.*, Oct. 22, 1866, at 4, col. 2.

35 *Cincinnati Commercial*, Aug. 31, 1866, at 2, col. 3.

36 *Philadelphia Press*, Sept. 18, 1866, at 8.

37 11 NCAB, *supra* note 12, at 236 (1909).

38 *Proceedings of the Republican Union State Convention* 35 (Sept. 5, 1866).

39 *Id.*

40 *Id.* at 41.

41 *Id.* See also the speech of Lyman Tremain: "The first [section of the Fourteenth Amendment] defines citizenship of the United States, and prohibits any State from denying to any person its privileges without legal process. . . . The first section is necessary to secure to the millions of newly created freedmen the rights of citizenship." *Id.* at 20. Tremain noted that the Civil Rights bill might be held unconstitutional or be repealed. "It seems, therefore, to be demanded by every consideration of justice and wise statesmanship that these persons should be secured in the immunities and privileges of citizenship, the right to sue, to make contracts, to hold and transmit property and to be witnesses, by an amendment of the constitution." *Id.* at 20–21.

42 *Albany Evening J.*, Sept. 21, 1866, at 1, col. 3.

43 *Id.* at col. 3.

44 *Id.* at col. 4.

45 *Id.* at col. 5.

46 *See* speech of Sen. Luke Poland to the Vermont legislature, reprinted in *Daily* (Burlington, Vt.) *Free Press*, Nov. 23, 1866, at 2, col. 1, and Nov. 24, 1866, at 2, col. 1 (suggesting that the Civil Rights bill embodied the same principles as § 1); speech of Sen. George Edmonds, reprinted in *Daily* (Burlington, Vt.) *Free Press*, Nov. 13, 1866, at 2, col. 2, and Nov. 14, 1866, at 2, col. 2 (summarizing §1 as extending the rights and privileges of citizens to blacks). *Compare* speech of Sen. Stewart in the *Daily Territorial Enterprise*, Sept. 16, 1866, at 1, cols. 2–3. Benjamin Butler in a speech, recorded in the *Daily Territorial Enterprise*, Sept. 20, 1866, at 1, col. 3, noted: "Therefore, it becomes the duty of every man to sustain the Congress, in sustaining first the Civil Rights Bill, which gives to everybody their rights in every State; and sustain Congress in giving protection to the negro, in holding these States where they are, and insisting that

free speech, a free press, civil and religious liberty, shall be guarantied until a change can be made, sustain the loyal men of the South." *See also* speech of Sen. Stewart reprinted in *Daily Territorial Enterprise*, Oct. 14, 1866, at 1, col. 1. For a few other campaign statements saying that the amendment covered the same ground as the Civil Rights bill and an argument that these vague statements show that the rights in the Bill of Rights were not incorporated, see Fairman, *supra* note 4, at 68–78. Of the statements Fairman collected, one seems inconsistent with incorporation of the Bill of Rights, a speech by Sen. John Sherman saying that the sum and substance of the first clause was the right to come and go, to sue, and to make contracts. Fairman, *supra* note 4, at 77.

47 *See* notes 165, 167, and 174–202, *supra* chapter 2, and accompanying text.

48 *Cincinnati Commercial*, Sept. 3, 1866, at 2, col. 3.

49 *See* note 168, *supra* chapter 2, and accompanying text.

50 *See, e.g.*, notes 192 and 193, *supra* chapter 2.

51 *See* notes 164–166, *supra* chapter 2, and accompanying text. *See also* Cong. Globe, 39th Cong., 1st sess., 1153 (Thayer) (1866).

52 Cong. Globe, 39th Cong., 1st sess., 3436 (1866).

53 *Id.* at 3437.

54 *Daily Territorial Enterprise*, Sept. 13, 1866, at 1, col. 2.

55 *See* notes 201–202, *supra* chapter 2, and accompanying text.

56 *Daily Territorial Enterprise*, Sept. 13, 1866, at 1, col. 2.

57 Oct. 4, 1866, at 1, col. 6.

58 *Cincinnati Commercial*, Sept. 9, 1866, at 8, col. 1.

59 *Id.* at col. 2.

60 *Id.*

61 *Brattleboro* (Vt.) *Record and Farmer*, Nov. 3, 1866, at 1.

62 *Id.*

63 *Cincinnati Daily Gazette*, Aug. 18, 1866, at 1, cols. 3–9.

64 Cong. Globe, 41st. Cong., 3d sess., 1245 (1871).

65 Cong. Globe, 43d Cong., 1st sess., 413 (1874).

66 *North American* (Pa.), Aug. 30, 1866, at 2, col. 3, cited in Bond, "The Original Understanding of the Fourteenth Amendment in Illinois, Ohio and Pennsylvania," 18 Akron L. R. 435 (1985). Bond concludes that selective incorporation was intended. *See also* Bond, "Ratification of the Fourteenth Amendment in North Carolina," 20 Wake Forest L. Rev. 89 (1984).

67 *Burlington* (Iowa) *Hawk Eye*, Sept. 13, 1866, at 1, col. 2.

68 *Dubuque Daily Times*, Sept. 8, 1866, at 1, col. 3.

69 *Cincinnati Commercial*, Aug. 27, 1866, at 1, col. 3.

70 *See* Fairman, *supra* note 4, at 68–78.

71 *See, e.g.*, notes 10–60 *supra*, and accompanying text.

72 For a survey of some of this material and a contrary opinion, *see* Fairman, *supra* note 4, at 81–126.

73 *Maine Senate Journal* 20–21 (1867).

74 *Journal of the Extra Session of the 22nd Senate of the State of New Jersey* 7 (1866).

75 *Senate Journal of the State of Nebraska*, 1st, 2d, and 3d sess., May 17, 1867, 57–58 (1867).

76 4 *The Messages and Proclamations of the Governors of the State of Missouri* 81 (1924).

77 *Journal of Vermont Senate 1866*, 24–25 (1866).

78 *Journal of Senate of State of Conn. (1866)* 44 (1866).

79 Biennial Message, State of Nevada, Jan. 10, 1867.

80 *Reports Made to the General Assembly of Illinois at its 25th Session*, Jan. 7, 1867, 29–30 (1867).

81 Fairman, *supra* note 4, at 96.

82 *See, e.g.,* Pa. Leg. Rec. *Appendix* LIII (1867) (Democratic racism); *id.* at XVI. State senator Bigham noted that § 1 of the amendment guarantied "State rights" to every human being, but not political rights. *Id.* at XVI. He also suggested that it put the Civil Rights bill in the Constitution. *Id.* at XVII. *See also id.* at XLV.

83 *Id.* at XXXI.

84 *Id.* at XXXII.

85 *Id.* at XXXIII.

86 *Id.*

87 *Id.* at XLV.

88 *Id.*

89 *Id.* at XLVIII.

90 *Id.*

91 *Id.* at LV.

92 *Id.* at LVI. *See also* remarks by Ewing: the first section of the Fourteenth Amendment would secure to the oppressed "all the privileges and rights of man," *id.* at LIX, and Landon: the amendment would "make liberty a reality," *id.* at LXXIX.

93 *Id.* at XCIX.

94 *Id.*

95 *Id.*

96 *See, e.g., id.* at XIII.

97 *Id.*

98 *Id.* at LII.

99 H. R. Doc. No. 149, Mass. Gen. Ct., at 1–4 (1867).

100 *Id.* at 2.

101 *Id.* at 2–4.

102 *Id.* at 25.

103 J. James, *Ratification of the Fourteenth Amendment* 143–44 (1984) (hereinafter cited as James, *Ratification*).

104 *Id.* at 142.

105 *See* notes 70–84, chapter 3, *supra.*

106 James, *Ratification, supra* note 103, at 17.

107 *Id.* at 60.

108 *Id.* at 75.

109 *Id.* at 106.

110 *Id.* at 151.

111 *Id.* at 189.
112 C. Fairman, *Reconstruction and Reunion (1864–88)* 254 (1971).
113 *Id.*
114 W. Brock, *An American Crisis, Congress and Reconstruction 1865–1867* 127–28 (1963).
115 *Id.*
116 *Id.*

Chapter 6

1   Fairman, "Does the Fourteenth Amendment Incorporate the Bill of Rights?" 2 Stan. L. Rev. 51, 126 (1949) (hereinafter cited as Fairman).
2   *Id.* at 126–32.
3   H. Trefousse, *The Radical Republicans* 408 (1975).
4   *Id.*
5   J. James, *The Ratification of the Fourteenth Amendment* 295 (1984).
6   Fairman, *supra* note 1 at 127.
7   Duncan v. Louisiana, 391 U.S. 145 (1968).
8   Fairman, *supra* note 1 at 127.
9   Williams v. Florida, 399 U.S. 78 (1970).
10 Fairman, *supra* note 1 at 128.
11 Cong. Globe, 42d Cong., 1st sess., 21, 154, 158 (1871); *see, generally,* K. Stamp, *The Era of Reconstruction 1865–77* (1965); V. Wharton, *The Negro in Mississippi 1865–1890* (1965).
12 P. Paludan, *A Covenant with Death* 238 (1975) (hereinafter cited as Paludan).
13 Cong. Globe, 42d Cong., 1st sess., 491 (1871).
14 *E.g., id.* at appendix 50, where portions are quoted.
15 For the text, *see* R. Carr, *Federal Protection of Civil Rights* at appendix 1, p. 241.
16 For the negative effect of devotion to federalism *see* Paludan, *supra* note 11, at 275–82.
17 Cong. Globe, 39th Cong., 1st sess., 1833 (1866).
18 Cong. Globe, 42d Cong., 1st sess., appendix 151.
19 *Id.* at appendix 78, 80.
20 *Id.* at 78. *See* Zeigler, "A Reassessment of the Younger Doctrine," 987 Duke L. J. (1983); Avins, "The Ku Klux Klan Act of 1871: Some Reflected Light on the Fourteenth Amendment," 11 St. Louis L.U.L.J. 331 (1967); Franz, "Congressional Power to Enforce the Fourteenth Amendment Against Private Acts," 73 Yale L. J. 1353 (1964).
21 See chapter 5, *supra.*
22 Act of September 28, 1850, sess. I, ch. 60, sec. 7.
23 Ableman v. Booth, 62 U.S. (21 How.) 506, 525 (1859).
24 Prigg v. Pennsylvania, 41 U.S. (16 Pet.) 539 (1842).
25 Cong. Globe, 39th Cong., 1st sess., 1294 (1866); *see* notes 26–28 *infra.*
26 41 U.S. (16 Pet.) 539 (1842); *see e.g.,* Cong. Globe, 42d Cong., 1st sess., 69–70 (1870).
27 41 U.S. (16 Pet.) 539 (1842).

28 41 U.S. (16 Pet.) 539 (1842); *compare* Cong. Globe, 42d Cong., 1st sess., H. appendix 70 (1871) with *id.* at H. appendix 115; S. appendix 252, 514.

29 The Civil Rights Cases, 109 U.S. 3 (1883).

30 Letter from Justice Bradley to Judge Woods (March 12, 1871), Bradley Papers, New Jersey Historical Society; U.S. v. Hall, 26 Fed. Cas. 79 (No. 15,282) (C.C.S.D. Ala. 1871).

31 Act of April 20, 1871, 17 Stat. 13.

32 *See* note 20 *supra.*

33 P. Paludan, *A Covenant with Death* (1975).

34 *Id.* at 3.

35 *Cf.,* Cong. Globe, 41st Cong., 2d sess., appendix 310 (1871); *see id.* at note 42d Cong., 1st sess., 515 (Fowler) (1870).

36 Cong. Globe, 42d Cong., 1st sess., appendix 84 (1871).

37 *Id.*

38 Berger, "Incorporation of the Bill of Rights in the Fourteenth Amendment: A Nine-Lived Cat," 42 Ohio St. L. J. 435, 463 (1981) (hereinafter cited as Berger, "Incorporation").

39 *See, e.g.,* Cong. Globe, 42d Cong., 1st sess., appendix 314 (1871).

40 Crosskey, "Charles Fairman, 'Legislative History,' and the Constitutional Limitations on State Authority," 22 U. Chi. L. Rev. 1 (1954) 1, 89–100 (hereinafter cited as Crosskey).

41 Cong. Globe, 42d Cong., 1st sess., 577 (1871).

42 Cong. Globe, 42d Cong., 1st sess., appendix 151 (1871) (Garfield).

43 *Id.* at 334.

44 *Id.*

45 *Id.* at 370.

46 *Id.* at 448.

47 *Id.* at 380.

48 *See, e.g., id.* at 382 (Hawley), 414 (Roberts).

49 *See* Cong. Globe, 41st Cong., 2d sess., 515 (1870) (Fowler), appendix 310 (Maynard) (1871). *See also* Berger, "The Fourteenth Amendment: Light from the Fifteenth," 74 Nw. U. L. Rev. 311, 346 n.217 (1979).

50 Cong. Globe, 41st Cong., 1st sess., at 475–76.

51 *Id.* at 476.

52 *Id.* at 475.

53 *Id.* at 42d Cong., 1st sess., 499 (1871).

54 *Id.* at 42d Cong., 2d sess., 844 (1872).

55 *Id.* at 843.

56 *Id.* at 844.

57 Cong. Globe, 41st Cong., 3d sess., 1244–45 (1871).

58 *Id.* at 1245.

59 *Id.*

60 *Id.*

61 59 U.S. (18 How.) 272 (1856); *see,* Crosskey, "Charles Fairman, 'Legislative History,' and the Constitutional Limitations on State Authority," 22 U. Chi. L. Rev. 1, 6–7 (1954).

62 Cong. Globe, 41st Cong., 3d sess., 1245 (1871).

63 *See* Crosskey, *supra* note 40 at 98–100; Cong. Globe, 42d Cong., 1st sess., 454 (Cox), 396 (Rice) (1871).

64 Cong. Globe, 42d Cong., 1st sess., appendix 314 (1871).

65 Ch. 99, 16 Stat. 433; *see, e.g.,* Cong. Globe, 42d Cong., 1st sess., 396, appendix 314 (1871).

66 2 Cong. Rec. 384 (1874).

67 *Id.* at 384–85.

68 *Id.*

69 *Id.* at appendix 241.

70 *Id.* at appendix 242.

71 *Id.*

72 *Id.*

73 *Id.*

74 *Id.*

75 *Id.* at 420 (Herndon) (1872). *Compare* Cong. Globe, 42d Cong., 2d sess., appendix 25 (1872) with 2 Cong. Rec. 4086 (1874) (Thurman).

76 *E.g.,* Cong. Globe, 39th Cong., 1st sess., 2765 (1866) (Howard); note 56 *supra* (Sherman).

77 H. R. Rep. No. 22, 41st Cong., 3d sess., 1 (1871), *reprinted* in A. Avins, *The Reconstruction Amendments' Debates* 466 (1967). Some statements in the Report are not consistent with the views Bingham expressed in March 1871. *See* Cong. Globe, 42d Cong., 1st sess., appendix 314 (1871).

78 H. R. Rep. No. 22, 41st Cong., 3d sess., 1 (1871).

79 *Id.*

80 *Id.*

81 Berger, "Incorporation of the Bill of Rights in the Fourteenth Amendment: A Nine-Lived Cat," 42 Ohio St. L. R. 435, 464 (1981) (hereinafter cited as Berger, "Incorporation"). *See also* Berger, "The Fourteenth Amendment: Light from the Fifteenth," 74 Nw. U. L. Rev. 311 (1979).

82 4 Cong. Rec. 175 (1875).

83 Berger, "Incorporation," *supra* note 81 at 464 (quoting F. O'Brian, *Justice Reed and the First Amendment* 116 [1958]).

84 *E.g.,* 4 Cong. Rec. 5581, 5583, 5592 (1876).

85 *See id.* at 5595; Meyer, "The Blaine Amendment and the Bill of Rights," 64 Harv. L. Rev. 939, 943 (1951).

86 *See* 4 Cong. Rec. 5581 (Kernan), 5583 (Whyte), 5592 (Eaton) (1876). *See also* Meyer, "The Blaine Amendment and the Bill of Rights," 64 Harv. L. Rev. 939, 943 (1951).

87 *See* Cong. Globe, 39th Cong., 1st sess., 2765–66 (Howard), 2542 (Bingham), 1034, 1089 (Bingham speaking of the prototype of his amendment) (1866). *See also* Cong. Globe, 42d Cong., 1st sess., appendix 84 (1871) (Bingham).

88 Berger, "The Fourteenth Amendment: Light from the Fifteenth," 74 Nw. U. L. Rev. 311, 347 (1979).

89 *See* notes 35–62 and accompanying text.

90 *See* note 86 *supra.*

91 4 Cong. Rec. 5561 (1876) (Frelinghuysen).

92 92 U.S. 542 (1876).
93 *Id.* at 553–54.
94 *Id.* at 559; Justice Clifford dissented.
95 92 U.S. 90 (1876).
96 *Id.* at 93.
97 *See* text accompanying notes 66–75 *supra.*
98 4 Cong. Rec. 5585 (1876).

Chapter 7

1   The Slaughter-House Cases, 83 U.S. (16 Wall.) 36 (1873).
2   Morrison, "Does the Fourteenth Amendment Incorporate the Bill of Rights?: The Judicial Interpretation," 2 Stan. L. Rev. 140 (1949).
3   L. Levy, *Judgments* 69 (1972).
4   *Id.*
5   26 F. Cas. 79 (C.C.S.D. Ala. 1871) (No. 15,282).
6   Filler, "William B. Woods," in 2 *The Justices of the United States Supreme Court* 1327, 1331 (L. Friedman and F. Israel eds. 1969) (hereinafter *Justices*).
7   *Id.* at 1334.
8   26 F. Cas. at 81–82.
9   R. Kaczorowski, *The Politics of Judicial Interpretation: The Federal Courts, Department of Justice, and Civil Rights (1866–1876)* 125–26, 129, 131 (1985) (hereinafter cited as Kaczrowski); letter from Justice Bradley to Judge Woods, March 23, 1871 (in Bradley Papers, New Jersey Historical Society).
10 J. Pomeroy, *Introduction to Constitutional Law* (1868). After *Slaughter-House*, the orthodox view appeared in almost all texts. For Cooley's views, *see* P. Paludan, *A Covenant with Death* 267–73 (1975).
11 Slaughter-House Cases, 83 U.S. (16 Wall.) 36, 71–72 (1873).
12 Maxwell v. Dow, 176 U.S. 581 (1900).
13 60 U.S. (19 How.) 393 (1857).
14 32 U.S. (7 Pet.) 243 (1833).
15 59 U.S. (18 How.) 272 (1856).
16 60 U.S. (19 How.) at 403, 449.
17 Crosskey, "Charles Fairman, 'Legislative History,' and the Constitutional Limitations on State Authority," 22 U. Chi. L. Rev. 1, 1–10 (1954) (hereinafter cited as Crosskey).
18 *Id.* at 4–10.
19 Murray's Lessee v. Hoboken Land & Improvement Co., 59 U.S. (18 How.) 272 (1856); Crosskey, *supra* note 17, at 6–7.
20 Twitchell v. Pennsylvania, 74 U.S. (7 Wall.) 321 (1869).
21 *Id.* at 325.
22 83 U.S. (16 Wall.) 36 (1873).
23 R. Cortner, *The Supreme Court and the Second Bill of Rights* 7 (1981) (hereinafter cited as Cortner).
24 Gillette, "Samuel Miller," in 2 *Justices, supra* note 6, at 1011.

25 *Id.* at 1018.
26 83 U.S. at 74.
27 *Id.* at 76.
28 *Id.* at 77–78.
29 *See* Cong. Globe, 39th Cong., 1st sess., 1202 (1864); 35th Cong., 2d sess., 982–84 (1859).
30 *E.g.,* Cong. Globe, 39th Cong., 1st sess., 1118–19, 1294, 1833 (1866).
31 83 U.S. at 79.
32 United States v. Cruikshank, 92 U.S. (2 Otto) 542 (1876).
33 *But see* Palmer, "The Parameters of Constitutional Reconstruction: Slaughter-House, Cruikshank, and the Fourteenth Amendment," 1984 U. Ill. L. Rev. 739.
34 83 U.S. at 116.
35 *Id.* at 118.
36 *Id.*
37 Cortner, *supra* note 23, at 8.
38 83 U.S. at 129.
39 Paludan, *A Covenant with Death* 236 (1975) (hereinafter cited as Paludan) (citing 2 C. Warren, *The Supreme Court in United States History* 541 [1928]).
40 1 J. Burgess, *Political Science and Comparative Constitutional Law* 228–30 (1890), *quoted in* Cortner, *supra* note 23, at 10.
41 Paludan, *supra* note 39, at 57.
42 5 P. Smith, *Trial by Fire* 816 (1982).
43 *Id.*
44 *Id.* at 827.
45 *Id.* at 851; Kaczorowski, *supra* note 9, at 125–26, 129, 131.
46 92 U.S. 542 (1876).
47 *Id.* at 551.
48 *Id.* at 552.
49 *Id.* at 551–53.
50 *Id.* at 554–55.
51 *Id.* at 549; Paludan, *supra* note 39, at 58.
52 Paludan, *supra* note 39, at 58.
53 United States v. Cruikshank, 25 F. Cas. 707 (C.C.D.La. 1874) (No. 14,897). Though retreating from the position he took as to *Hall*, Bradley still held to a broader view of national power to protect blacks than the Court would later take.
54 92 U.S. 90 (1876).
55 *Id.* at 92.
56 *Id.* at 93.
57 92 U.S. 214 (1876).
58 *Id.* at 220.
59 J. McPherson, *Ordeal by Fire: The Civil War and Reconstruction* 602–606 (1982).
60 United States v. Harris, 106 U.S. 629 (1883). *Harris* left open the possibility of legislation supplying protection if the state failed to supply it. For a thoughtful discussion of Waite Court decisions and the thesis that they

were products of Republican ideas of federalism, *see* Benedict, "Preserving Federalism: Reconstruction and the Waite Court," 1978 *Supreme Court Review* 39. For a more critical view, *see* C. P. Magrath, *Morrison, R. Waite: The Triumph of Character* 110–71 (1963).

61 The Civil Rights Cases, 109 U.S. 3 (1883).
62 190 U.S. 127 (1903).
63 110 U.S. 516 (1884).
64 Davidson v. New Orleans, 96 U.S. 97 (1878).
65 Cortner, *supra* note 23, at 13.
66 110 U.S. at 517–18.
67 Murray's Lessee v. Hoboken Land and Improvement Co., 59 U.S. (18 How.) 272 (1856).
68 *Id.*
69 A. Howard, *The Road from Runnymede: Magna Carta and Constitutionalism in America* 158–59 (1968) (hereinafter cited as Howard); *cf. id.* at 352–53.
70 *Id.* at 412, 416.
71 *Id.* at 419, 422.
72 *Id.* at 158–59.
73 *Id.* at 352–53.
74 C. Miller, *The Supreme Court and the Uses of History* 43 (1969) (hereinafter cited as Miller).
75 *Id.*
76 Filler, "Stanley Matthews," in 2 *Justices, supra* note 6, at 1351–60.
77 110 U.S. 516, 521–27 (1884); Howard, *supra* note 69, at 352–53.
78 110 U.S. at 528–29.
79 Miller, *supra* note 74, at 50.
80 R. Berger, *Government by Judiciary* 134–56 (1977).
81 Howard, *supra* note 69, at 354–55.
82 110 U.S. at 531–32.
83 *Id.* at 535.
84 *Id.* at 534–35.
85 *Id.* at 550.
86 Filler, "John M. Harlan," in 2 *Justices, supra* note 6, at 1281.
87 *Id.* at 1283.
88 *Id.* at 1283–84.
89 109 U.S. 3, 26 (1883).
90 163 U.S. 537, 552 (1896).
91 110 U.S. 516, 539–40 (1884).
92 *Id.* at 546.
93 *Id.* at 557–58.
94 Fairman, "Does the Fourteenth Amendment Incorporate the Bill of Rights?" 2 Stan. L. Rev. 5, 84 (1949).
95 *Id.* at 101.
96 *Id.* at 106.
97 *Id.* at 82–83.
98 123 U.S. 131 (1887).
99 19 *Dictionary of American Biography* 34–35 (1927).

100 *Id.*
101 83 U.S. (16 Wall.) 36 (1873).
102 110 U.S. 516 (1884).
103 123 U.S. at 148–49.
104 *Id.* at 150–52.
105 *Id.* at 153.
106 *Id.* at 166.
107 166 U.S. 226 (1897).
108 Cortner, *supra* note 23, at 26.
109 *Id.* at 28.
110 144 U.S. 323 (1892).
111 *Id.* at 338–39 (Field, J., dissenting).
112 *Id.* at 366, 370.
113 *Id.* at 361.
114 *Id.* at 362–63.
115 *Id.* at 363.
116 United States v. Hall, 26 F. Cas. 79 (C.C.S.D.Ala. 1871) (No. 15,282).
117 83 U.S. (16 Wall.) 36, 116 (1873).
118 144 U.S. 323, 361.
119 McCloskey, "Stephen J. Field," in 2 *Justices, supra* note 6, at 1069, 1077.
120 *Id.* at 1084 (quoting *Ex parte* Wall, 107 U.S. 265, 302 [1883]).
121 *Id.* at 1084–85.
122 *Id.*
123 *Id.* at 1086.
124 W. Guthrie, *Lectures on the Fourteenth Article of Amendment* 60–65 (1898), *quoted in* Cortner, *supra* note 23, at 29.
125 *Id.*
126 176 U.S. 581 (1900).
127 Cortner, *supra* note 23, at 30.
128 *Id.*
129 170 U.S. 343 (1898).
130 176 U.S. 581 (1900).
131 *Id.* at 584.
132 Skolnik, "Rufus Peckham," in 3 *Justices, supra* note 6, at 1685, 1696–1702.
133 *Id.* at 1697.
134 *Id.*
135 176 U.S. at 593.
136 *Id.*
137 *Id.* at 594–600.
138 *Id.* at 595.
139 *Id.* at 601.
140 *Id.* at 601–602.
141 *Id.* at 602.
142 *See* notes 80–102, chapter 3, *supra.*
143 176 U.S. at 602–603.
144 *Id.* at 612.
145 *Id.* at 612.

146 *Id.* at 617.
147 *Id.* at 614.
148 198 U.S. 45 (1905).
149 *Compare* Williamson v. Lee Optical Co., 348 U.S. 483 (1955) *with* Board of Education v. Barnette, 319 U.S. 624 (1943).
150 211 U.S. 78 (1908).
151 *Id.* at 98.
152 *Id.* at 114.
153 *Id.* at 96–99.
154 6 F. Cas. 546 (C.C.E.D.Pa. 1823) (No. 3230).

Chapter 8

1 Chicago, Burlington & Quincy Railroad Co. v. Chicago, 166 U.S. 226 (1897).
2 268 U.S. 652, 666 (1925).
3 283 U.S. 697 (1931).
4 283 U.S. 359 (1931).
5 Hendel, "Charles Evans Hughes," in 3 *The Justices of the United States Supreme Court* 1893 (1969) (hereinafter cited as *Justices*); D. Burner, "Owen J. Roberts," in *id.* at 2253.
6 283 U.S. at 722–23.
7 287 U.S. 45 (1932).
8 *Id.* at 65–66.
9 Chicago, Burlington & Quincy R. Co. v. Chicago, 166 U.S. 226 (1897).
10 Gitlow v. New York, 268 U.S. 652 (1925).
11 Near v. Minnesota, 283 U.S. 697 (1931).
12 287 U.S. at 67.
13 299 U.S. 353 (1937).
14 R. Cortner, *The Supreme Court and the Second Bill of Rights* 89–90 (1981).
15 299 U.S. at 364–66.
16 *Id.* at 366.
17 302 U.S. 319 (1937).
18 *Id.* at 321–22.
19 *Id.* at 325–26.
20 *Id.*
21 *Id.*
22 *Id.* at 319–25.
23 *E.g.*, Palko v. Connecticut, 302 U.S. 319, 325–26 (1937); Boyd v. United States, 116 U.S. 616, 618 (1886). *See also* Shuttlesworth v. Birmingham, 394 U.S. 147, 152 (1969).
24 W. Crosskey, *Politics and the Constitution in the History of the United States* 514 (1953), *quoted in* Anastaplo, "Mr. Crosskey, the American Constitution, and the Nature of Things," 15 Loy. U. Chi. L. J. 181, 186 (1984).
25 Cantwell v. Connecticut, 310 U.S. 296 (1940); Everson v. Board of Education, 330 U.S. 1 (1947).
26 332 U.S. 46 (1947).

27 Frank, "Hugo L. Black," in 3 *Justices, supra* note 5, at 2321, 2326 (1969).
28 *Id.* at 2326–27.
29 *See* Frankfurter, "Memorandum on 'Incorporation' of the Bill of Rights into the Due Process Clause of the Fourteenth Amendment," 78 Harv. L. Rev. 746 (1965).
30 332 U.S. 46, 71–72 (1947) (Black, J., dissenting).
31 *Id.* at 68–123.
32 332 U.S. at 124 (Murphy, J., dissenting).
33 *But see* Younger v. Harris, 401 U.S. 37 (1971) (an early Burger court decision joined in by a number of Justices from the Warren Court).
34 347 U.S. 483 (1954).
35 *E.g.*, Near v. Minnesota, 283 U.S. 697 (1931); Powell v. Alabama, 287 U.S. 45 (1932); Schneider v. Town of Irvington, 308 U.S. 147 (1939); Thomas v. Collins, 323 U.S. 516 (1945); Cantwell v. Connecticut, 350 U.S. 296 (1940); West Virginia Board of Education v. Barnette, 319 U.S. 624 (1943).
36 Mapp v. Ohio, 367 U.S. 643 (1961).
37 Gideon v. Wainwright, 372 U.S. 335 (1963).
38 Malloy v. Hogan, 378 U.S. 1 (1964).
39 391 U.S. 145 (1968).
40 *Id.* at 166 (Black, J., concurring).
41 *Id., see* Adamson v. California, 332 U.S. 46, 92–123 (1947) (Black, J., dissenting).
42 391 U.S. 145 at 174, 188 (Harlan and Stewart, dissenting).
43 395 U.S. 784 (1969).
44 *Id.*
45 *See* United States v. Guest, 383 U.S. 745 (1966).
46 Brown v. Board of Education, 347 U.S. 483 (1954).
47 Katzenbach v. Morgan, 314 U.S. 641 (1966).
48 Edwards v. South Carolina, 373 U.S. 229 (1963).
49 *E.g.*, Engel v. Vitale, 370 U.S. 421 (1962).
50 *E.g.*, Yates v. United States, 354 U.S. 298 (1957).
51 *E.g.*, Brown v. Board of Education, 347 U.S. 483 (1954).
52 42 U.S.C. § 1983 applied in Monroe v. Pape, 365 U.S. 167 (1961).
53 *E.g.*, Monroe v. Pape, 365 U.S. 167 (1961).
54 Pierson v. Ray, 386 U.S. 547 (1967) (immunity of judges); Imbler v. Pachtman, 424 U.S. 409 (1976) (immunity of prosecutors).
55 Connick v. Myers, 103 S. Ct. 1684 (1983); Perry v. Sinderman, 408 U.S. 593 (1972).
56 Williams v. Florida, 399 U.S. 78, 118 (1970) (Harlan, J., dissenting); Duncan v. Louisiana, 391 U.S. 145, 171 (1968) (Harlan, J., dissenting).
57 Duncan v. Louisiana, 391 U.S. 145 (1968).
58 399 U.S. 78 (1970).
59 Apodaca v. Oregon, 406 U.S. 404 (1972); Johnson v. Louisiana, 406 U.S. 356 (1972).
60 *See* Ballew v. Georgia, 435 U.S. 223 (1978).
61 *See* J. Smith, *Freedom's Fetters: Alien and Sedition Laws* (1956); Prigg v. Pennsylvania, 41 U.S. (19 Pet.) 539 (1842); Dred Scott v. Sandford, 60 U.S.

(19 How.) 393 (1857); Berea College v. Kentucky, 211 U.S. 45 (1908); Whitney v. California, 274 U.S. 357 (1927).

62 W. Van Alstyne, *Interpretations of the First Amendment* (1984).

63 *See* Curtis, "The Fourteenth Amendment and the Bill of Rights," 14 Conn. L. Rev. 237, 241–58 (1982).

64 A. Singer, *Campaign Speeches of American Presidential Candidates 1928–1972* 361 (1976).

65 *See Impeachment, Selected Materials* (House Doc. 93-7) *Committee on the Judiciary*, 93d Cong., 2d sess., pursuant to H. Res. 803 (House Impeachment Inquiry) (1973).

66 *E.g.*, United States v. Leon, 104 S. Ct. 3405 (1984).

67 *E.g.*, Dunaway v. New York, 442 U.S. 200 (1979).

68 *See* Ohio v. Johnson, 104 S. Ct. 2536 (1984).

69 104 S. Ct. 3405 (1984).

70 *Id.* at 3419–20.

71 104 S. Ct. 3430, 3452–53 (1984) (Stevens, J., dissenting).

72 *Id.* at 3456–57.

73 Fisher v. United States, 425 U.S. 391 (1976).

74 116 U.S. 616 (1886).

75 Paul v. Davis, 424 U.S. 693 (1976).

76 Hudgens v. NLRB, 424 U.S. 507 (1976).

77 Dolbert v. Florida, 432 U.S. 282 (1977).

78 Williams v. Florida, 399 U.S. 78 (1970).

79 Rummel v. Estelle, 445 U.S. 263 (1980). The holding was severely limited in Solam v. Holm, 103 S. Ct. 300 (1983).

80 381 U.S. 479 (1965).

81 381 U.S. 479, 507 (1965) (Black, J., dissenting).

82 410 U.S. 113 (1973).

83 *See* L. Levy, *Legacy of Suppression* (1960) for an argument that the First Amendment did not substantially change English common law. For the contrary argument, *see* Mayton, "Seditious Libel and the Last Guarantee of a Freedom of Expression," 84 Col. L. Rev. 91 (1984).

84 *See* note 66 *supra*.

85 436 U.S. 547 (1978).

86 387 U.S. 294 (1967).

87 436 U.S. at 577–78 (Stevens, J., dissenting).

88 *E.g.*, State v. Granberry, 491 S.W. 2d 528 (Mo. 1973); State v. Collins, 297 A. 2d 620 (Me. 1972); State v. Santiago, 492 P. 2d 657 (Hawaii 1971).

89 *See* Wilkes, "The New Federalism in Criminal Procedure: State Court Evasion of the Burger Court," 62 Ky. L. J. 421 (1974).

90 Elison and NettikSimmons, "Federalism and State Constitutions: The New Doctrine of Independent and Adequate State Grounds," 45 Mont. L. Rev. 177, 198–99 (1984).

91 Brennan, "Some Aspects of Federalism," 39 N.Y.U.L. Rev. 945, 955 (1964), *quoted in* Elison and NettikSimmons, *supra* note 90, at 198.

92 Brennan, "State Constitutions and the Protection of Individual Rights," 90 Harv. L. Rev. 489, 491 (1977), *quoted in* Elison and NettikSimmons,

supra note 90, at 199.

93 Florida v. Casals, 103 S. Ct. 3100, 3102 (1983) (Burger, C. J., concurring), *quoted in* Elison and NettikSimmons, *supra* note 90, at 199.

94 Elison and NettikSimmons, *supra* note 90. *See, e.g.*, Michigan v. Long, 103 S. Ct. 3469 (1983).

95 Pruneyard Shopping Center v. Robins, 447 U.S. 74 (1980).

96 *Id.*

97 Food Employees v. Logan Valley Plaza, 391 U.S. 308 (1968).

98 Hudgens v. NLRB, 424 U.S. 507 (1976).

99 Robins v. Pruneyard Shopping Center, 23 Cal. 3d 899, 910, 592 P. 2d 341, 347 (1979).

100 447 U.S. at 91 (Marshall, J., concurring).

101 406 U.S. 404 (1972).

102 435 U.S. 223 (1978).

103 435 U.S. at 246 (Powell, J., concurring).

104 *Id.* at 245–46.

Conclusion

1 *Compare* R. Cover, *Justice Accused* 42–61 (1975) (hereinafter cited as *Justice Accused*) *with* Prigg v. Pennsylvania, 41 U.S. (16 Pet.) 539 (1842) and Dred Scott v. Sandford, 60 U.S. (19 How.) 393 (1857).

2 *Justice Accused, supra* note 1, at 259.

3 J. Tiffany, *A Treatise on the Unconstitutionality of American Slavery* (1849). For a thought-provoking essay, *see* Perry, "The Authority of Text, Tradition, and Reason: A Theory of Constitutional Interpretation," 58 So. Cal. L. Rev. 551 (1985).

4 *Justice Accused, supra* note 1, at 120–32.

5 41 U.S. (16 Pet.) 539 (1842).

6 *Id.*

7 D. Fehrenbacher, *The Dred Scott Case* 44 (1978).

8 *Id.* at 45.

9 *Justice Accused, supra* note 1, at 168.

10 P. Angle and E. Miers eds., *The Living Lincoln* 275 (1955).

11 Cong. Globe, 39th Cong., 1st sess., 1294 (1866).

12 Cong. Globe, 42d Cong., 1st sess., 499 (1871).

13 *See* notes to chapters 2 and 5 *supra*.

14 Cong. Globe, 39th Cong., 1st sess., 1089–90 and 2765–66 (1866).

15 Fairman, "Does the Fourteenth Amendment Incorporate the Bill of Rights?" 2 Stan. L. Rev. 5, 51 (1949) (hereinafter cited as Fairman).

16 *Id.* at 43–134.

17 Cong. Globe, 39th Cong., 1st sess., at 3167, 3201 (1866).

18 *Id.* at appendix 256.

19 *Burlington* (Iowa) *Hawk Eye*, Sept. 28, 1866, at 1, col. 2.

20 *Dubuque Daily Times*, Nov. 21, 1866, at 2, col. 1.

21 *Id.*, Dec. 3, 1866, at 2, col. 2.

22 *Philadelphia Inquirer*, Sept. 5, 1866, at 8, col. 3.

23 (Springfield) *Daily Ill. St. J.*, Sept. 21, 1866, at 2, col. 6.

24 *Cincinnati Commercial*, Sept. 3, 1866, at 2, col. 3.

25 Fairman, *supra* note 15, at 96.

26 Pa. Legis. Rec., appendix XXXI (1867).

27 *Id.* at XLVIII.

28 *Id.* at XCIX.

29 *N.Y. Tribune*, Sept. 4, 1866, at 1, col. 4.

30 Fairman, *supra* note 15, at 76–77.

31 332 U.S. 46, 89 (1947) (Black, J., dissenting).

Index

Absolute rights, 76, 119–20. *See also* Fundamental rights

Adams, John, 107, 181

Adamson v. California, 4–5, 201–202, 220

Aliens: due process and, 107

Allison, William Boyd, 144

Ames, Adelbert, 157

Anderson, George, 48

Antieau, Chester, 65

Antislavery: actions of state legislatures, 30–31; Garrisonian, 23, 44, 45; judicial response to, 212; moderate political, 6, 42, 45; origins of Fourteenth Amendment, 6–7, 107, 110; publications, suppression of, 30–31; Radical political, 42, 43, 213; Republican, 45, 46. *See also* Republican legal thought

Arms, right to bear, 24, 170, 203; Supreme Court on, 170, 203

Arnold, Isaac Newton, 37, 40, 50

Articles of Confederation: use of words *privileges* and *immunities* in, 65

Assembly, freedom of, 56, 135, 137, 140, 150, 164, 170, 199

Baker, Jehu, 90–91

Baldwin, John, 56

Ballew v. Georgia, 210

Barron v. Baltimore, 29, 42, 48, 51, 61, 70, 81, 83, 84, 91, 96, 97, 101, 109, 112, 121, 123, 126, 127, 130, 150, 173–74, 204, 218, 233 n.201; antislavery context of, 23; Bill of Rights not applied to states, 7; Marshall's decision in, 22–23

Beccaria, Marquis: quoted by Continental Congress, 18–19

Belz, Herman, 34–35

Benedict, Michael: on New Orleans massacre, 136; study of Reconstruction politics, 34, 37, 38, 59, 68, 73

Benton v. Maryland, 203

Berger, Raoul: attack on Bingham, 120–26; attack on Howard, 126–28; *Government by Judiciary*, 3, 113, 114, 116–17, 128; influence of Fairman on, 113–19; on privileges and immunities clause, 114–17; rejection of incorporation, 113

Bill of Rights: applicable to states, 1–4, 22–25; congressional debate on, 21–22; Court decisions narrowing protections of, 222 n.29; criminal procedure guaranties of, 203; intentions of founding fathers, 1–2; legal scholars on,

Michael Kent Curtis is a practicing attorney for the Greensboro law firm, Smith, Patterson, Follin, Curtis, James, and Harkavy. He has been an instructor in constitutional law, criminal law, and evidence at Guilford College, concurrently with his law practice. He continues to serve as a cooperating attorney for the North Carolina Civil Liberties Union and is the author of several articles on the question of the Bill of Rights and the Fourteenth Amendment.